Beyond Two Parties

Why America Needs a Multiparty System
and How We Can Have It

Dan Eckam

Table of Contents

List of Tables and Figures

Tables:

Figures:

Note: Some of the charts in this book rely heavily on color. If you are reading this book in black-and-white, you may not get the full effect. You can view full-color versions of these charts on my website, at **daneckam.com/book/btp/figures**.

Acknowledgments

I want to thank all those who took the time to talk to me about our political system and about the ideas contained in this book. Thank you to my colleagues in Common Ground for Texans, including Joanne Richards, Hamilton Richards, Saundra Ragona, and Rick Hastie, for discussing these ideas with me. I'm also grateful to members of the philosophy discussion group I'm a part of for their interest and feedback, especially Gary Bjerke, Milton Wright, George Hoekstra, Harold Collins, Jon Meador and Ted Brown. I'm grateful to professors Kurt Weyland and Daron Shaw of the University of Texas at Austin, and to Richard Winger of *Ballot Access News*, for sharing thoughts and relevant information with me. For advice on the writing and production processes, I'm grateful to Laura Creedle and James Galloway.

My experience as an activist and organizer for the Justice Party of Texas, from 2012 to 2014, helped prepare me for writing this book. I'm grateful to lead organizer Ben Shaw (R.I.P.) for his friendship and encouragement, and to Rocky Anderson for inspiration.

Finally, I'm grateful to friends and family who discussed these ideas with me, supported this effort, and/or gave valuable feedback. These include Eric Lawrence, Dan Gillotte, Rob Nylund, Gregory Foster, Alan Watts, Matt Pyle, Srinivas Nedunuri, Naiman Rigby, Lawson Reilly, David Downman, Susan Downman, John Dudas, Jarrett Paschel, Henry Reynolds, and my sister, Cindy Gray.

0. Introduction

Imagine that you're taking a painting class, and the teacher assigns you the exercise of painting a still from your favorite black-and-white movie. You can only use black paint and white paint — with *no mixing allowed*. That last part is a real kicker, you realize, because it means there will be no shades of gray, just pure black and pure white. You were thinking of *Casablanca*, of maybe taking a still from the scene at the airport. But without grays? It seems impossible to depict so as to be recognizable.

This is a bit like the problem of representation in American politics, where a vast mosaic of different viewpoints and values are reduced to just two parties. Our two-party system systematically excludes parties other than the dominant Republican and Democratic ones — so it can fairly be described as a *duopolistic* system. At the national level, it's been many decades since someone from another party held a seat in Congress.

I think this is a big part of the reason for the dysfunction in our politics. We're the only major democratic country in the world that has such a duopolistic system. It seems to me that we don't often consider how strange this is. We take the two-party system for granted, and don't consider how it might be connected to our political maladies.

But stop and think about it for a moment. In such a big, diverse country, does it really make sense that we could be effectively, accurately represented by just two parties? We are trying to run a *representative* democracy, aren't we? Do these parties really stand for anything, consistently — other than "not the other party"? In recent times, we've seen a lot of negativity in politics, a lot of one side vilifying the other. There's a lot of motivating the party base by fearmongering about what the other party will do if it wins power. Our politics have been hollowed out by these tendencies.

It's strange, too, that some of us (including those who defend the two-party system) don't seem to mind a lack of choices. Historically, Americans have famously valued free enterprise and competition. Go to a typical supermarket and you'll find many, many options within most categories of product. But in politics, we accept it as normal that there are only two real choices — unless you want to "throw away" your vote by casting it for a minor party. Many of us tend to think that we've always had the two-party system we have today, even if the two haven't always been the same. And although we'd like to have more parties, we often think there's no practical way we can get there — that it would require a constitutional amendment, or so many reforms to the law that it stands no chance of getting done.

These viewpoints are largely based on lack of information — about our history, our Constitution, and most importantly about how our choice of voting methods has a major influence on the character of the party system. This book is intended to supply some of this missing info.

I decided to write this book for a few reasons. The first is because I care about the dire state of American politics, and I want it to do better. I think it has the potential to do *a lot* better, and fulfilling this potential would make a big difference in people's lives. There are big problems in the world that our political systems should be dealing with, yet are mostly failing to. And the problems are set to get bigger — problems like climate change, pollution, healthcare, the automation of jobs due to artificial intelligence, and other challenges brought on by advancing technology, including genetic engineering, bio-hacking, and much more. These issues require government involvement, and managing them in the interests of the public requires a healthier, more functional system of politics than what we've been seeing in recent decades.

I'm not going to be making a partisan argument in this book. I do have opinions on political matters, but the point of this book is not to push them on others. I just want us to be able to debate them honestly. I want a real, vital, engaged system of politics, where voices are heard and the interests of the people are taken seriously by elected leaders.

I've been thinking about the two-party system for a long time. I cast a third-party vote in several presidential elections, beginning with the second one I voted in, the election of 1992. I have always appreciated having choices. I've intuitively understood that without choices, accountability is much harder to achieve. Just as a company with monopoly power can afford to be unresponsive to the demands of its customers, parties in a duopolistic system have an easier time avoiding accountability. Duopoly is better than monopoly, it's true — but not by that much — or, at least, not by *enough*. (And in fact, many of our electoral districts are so lopsided for one party or the other that they are essentially "captured" by that party — a local monopoly.)

So many times, as I've watched the political news, I've wondered how things would be different if we had a multiparty system instead of our two-party duopoly. When a party forces the government to shut down, for example — as has become almost commonplace in the United States over the last few decades — how might that process unfold differently if we had more than two parties in government? When a president deserves to be investigated and possibly impeached, and the opposing party leadership decides against pursuing it for political reasons, how is that connected to our party system, and how might it work differently in a different system? Time and time again, when I asked myself such questions, and played out the scenario in my mind, the exercise suggested that we'd be a lot better off with a multiparty system.

So that's the second reason I'm writing this book: I think I've had enough insights about the subject matter that I can make a strong argument for a multiparty system, which, if it convinces enough people, would help us to make changes that would significantly improve American politics.

But why should you believe anything I have to say? I am not a degreed professional in political science or government. I have taught myself what I know of it. I am, essentially, an amateur. So, the first answer is, don't take my word for anything. Read skeptically and decide for yourself if my reasoning makes sense. Check my references — I've included enough of them to back up my claims resoundingly. I am writing in a tradition of outsiders tackling subjects that are of public concern, grounded in an Enlightenment ideal that facts and logic are open to anybody to use. Occasionally, such an outsider perspective can be valuable because it is not steeped in the conventions of a given profession. I don't know if that's true of this book, but it could be. Read with an open mind and judge for yourself.

There is, perhaps, an additional reason why my thoughts about our party system could be worth considering — it has to do with my academic and professional background, and my intellectual orientation. I have always been curious about the world, about the place of humans in it, and the values that we hold dear as we try to navigate through it. This has led me to a strong appreciation of both science and philosophy. I was fortunate enough to be raised in a middle-class household with access to good public schools. I excelled in high school academics and won enough in college scholarships that I was able to attend college full-time for eight years (while working part-time). I struggled to pick a major, not wanting to pin myself down; eventually I got a bachelor's degree in studio art, from the University of Texas at Austin. It was an odd choice for someone who had not exhibited any real interest in drawing or painting before college, and in part, it was the product of feeling somewhat directionless at that time in my life. But it was very rewarding intellectually — for it turns out that modern art is, or can be, about manipulating ideas as much as about imagery or media. In studying art, I learned how to think about problem-solving. And not just solving a problem, but *choosing* a problem to solve. Understanding that questions matter as much as answers. I was exposed to interesting theories of art and its functions in society. I learned how to take a concept and *develop* it — extending, enhancing, building, but also refining, whittling, subtracting — and to consider carefully how the artist's expression would be *perceived* by the viewer.

In my last three years of college I earned a second bachelor's degree, this one in computer science. I have worked in the tech industry since then, as a software and website developer. This has given me plenty of exposure to complex systems — which is highly relevant to this book, for our systems of self-government, including the party system, are connected in subtle and complex ways, and structure makes a huge difference.

I think I've always been a kind of "structuralist" — by which I mean someone who sees how systems operate in terms of how they are structured. I understand that making changes to a structure has consequences for how it works, both intended and unintended. How incentives are structured, for example, can have profound effects on human behavior. How we organize elections can have profound effects on the kind of leadership we get from elected leaders. This book is largely about the effects of political structure, and why we should make some structural changes in order to produce a better, more fair and more representative system.

It's basically an *engineering* problem — how to shift from a two-party system to a multiparty one. It has struck me, sometimes, that it's too bad that we don't have academic departments of "political engineering" instead of (or in addition to) "political science". Science is a *descriptive* enterprise — a study of what exists, and the laws and principles it follows. Engineering, on the other hand, is about how to use scientific knowledge to build things. Our systems of representation, of democracy, and of governance are things that we've built, over centuries: They're social and legal constructs. So if we want to improve them, as constructions, we need engineering to do it. Don't get me wrong, science is very important too. We need to have the clear understanding of reality that only a rigorously descriptive project can give us. We need solid, objective political science. But if we are trying to improve our republic, if we want to become the best democratic country we can be, we also need political engineering to get us there.

Get where, though? How do we know which direction we want to move, from the current status quo? This is where the *normative* component comes in, to complement the descriptive. So this is where we need philosophy to help us understand what is best. I see political philosophy as ethics extended to the realm of society and how it is regulated by government. At the highest level, this book is a work of political philosophy. But really it's about engineering, which is based both on science — where are we, and what moves are possible? — and ethics — where should we want to go from here?

So, because I've worked in the field of software engineering, and continually had to understand and manipulate structures of program code, and because I have a solid grounding in the principles of science, and because I also know some things about political philosophy, and because I have experience in analyzing and solving problems creatively, perhaps, for all these reasons, I'm in a good position to explain both how and why we should move beyond the two-party system and adopt multiparty politics.

I have also given a lot of thought to pragmatic issues. My aim, in this book, is to sketch out a plan of action that can actually be carried out. As I'll explain, it does not depend on any amendments to our Constitution. Some simple, statutory changes would be enough to set us on a clear path towards multiparty democracy. The main difficulties lie in convincing elected officials to make the changes. Being well-informed about the comparative advantages of a multiparty versus two-party system is a big part of the battle.

I want to point out that I'm making some basic assumptions in this book. Maybe the biggest and most basic is that we should continue as a democratic country — a *representative* democracy, of course, which is to say a republic: I mean "democracy" in a broad sense. There seem to be some serious thinkers today expressing skepticism that democracy is capable of dealing with the massive challenges we have begun to face as a species — the threat of extinction from climate change, for example. They seem to think that maybe only an authoritarian (or heavily surveillance-oriented) government will be capable of acting quickly and decisively enough to avoid worldwide catastrophe.[1] It's not a happy thought, but maybe they are right. Maybe things really are that grim, and liberal-democratic self-government is too fraught with difficulties to do the job. And maybe the good things about authoritarianism outweigh the well-known bad things — the risk of tyranny, for example.

---

[1] E.g. Bostrom 2018.

I don't know. I'm doubtful of this logic, because we've seen that authoritarian government almost always leads to tyranny. Some dictators may be benevolent, but others are anything but. And it's not easy to know which is which until it's too late. It's also not easy to restore democratic government after a benevolent dictatorship has outlived its usefulness. I don't think we're at the end of the era of democracy. I think it can work well, and does work in some countries a lot better than it is currently working in the U.S. But I could be wrong. Anyway, in this book I take for granted that we'll continue in the paradigm of representative democracy. (Even if we don't, an improved party system could conceivably be very useful, in whatever new system we adopt.)

Outlining the argument

So, how can we have a multiparty system in the United States? The main thing is to change how we vote. As I describe in chapter 1, we should elect congressional representatives from multi-member districts, using proportional representation. In this country, most elections are decided either by a plurality of votes (i.e. whoever has the most, even if less than a majority), or by a two-round voting system. We could be doing a lot better than these voting methods. As we'll see, there are many ways to vote — such as ranked-choice voting, in which voters list their choices in order of preference. And the selection of voting method has a big influence on the type of party system a country has. Proportional representation tends to lead to a multiparty system.

Chapter 1, on its own, specifies the structural changes needed to bring about a multiparty system. But we cannot make those changes if we, as a people, are not convinced that we should make them. So understanding *why* we should have a multiparty system is an essential piece of how we'll be able to get there. This begins with an understanding of why parties are important in democratic countries — and that's the main subject of chapter 2, where I explore elements of democratic theory, and draw some comparisons between our exceptional party system and those found in other parts of the world.

In chapters 3 and 4, I tear into the two-party system, pointing out just how bad it is — how high the price we're paying, in terms of good governance. This is a crucial part of the argument that we'd be better off ditching the duopoly. It includes some thoughts about what our Founders expected when they wrote the Constitution: As many people know, they were not big fans of political parties, and hoped that we could be governed without them. They were mistaken about that, for parties are essential to the healthy operation of any representative democracy. But if they had known that we'd have political parties, would they have wanted a two-party system, or a multiparty one? I think they would have preferred the latter, and I will make the case for that view.

In chapter 5, I consider some of the major objections people have to a multiparty system in the United States, and how to convince elected leaders, activists, and others that we should make the shift. Chapter 6 extends this discussion, explaining how to answer misconceptions about alternative voting methods and proportional representation. Finally, in chapter 7 I summarize the argument of the book.

I hope all concerned Americans, and interested citizens of other nations, will find something of value in this book, especially activists, for whom it may be a useful resource. For those who are unconvinced of the need to change to a multiparty system, I hope to convince you — and if I don't manage to do so, I hope at least you'll have found some interesting insights along the way.

1. A Path to Multiparty Democracy
or How, Part 1: The Mechanics

"A long habit of not thinking a thing wrong, *gives it a superficial appearance of being* right.*" — Thomas Paine*

Many Americans are thoroughly disillusioned and appalled by the political dysfunction in Washington, D.C., and in our state capitals. But we don't agree on how to fix things. Is the answer to institute term limits for all public offices? Use the internet to let the people vote directly on policy proposals? Get big money out of politics?

In this book, I argue that the two-party system — the electoral duopoly by which the two main political parties maintain a stranglehold on electoral competition — is to blame for much of the overall system's dysfunction. The key to more accountability and better representation is to give people more choices, and clearer ones. As in an economic marketplace, competition in the political "marketplace" of ideas helps keep the competing organizations more responsive and accountable to voters. The people are empowered by a greater range of choice — more of them engaged in the political process since more will be able to find a party they actually like, rather than having to choose "the lesser of two evils". When we are able to more clearly express ourselves in the electoral process, we'll get more of what we want and less of what we don't.

Unfortunately, many people take the two-party system for granted — as if it's a necessary part of American political practice. It isn't — in fact, the Constitution doesn't mention political parties at all, and our party system hasn't always been as exclusive as it is today. It's time to broaden our horizons, to consider solutions we might not have considered before, to deal with the deep problems we face.

The measures we need for the switch to a multiparty system are fairly straightforward, and mostly statutory, not constitutional. But we'll never get them done unless we find the political will to do so — unless millions of us recognize the failure of the two-party system, and how more parties would help. We need to understand both *why* we should change our party system and *how* we can do it.

Explaining why will take some time, as there are a lot of strands to pull together. So I'm going to begin by explaining how, because a specific program of structural changes can be outlined concisely, and doing so will give us a concrete benchmark to keep in mind when we get to the details of why. While it's crucial to point out problems with the current system, it's not sufficient — we also need a better alternative, and this chapter will explain what it could look like. I'm pointing out the path before explaining why we should follow it.

To understand how we can move beyond the two-party system, we first need to understand what supports it. What blocks new parties from becoming serious players in the political game? Once we know the answer to this question, we'll be able to dismantle the obstacles and create the conditions necessary for a multiparty system.

A key influence on the shape of any party system is the method of voting — that is, the *electoral system*. There are many different methods of choosing leaders, and their details can make a big difference. So that's the main focus of this chapter.

The spoiler effect

Perhaps the biggest impediment to third parties in our system is the *spoiler effect* — the fact that by drawing votes away from a major-party contender, a third-party or independent candidate can help the other side, resulting in a worse outcome from his perspective than if he had not run for office. A classic example of this potential comes from the presidential election of 2000: the case of Ralph Nader.

Nader was born in 1934 to Lebanese immigrants; he grew up in Connecticut, attended Princeton and Harvard, and began practicing law in 1959. In 1965, he published a famous exposé of the American auto industry, *Unsafe at Any Speed*, which became a best seller and helped make him a household name by the 1970s, as a consumer advocate. He founded several nonprofit advocacy groups, including Public Citizen and the Public Interest Research Group. He played a leading role in the passage of major legislation such as the Clean Air Act, the Clean Water Act, and the Freedom of Information Act. He helped end smoking on airliners.

By the 1990s, Nader was a hero to many on the left. In 1996, he ran for president with the support of the Green Party, getting on the ballot in 22 states, including the District of Columbia. He won nearly 700,000 votes — 0.71 percent of the popular vote.

In 2000, he ran again, this time getting on the ballot in 44 states. In the crucial swing state of Florida, he got 97,488 votes, or 1.63 percent, compared with 48.85 percent for George W. Bush, 48.84 percent for Al Gore, and 0.29 percent for Pat Buchanan. About 0.39 percent went to an assortment of other minor candidates.

If Nader's votes had all gone to Gore instead, Gore would've had more votes than Bush and won Florida and the presidency. So, it seems that Nader's presence on the ballot spoiled what would otherwise have been a victory for Gore, which for most Nader voters would have been preferable to Bush winning. He didn't do it intentionally.[2] And we can't be absolutely certain that he actually did it. Maybe his voters would have stayed home, had he not been a candidate. Maybe some of them would have voted for Buchanan, or another minor-party candidate, rather than voting for Gore. But the consensus among political scientists seems to be that he was one of several factors that cost Gore the win.[3]

Regardless, the episode serves as a good illustration of the spoiler effect. Whether or not Nader truly spoiled the election for Gore, many people believe that he did — so many, in fact, that the spoiler effect has also been described as the "Nader effect".[4] Crucially, this belief itself leads to changes in voting behavior.

When people believe that voting their honest preference may result in victory for a candidate they don't like, it steers them away from that choice towards one with a better chance of winning. No doubt

---

[2] See Burden 2005.

[3] See, for example, Scher 2016.

[4] Resnick 2016.

some Nader voters regretted their decision when they saw how close Gore came to defeating Bush in Florida. And no doubt some of them decided that they'd vote Democratic in the future. That's the spoiler effect at work — sharply limiting the possibility of small or new parties gaining a foothold in the electorate. The threat of a minor-party candidate spoiling an election crops up often enough that many voters are wary of the danger, and refuse even to consider options other than those most likely to win. The media likewise give second-tier candidates very little consideration.

But what gives rise to the spoiler effect in the first place? The answer is that our voting method allows a winner to be declared without requiring a majority. After all, if one candidate has more than 50 percent of all the votes, then it doesn't matter if the third-place finisher's votes had gone instead to the second-place finisher; the winner would be the same.

There's a very simple way to ensure that the winner of an election has a majority of the votes: hold a runoff. Or, better yet, a series of runoffs: At every round, if no candidate has a majority, eliminate the last-place finisher, then vote again. Continue in the same way until somebody has a majority. Such a series of runoffs, dropping only one candidate off the ballot at a time, is called the *exhaustive* ballot. It has long been used in group-level settings. The Republican National Committee, in choosing its chairman, uses a similar system of repeated ballots, where no candidate need drop out between rounds.[5] The show *American Idol* apparently uses a system like exhaustive voting.

Deciding elections by plurality vote (that is, not requiring an absolute majority) opens the door to the spoiler effect. As long as there are only two choices, there's no problem; but the minute a third party comes along, the spoiler effect is ready to wreak havoc. Plurality voting is one of the most important problems to be dealt with in moving to a multiparty system.

The exhaustive ballot works great on a small scale, say at a meeting, but on a large scale is far less practical. It's expensive for governments

---

[5] FairVote 2009.

to hold elections. To ask voters to return to the polls at each of an unknown number of voting rounds would make the price exorbitant.

Two-round runoff voting

Runoff elections are common in the United States, but are typically only two rounds — every candidate other than the top two is dropped after the first round. This format is much better than plurality voting in terms of the spoiler effect, but not as good as exhaustive balloting. It greatly reduces the chances for minor-party candidates to play a spoiler role, but doesn't eliminate them.

Why? Because the danger of "spoiling" moves to the first round: one minor party can spoil another's chances to make it to the second round, in a way that doesn't happen under exhaustive voting. Consider the example of the 2002 French presidential election, which is held in two rounds. Sixteen parties fielded a presidential candidate that year. The most prominent leftist party was the Socialists, led by Lionel Jospin. On the center-right was the RPR (Rally for the Republic), led by Jacques Chirac. On the far right was National Front candidate Jean-Marie Le Pen, long a force in French politics but never a leading contender for the presidency.

Despite the fragmentation, most knowledgeable observers expected Jospin to face Chirac in the second round. They were wrong. In the first round, Chirac won 19.9 percent, Jospin 16.2 percent, and Le Pen 16.9 percent, enough for second place. This result sent shock waves through France, which had never before seen a far-right candidate come so close to being elected president. In the second round the nation rallied around Chirac, who defeated Le Pen by a whopping margin, 82.2 percent to 17.8. In other words, it was no contest — meaning that the most consequential piece of the decision was made at the first round, where the spoiler effect was huge.

Had the French used exhaustive balloting instead of limiting the vote to two rounds, Jospin almost certainly would've made it to the final round to face off against Chirac. The early rounds would've seen some marginal leftist candidates eliminated, whose votes would then have gone to Jospin. Would the country then have elected a different president? It's quite possible. Thanks to the spoiler effect, and the voting method used, we'll never know.

This episode illustrates the limits of the two-round election format in dealing with the spoiler effect when there are many candidates competing. Had there been only three candidates, Jospin, Chirac and Le Pen, the spoiler effect would not have been a factor. Had there been four, five, or six candidates, it's quite possible that Jospin would still have had enough strength to fend off Le Pen and reach the second round. But with sixteen candidates, it was too much.

Another example of the problem is the 1961 special Senate election in Texas to fill the former seat of Lyndon B. Johnson, who had been elected vice president. Of 71 candidates, six were considered serious — five Democrats, including incumbent William Blakley, who had been appointed to the seat by the governor, and one Republican, John Tower, who had just lost the contest for the same seat to LBJ the previous fall. In the first round, Tower came first with 30.9 percent of the vote; Blakley placed second with 18.0 percent. In the second round, Tower won a narrow victory of 50.6 to 49.4 percent, becoming the first Republican senator from Texas since the Reconstruction era.[6] With so much division among the Democrats, it seems likely that if there had been more rounds, one of their number would've been elected — maybe future Speaker of the House Jim Wright, who had come third in the first round and who had "the private backing of both Lyndon Johnson and Sam Rayburn".[7]

There seems to be a pattern in how the spoiler effect arises in different election methods. With plurality voting, i.e. a single round, the spoiler effect is potentially an issue whenever there are more than two candidates. In a two-round election, the spoiler effect can only be an issue when there are more than three candidates. Extending this logic would suggest that an N-round election is safe from the spoiler effect for up to $N+1$ candidates. While I can't prove this is true, I believe it is, at least for the main cause of "spoilage". But as we'll see

---

[6] "Senatorial Elections ..."
[7] "Senate, Everyone?"

later, adding rounds may not be enough to eliminate all possible spoiler-like effects.

Instant-runoff voting

This brings us to an innovation in voting methods: What if we could *simulate* the exhaustive ballot by asking voters to specify their preferences in advance? If they could somehow indicate how they would vote under exhaustive balloting, then we could use that information to arrive at the same result. This is the idea of instant-runoff voting (IRV), also known as the alternative vote, or as (single-winner) ranked-choice voting. It was invented by an American architect, William Robert Ware, in 1871, but first used for elections in Australia in the early 20th century.[8]

Under IRV, a voter ranks her choices from first to last on her ballot. Typically, it's optional to name second or third choices or beyond, so a voter who only knows who her favorite is, and knows little about the comparative strengths of other candidates, can simply vote for that one. In the first round of counting, voters' top choices are tallied. If any candidate wins a majority of votes, he wins the election. Otherwise, the last-place finisher is eliminated, and ballots that were counted for him are updated to go to the next preference. (At all times, a ballot's full vote goes to its topmost uneliminated candidate.) Votes are then re-tallied. Rounds continue in this way until one candidate has a majority of votes.

Let's consider an example, with four candidates, Smith, Jones, Kim, and Turner, and nine voters, whose ballots are as shown:

---

[8] Reilly 2004.

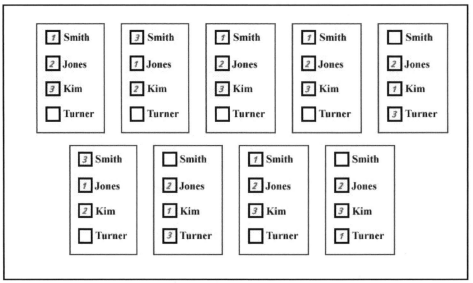

Figure 1.1. Example of IRV ballots in a four-way race

This set of ballots can also be represented as follows:
- 4 ballots: Smith > Jones > Kim
- 2 ballots: Jones > Kim > Smith
- 2 ballots: Kim > Jones > Turner
- 1 ballot: Turner > Jones > Kim

(Note: omitting a preference for one or more candidates, as most of these ballots did for Turner, effectively means the voter ranks those candidates last.)

In the first round, Smith has four votes out of nine. In a plurality election, he would win. But since five votes are needed for a majority, we must eliminate the candidate with the fewest votes — Turner — transfer his votes according to the preferences of those who voted for him, and count again. Turner got only one vote, and that voter chose Jones as a second preference. So the second-round tally is four votes for Smith, three for Jones, and two for Kim. Still no one has a majority of votes, so we eliminate Kim and transfer her votes according to the preferences of those who voted for her. Both of those voters ranked Jones second; so the third-round tally comes out to four votes for Smith and five for Jones, who is declared the winner.

If this result seems unfair to Smith, who was way ahead in the first round, remember that more voters chose not-Smith than chose him. Smith has only minority support in this electorate, but the opposition is not unified. Under plurality voting, there would have been pressure on Kim and Turner — the two who didn't reach the final round — not to run at all. Or would Jones have felt pressured not to run? Since both Jones and Kim got two votes in the first round, it's not altogether clear who should stand aside. Under IRV there would be no need to solve this coordination problem, and voters would have more choices.

Here's a simple flowchart representing how IRV ballots are counted:

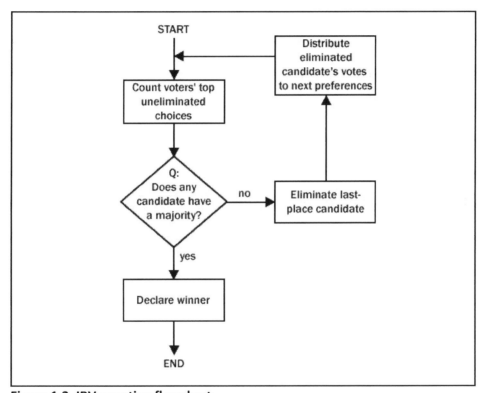

Figure 1.2. IRV counting flowchart

When we don't insist that a candidate have a majority of votes to be elected, it means that he may be opposed by more people than support him. That's hardly fair representation, as our nation's founders understood. In *Federalist* no. 68, Alexander Hamilton wrote:

[A]s a majority of the votes might not always happen to centre in one man, and as it might be **unsafe to permit less than a majority to be conclusive**, it is provided that, in such a contingency, the House of Representatives shall select out of the candidates who shall have the five highest number of votes, the man who in their opinion may be best qualified for the office. [emphasis added]

Leave aside the fact that he is writing about the electoral college, which is a step (or two, at the time) removed from the citizenry. The point here is that Hamilton thought it unwise for an elected official to win election with less than a majority of votes. And he was right. Not only does it mean that the winner is opposed by a majority, it also adds to incentives for politicians to divide the opposition.

Despite this, we often elect someone with much less than a majority. Governors Rick Perry of Texas, Mark Dayton of Minnesota, Lincoln Chafee of Rhode Island, Paul LePage of Maine, and Jesse Ventura of Minnesota were all elected with significantly less than 50 percent. Bill Clinton was elected President in 1992 with only 43.0 percent. Woodrow Wilson won in 1912 with only 41.8 percent. This is merely a sample; the full list is very long. According to the electoral reform group FairVote, 28 percent of the 39 governors elected in 2010 or 2011 won without a majority of votes.[9]

Duverger's law

The logic of the spoiler effect described above is well-known in political science as *Duverger's law*, named for Maurice Duverger (pronounced "doo-ver-zhay"), who wrote about this dynamic starting in the early 1950s. (He wasn't the first to notice it, but "he was the first to dare to claim that it was a law"[10]). Essentially, it says two things:

1. A single-member-district, plurality voting system tends to lead to a two-party system, and
2. The two-round majority voting system and proportional representation tend to lead to a multiparty system.

---

[9] Needham 2012.
[10] Riker 1982b.

The first part relates to what I described above as the spoiler effect, and it has been recognized for a long time. The political scientist Arthur Holcombe wrote in 1911 that "The tendency under the system of plurality elections toward the establishment of the two-party system is... almost irresistible". As E.E. Schattschneider wrote in 1942:

> [I]t is clear that the operation of the system [of single-member-district plurality elections] is to exaggerate the victory of the strongest party and to discriminate radically against lesser parties. The system discriminates moderately against the second party but against the third, fourth, and fifth parties the force of this tendency is multiplied to the point of extinguishing their chances of winning seats altogether.[11]

It seems clear enough how this effect works in the U.S. But how do we know that it applies universally? Critics have objected to it on the basis of the examples of Canada and India, both of which have more than two parties even though they use plurality elections. Let's take a quick look at these two cases.

Canadian government is highly decentralized, and regional parties can be very important. For example, the Parti Québécois has been a strong nationalist force in the province of Quebec, and has a strong influence on federal politics through its federal ally, the Bloc Québécois. The New Democratic Party has been, for most of its history, the third or fourth largest party in Canada, with a historic stronghold in the country's west. Both parties have shown their staying power despite plurality elections.

If you think about it, the logic of the spoiler effect really only applies to one jurisdiction at a time. It pressures voters in that electoral district to choose from between the two leading contenders there. But couldn't one district be between party A and party B, while another is between parties C and D? That is, why should the top two parties in one area be the same as the top two in another? The answer is that they don't have to be; there is only a tendency in that direction. This explains the apparent exception of Canada, where parties can be

---

[11] Schattschneider 1942, p. 75.

"the main parties in some provinces while they are third parties nationally".[12]

In India, at least for the first few decades after independence, many minor parties coexisted along with one dominant party, Congress (full name Indian National Congress). Riker proposes that the reason the Indian party system has not had to consolidate further is that Congress, occupying the center of the political spectrum, has usually been the second choice of voters both on the right and the left — thus it has probably been a *Condorcet winner* most of the time. (A Condorcet winner is, roughly, a consensus candidate. I'll explain the concept later in this chapter.) This fact seems to have reduced the incentives for minor parties to consolidate against the Congress Party. (Note: In more recent times, the Indian party system has become more varied.)

Taking these and other exceptional cases into account, Riker arrives at a revised form of Duverger's first proposition which, he says, holds true universally:

> Plurality election rules bring about and maintain two-party competition except in countries where (1) third parties nationally are continually one of two parties locally, and (2) one party among several is almost always the Condorcet winner in elections.[13]

(Note: Three and a half decades after Riker's paper, we may wonder whether Britain should be viewed as another exception. The country uses plurality rules [known there as "first past the post"] and single-member districts, yet in the 56th Parliament [2015-2017] no fewer than eleven parties had seats. Some of these, including the Scottish National Party with the third highest number of seats, are regional parties, which the revised Duverger's law accounts for. Others, such as the Greens, have a very small number of seats. But one party has convincingly defied Duverger's law — the Liberal Democrats, who won 62 seats in the 2005 elections and in 2010, with almost as many seats, were able to force the Tories into a coalition government. They

---

[12] Riker 1982b, p. 760.
[13] Riker 1982b.

are not a regional party. How can their strength be explained? The answer is that Duverger's law is only a *tendency* acting over a period of several election cycles. It acts like a headwind against parties like the Lib Dems; at times, sociopolitical forces may be enough to neutralize it, but eventually, if the party fails to displace one of the top two, its power is suppressed. Subsequent elections in which the Lib Dems were greatly reduced in number — eight seats in 2015, twelve in 2017 — seem to support this theory.)

Let's move on to Duverger's second proposition: "The double ballot majority system and proportional representation tend to multipartism".[14] When we speak of plurality elections, we're talking about electing one person to office. So we are speaking of single-member districts. That's also true when we're talking about the "double ballot majority system", which is the system used in France — i.e. the two-round runoff system. As discussed above, such a system is perfectly compatible with three major parties, and might be friendly enough to four or five, though not to sixteen. But saying that two-round voting systems tend to multipartism is not a very big claim if "multi" can mean as few as three.

Where things really get interesting is where Duverger's second proposition mentions proportional representation. Here, we move from single-member districts — filling one seat for each election — to filling several seats at once in the same election.

Multi-member districts and proportional representation

Proportional representation (PR) is a term that describes any electoral system of representation designed to make sure that various parts of an electorate are represented in proportion to their strength. For example, if 18 percent of people belong to a certain political grouping, and they all identify closely with it and would prefer to vote accordingly, then a proportional system would give about 18 percent of the seats in an elected body to representatives of that group.

There's no way to achieve this goal in a single-member district, because one person cannot be divided into parts. When a diverse

---

[14] Duverger 1954, translation by Sartori [1997, p. 29].

electorate has to choose just one person to represent them, they inevitably stand for the preferences of one part over others; they cannot effectively represent conflicting interests. Diversity is suppressed, or filtered out of the system. The majority — or, worse, merely a plurality — gets all of the representation.

So, what electoral method can be used to achieve proportional representation? Imagine an election in which eight parties are competing to fill 50 seats in a legislature. Each party has a stable of candidates ready to serve as elected representatives. At the election, 38 percent of voters choose the leading party, 22 percent choose the second party, 18 percent the third, 15 percent the fourth, and 7 percent choose one of the other parties. The voters make this choice just once — the 50 seats will be filled proportionally based on this one vote, not by means of a separate election for each seat.

Most PR systems have some sort of minimum threshold: Let's imagine that in this election a party needs at least 5 percent of the vote to get any seats. Since the last 7 percent of the vote was split among the smallest parties, let's assume that none of them reached this threshold, so the seats will be split among the top four parties. (Yes, this is a reduction of diversity and of proportionality, but it's reasonable to have a threshold like this, and it's still fair to call it proportional representation as long as the threshold isn't too high.)

Since the top four parties only account for 93 percent of the vote, we can't simply multiply the seats available by the vote share of each party to figure out how many seats each party should get. Instead, there are various methods of figuring this out. One of them is the D'Hondt method, named for a Belgian mathematician, Victor D'Hondt, who described it in 1878. The method involves computing a set of numbers for each party that represents the number of votes it received divided by 1, then by 2, by 3, by 4, etc. up to the number of seats being decided in the election — in the above example, 50. Then, looking at all the numbers thus generated for all the parties that meet the threshold, we identify the 50 biggest numbers by party and allocate each party one seat per "big number".

To make this process clearer, let's take a simpler example: a contest among three parties, to fill six seats, with 10,000 votes cast. Let's say

Party A gets 4,000 votes, Party B gets 3,800, and Party C gets 2,200. As shown in the following table, these numbers are divided by 1, then by 2, then by 3, and so on up to 6. From all these quotients, we choose the top six, since that's the number of seats we're filling — those numbers are shown in bold. And each party gets as many seats as it has boldface numbers. Since Party A has three of the top six quotients, it gets three seats; likewise Party B gets two and Party C, one.

Party	Votes/1	Votes/2	Votes/3	Votes/4	Votes/5	Votes/6	Seats won
Party A	**4,000**	**2,000**	**1,333**	1,000	800	666	3
Party B	**3,800**	**1,900**	1,266	950	760	633	2
Party C	**2,200**	1,100	733	550	440	366	1

Table 1.1. Example of seat allocation using the D'Hondt method

Incidentally, the D'Hondt method is mathematically equivalent to one described by Thomas Jefferson in 1792 to allocate seats in the House of Representatives among the various states.

So that explains how the votes in a PR election are translated into seats for the various parties involved. But I haven't explained how individual persons are selected to actually sit in them. That depends on the details of the system.

Types of proportional representation

In the type of PR I've been describing, known as *party-list* PR, there are two main versions. In "closed list" PR, the parties preselect their candidates and put them in order; if they win N seats, then the first N candidates on the party list are seated. The voters have no say over who the candidates are, only which parties win seats.

In "open list" PR, the voters are given some say in who is selected from the parties. By indicating a preference for one or more candidates over others, voters can essentially move some of them ahead of their colleagues in the party list.

Party-list PR is the "classic" version of proportional representation, the one that most students of political science think of first. It is the most commonly used type of PR for national legislative seats. Most European and Latin American countries use it.

Another version of PR is known as the *single transferable vote*, or STV for short. First invented in 1819, and first used in Denmark in 1855, it's actually older than party-list PR. But since it's a ranked-choice method like instant-runoff voting, its mechanism is arguably more complicated.

STV ballots are essentially the same as IRV ballots, with candidate choices ranked from most preferred to least. As in IRV, vote tallying proceeds round by round, and each voter's vote goes to a single candidate in each round. A *quota* is calculated for the election, representing the number of votes a candidate needs to win a seat. When, in a given round, no candidate meets this quota, one of them is eliminated. As in IRV, the votes given to that candidate transfer to the next candidate on those voters' ballots.

Unlike in IRV, a candidate's votes may transfer to another candidate not only when he is eliminated, but also when he wins a seat with a *surplus* of votes — that is, more than the quota. So, if your first choice easily wins a seat, your second choice also is considered, and so on if she wins with a surplus. Tallying and transferring votes continues round by round until all the seats are filled.

Let's consider an example to make the process clearer. (The following is taken from a pamphlet by the U.K.-based Electoral Reform Society, "What Is STV?".)

Suppose there are nine candidates running to fill five seats, and there are 647 valid votes. The *Droop quota* — the most common way to compute the quota — is the number of votes divided by one more than the number of seats, rounded down, plus one. 647 divided by six is 107.83; dropping the fraction and adding one, we get 108. The rounds proceed as follows:

Cand.	1st stage	2nd stage	3rd stage	4th stage	5th stage	6th stage
	Votes	Transfer of Evans's surplus	Exclusion of Pearson	Exclusion of Lennon	Transfer of Stewart's surplus	Exclusion of Wilcox
Evans	**144**	**108**	**108**	**108**	**108**	**108**
Augustine	95	95	96	96	96	**128**
Harley	91	92	93	93	94	**109**
Stewart	66	68	69	**115**	**108**	**108**
Wilcox	60	60	60	60	60	-
Lennon	58	58	58	-	-	-
Cohen	55	64	69	71	73	74
Vine	48	68	91	97	101	**108**
Pearson	30	34	-	-	-	-
Non-transferable			3	7	7	12
Total	647	647	647	647	647	647

Table 1.2. Example of STV election to fill five seats

In the first stage, Evans wins more than the quota and is elected. Her surplus of 36 votes transfers to her voters' second choices, in proportion to how often they were named. Of the 144 voters who picked Evans as first choice, 80 chose Vine as their second choice; since the surplus of 36 is one-quarter of 144, we give 20 (one-quarter of 80) of this surplus to Vine. And likewise for the other candidates named second by Evans voters. This gives us the vote tallies for the second stage. Still only one candidate has met the quota.

In the third stage, since no one new has met the quota and there is no surplus to redistribute, we eliminate the candidate with the smallest number of votes — Pearson. She has 34 votes, 30 of which were first-preference votes and the other four of which were transferred from Evans. These 34 transfer to the next uneliminated candidate on those voters' lists. In three cases, the ballots did not specify a next choice — meaning essentially that those voters don't have a preference among the remaining candidates. Those three ballots are considered *exhausted*, and show up as "non-transferable".

Pearson's elimination and the transfer of her votes don't give any candidate a quota, so we still have awarded only one seat out of the five. So in the fourth stage, we again eliminate the candidate with the least votes — which is now Lennon. Her votes transfer to other candidates, except for four which become exhausted; this gives Stewart enough to meet the quota and be elected with a surplus of 7 votes.

These surplus votes are transferred in the 5th stage to other candidates, just as Evans's surplus was earlier. This is too few to put any other candidate over the top, so we then eliminate the last-place candidate (Wilcox), in the 6th stage, redistributing her votes to the next candidates on those ballots. This gives Augustine, Harley, and Vine enough votes to meet the quota. We have now filled all five of the seats up for grabs, and the election is over.

By transferring surplus votes as well as those from eliminated candidates, STV avoids wasting votes on those who already have enough to win as well as those who cannot win. It allows voters to select candidates individually instead of just a party — something many people appreciate (especially Americans, who are used to it). For these and other reasons, it's used fairly widely: Ireland, Northern Ireland, India, Pakistan, and Australia all use it on a national level. In the U.S., it has been used for many years to elect the city council in Cambridge, Massachusetts, and is used in several other local jurisdictions. New York City used it from 1937 to 1945.[15] Scotland and New Zealand also use it on a regional or local level.

In almost every country that uses proportional representation on a national or federal level, there are more than two viable parties. (The exception is Malta, which is basically a city-state with around half a million people.) The main reason is that PR does not obstruct the participation of more parties, as a system of single-member districts with plurality voting does.

Parties naturally come into existence to cater to the shifting demands of the electorate — and of non-voters who might be convinced to join the electorate. Parties are vehicles of representation.

---

[15] Rosa-Clot 2007.

And proportionality of representation is a highly desirable thing. As John Adams wrote in 1776:

> The principal difficulty lies, and the greatest care should be employed in constituting this Representative Assembly. It should be in miniature, an exact portrait of the people at large. It should think, feel, reason, and act like them. That it may be the interest of this Assembly to do strict justice at all times, it should be an equal representation, or in other words equal interest among the people should have equal interest in it.[16]

In a proportional system, minority interests of all kinds — racial, ethnic, political, religious — are taken into account, in a more accurate "portrait" of the people. It's noteworthy that Adams connects this simple principle to the interests of "strict justice". In a system of representative democracy, where decisions are made for the people by a few selected individuals, how can there be justice if the selection does not accurately (i.e. proportionally) represent the people?

To achieve proportionality, there's no better way than electing representatives in multi-member districts. (Eliminating districts altogether would allow for the highest degree of proportionality, but the United States is unlikely to go that far, and considering the size of the country, it might be too far anyway.) The question is, how many representatives should districts elect? For instance, Texas currently sends 36 elected reps to the House of Representatives. Instead of electing each of these from a single-member district, should it elect all of them from one statewide district? Or twelve from each of three districts? Or maybe four reps from each of nine districts?

The number of reps elected by a district is known as the *district magnitude*. The higher the magnitude, the less the system restricts the number of parties. So this is an important parameter for tuning the system. Say we adopted a high district magnitude like twelve, and subsequently 33 parties took seats in Congress, and it was a disaster. That could happen — there is a balance to be found between too few parties and too many. The answer, in that case, might well be to reduce the district magnitude.

---

[16] Adams 1776.

Of course, not every state has to use the same magnitude. In fact, even within one state there may be different-sized districts: Imagine a state with ten reps, in which 60 percent of the population lives in one section and the other 40 percent live in another — it might very reasonably have two districts, one with six reps and the other with four. Every state with more than one representative can decide on its own district magnitude. Personally, I think five seems about right — big enough to be a major reduction of impediments against small parties, but not so big as to encourage an over-proliferation of parties.

The history of multi-member districts in the United States

As it turns out, multi-member districts were used for many years, in many jurisdictions, in the U.S. Until 1842, when Congress mandated that states use single-member districts, they were actually quite common, as figure 1.3 (below) shows.

As you can see in this chart, districts electing up to thirteen members have existed in our past. For example, in the Third Congress of 1793-1795, Pennsylvania elected all of its thirteen Representatives at large. (To view an interactive version of this chart [and the next one] with more information, see Eckam 2016a.)

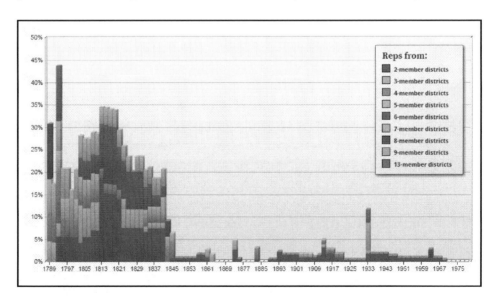

Figure 1.3. Representatives from multi-member districts in the U.S. House, 1789-1981, % of total (Full-color version: daneckam.com/book/btp/figures.)

This brings us to an important issue: *at-large* elections. This term is used in a variety of ways; the essence is that an official elected "at large" represents an undivided whole — that is, not from a district which is only part of the whole. For instance, in the 53rd Congress of 1891-1893, Pennsylvania sent 30 representatives to Washington, D.C. Twenty-eight of them were elected from single-member districts. The other two were elected statewide — these were at-large representatives.[17] So, a citizen of Pennsylvania at the time was a constituent for three reps: one from his local district and two representing everyone in the state.

In at-large by place, candidates run for a labeled seat — for example, "seat 1", "seat 2", and so on, or "place 1", "place 2", and so on. They do not compete against each other; rather, each seat is filled in a separate contest. So although we're not talking about a single-member district, we are talking about something with a very similar problem, that an electorate is choosing one person to represent it for each seat.

In another type of at-large voting, each voter is given a number of votes equal to the number of seats to be filled (let's call it M). There is just one race, with all candidates competing against each other. The winners are the top M vote-getters. In this system, sometimes called *block voting*, a majority party can run a slate of candidates and win all of the seats.

Some writers suggest further refinements in using the term "at large". The political geographer Kenneth C. Martis, in his extraordinary 1982 atlas, draws a distinction between states which had districts, but also elected one or more officials statewide, and states which elected their entire Congressional delegations statewide — that is, had no districts. Only in the former case does he apply the term "at large". The latter case he calls the "general ticket".

Others include proportional representation within the broad category of "at large" elections, especially when there are no districts.

---

17 Martis 1982, p. 5.

And sometimes, the term "at large" is applied to a single-member district, as in states with just one congressional representative, such as Wyoming or Alaska. I primarily use the term to describe multi-member elections that are *not* proportional, and are either run separately for each seat (i.e. by place) or block-voting style. Such elections are still very common in the U.S. for things like city councils, school boards, state judges (in those states that elect their judges), and so on.

Understood in this way, at-large elections are one of the *worst* ways to choose a body of representatives. They are prone to the spoiler effect, unless they are run using the exhaustive ballot or instant-runoff voting (seat by seat) — and as far as I know, none are. Even if an at-large election were conducted with IRV, the outcome would reflect the interests of the majority and give little or no representation to political minorities. And this problem is compounded by the fact that the same electorate is also voting in parallel separate elections. When two seats of a representative body are elected at-large, the majority tends to be overrepresented twice. When three seats are so elected, they tend to be overrepresented three times. And so on: The first overrepresentation comes with the majority getting 100 percent of the first seat; each additional seat they win adds to that. At-large representation is anathema to the principle of proportionality.

In the chart above, we see a drastic decline in multi-member districts in the 1840s, following the 1842 congressional mandate to use only single-member districts. But they don't disappear completely — why not? Martis[18] explains that in many of these cases, either a new state had joined the union, or a state's number of representatives changed after a census and the state legislature either lacked enough time to redistrict or could not agree on a new redistricting plan. In the immediate aftermath of the mandate, four states — New Hampshire, Georgia, Mississippi, and Missouri — simply dragged their feet on switching, amid questions about the law's constitutionality.[19] In 1932, the Supreme Court ruled in *Wood v. Broom* that, because the

---

[18] Martis 1982, pp. 4-5.
[19] Flores 1999, chapter 3.

Reapportionment Act of 1929 had not mentioned single-member districts, they were no longer required.

In 1967, Congress passed another mandate for single-member districts. The last representatives to be elected from a multi-member, at-large district were sent by Hawaii to the 91st Congress (1969-1971). This, but nothing beyond the 91st, was allowed by the 1967 act.[20]

State legislatures have also used at-large multi-member districts in many cases. Below is a chart similar to the one above, but for the House of Representatives of my home state of Texas. Notice that while the number of U.S. reps elected from multi-member districts never exceeded 45 percent, in Texas they were at times 100 percent of the total.

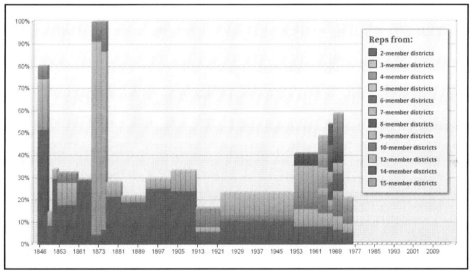

Figure 1.4. Representatives from multi-member districts in the Texas House, 1846-2015, % of total (Full-color version: daneckam.com/book/btp/figures.)

Why did Congress pass this 1967 mandate requiring all states to use single-member districts? Probably, for some incumbents, it was a matter of simple self-interest: They didn't want any change in the districts that had landed them in office. But the biggest part of the

---

[20] GPO 1967.

story seems to have been a concern that after the Voting Rights Act of 1965, some states might use at-large elections "to dilute the voting strength of newly-enfranchised blacks in the South".[21] Notably, then, one of the goals was to protect minority representation.

On the surface, this seems to contradict my argument that multi-member districts would actually *improve* representation of minorities, whether ethnic, political or otherwise. Indeed, the Supreme Court, in *Thornburg v. Gingles* (1986), overturned North Carolina's multi-member districts because of their negative impact on racial minorities. As Sandra Day O'Connor wrote, "[T]he at-large or multi-member district has an inherent tendency to submerge the votes of the minority."

The apparent conflict is resolved when we realize that none of these multi-member districts used proportional representation. There's been an unfortunate tendency to conflate multi-member districts with non-proportional at-large voting, because that's the way it's mostly been done in this country. But multi-member districts aren't necessarily at-large, and they're not necessarily disadvantageous to minorities. Used with a proportional electoral system like STV, they *support* minority representation.

The 1967 mandate for single-member districts is clearly a problem. For now, let me just say that it may not be as difficult to solve as it may seem. I'll address the issue further in chapter 5.

How district boundaries are drawn

Districting — the drawing of electoral district boundaries — is a very significant process in our representative democracy. It also happens to be very manipulable. By "cracking" — breaking up the opposition into separate districts — and "packing" — concentrating the opposition into one district to weaken their power in others — a political party that controls the districting process can give itself extra seats beyond its proportional strength in the electorate. Districting is so powerful that it can actually give a majority of seats to a party that runs second-place to another party statewide. And this *gerrymandering*

---

[21] Mast 1995.

— named for Elbridge Gerry, who was governor of Massachusetts from 1810 to 1812, and later served as Vice President under Madison — is by no means rare in the U.S. In a few states, the job of drawing district lines is given to an independent commission, but in most, it's up to the state legislature.

Examples from the 2012 elections will show how badly districting can distort representation. The states shown in the table below all had Republican-dominated legislatures after the success of that party in the 2010 elections — and the party used that power to redistrict to its advantage.

Legislative body or delegation	Popular vote two-party split*	Elected seats split	Δ seat share, vote share (R)
Michigan — state House of Representatives	D: 2.4m (54.0%) R: 2.0m (46.0%)	D: 51 (46.4%) R: 59 (53.6%)	+7.6%
Michigan — U.S. House of Representatives	D: 2.3m (52.7%) R: 2.1m (47.3%)	D: 5 (35.7%) R: 9 (64.3%)	+17.0%
Wisconsin — U.S. House of Representatives	D: 1.4m (50.8%) R: 1.4m (49.2%)	D: 3 (37.5%) R: 5 (62.5%)	+13.3%
Virginia — U.S. House of Representatives	D: 1.8m (49.0%) R: 1.9m (51.0%)	D: 3 (27.3%) R: 8 (72.7%)	+21.7%
Pennsylvania — U.S. House of Representatives	D: 2.8m (50.8%) R: 2.7m (49.2%)	D: 5 (27.8%) R: 13 (72.2%)	+23.0%
Ohio — U.S. House of Representatives	D: 2.4m (47.9%) R: 2.6m (52.1%)	D: 4 (25.0%) R: 12 (75.0%)	+22.9%

Table 1.3. Effects of partisan districting on representation in 2012

* Other parties not included.

Source: Wikipedia, Federal Election Commission, Groeger et al 2012.

As the table shows, in all of these five states in 2012, about half the voters voted Democratic, yet more than half the seats (in some cases, considerably more) were filled by Republicans. That's gerrymandering at work — and it's practiced by both parties. For example, Maryland's 3rd congressional district has gained notoriety as an extremely odd-shaped district designed to help elect Democrats.[22] Ronald Reagan complained about Democratic gerrymandering in the 1980s:

> In 1984, there were 367 congressional races contested by both parties. In the races, Republicans won half a million more votes than the Democrats. But the Democratic Party won 31 more seats. In California, one of the worst cases of gerrymandering in the country, Republicans received a majority of votes in the '84 congressional races, but the Democrats won 60 percent more of the seats. The fact is gerrymandering has become a national scandal. The Democratic-controlled State legislatures have so rigged the electoral process that the will of the people cannot be heard. They vote Republican but elect Democrats.[23]

Single-member districts help make this distortion possible. The idea that one person can accurately represent the interests of a large, diverse community is simply unrealistic. It's similar to the problem with winner-take-all states in presidential elections (of which I'll have more to say later). Single-member districts are winner-take-all on the district level, instead of the state.

Think of it like digital sampling with a rate that's too slow. Compact discs are recorded with a sampling rate of 44.1 KHz — that means each second of audio is divided into 44,100 slices. Each slice consists of a pair (for left and right channels) of 16-bit encodings of the signal. Imagine, though, that each second of signal were compressed into just one sample — i.e. that the sample rate was just once per second, or 1 Hz. The music would be unrecognizable. The granularity of the sampling process would be insufficient for the task of representing the audio signal with any degree of fidelity. Likewise, a single-

---

[22] Johnson 2014.
[23] Reagan 1988.

member district has insufficient granularity to represent the political interests of its residents.

With increased district magnitude comes greater potential for representative fidelity — for a more accurate "portrait of the people", as John Adams put it. I don't think it can ever be an "exact" portrait — the minute we move from direct to representative democracy, we lose some exactness. And if district magnitude is too high, it might overwhelm the system. But clearly, a district magnitude of one won't cut it. We need multi-member districts, along with a proportional voting system like STV, to ensure accurate representation.

There's a vast literature on districting and gerrymandering. It's a tangle of complicated issues, and what makes it so thorny is that competing values are involved. People want their districts to be compact, that is, a more-or-less convex shape that can be easily pictured or described, and they want them to be competitive between parties. They want to keep neighborhoods intact, and to follow natural boundaries. And this is all on top of keeping roughly equal population in each district, of course.

Satisfying all these demands, as well as giving suitable representation to minorities, can be impossible. But when we give up on the assumption of single-member districts, the problem is greatly alleviated. I'll have more to say about how this works in chapter 4. But in short, we took a wrong turn when we collectively opted for single-member districts as the best alternative to at-large districts. They are not. Proportional representation is.

A plethora of voting methods

There's almost no limit, other than our imaginations, to the number of ways to make a collective decision through voting. Many systems have been described, and many have been used. I've already mentioned plurality, two-round runoff, the exhaustive ballot, IRV, party-list PR, STV, and at-large voting (both by-place and block). Let me mention a few more:

The **Borda count** (named for the 18th-century French mathematician Jean-Charles de Borda), uses a ranked ballot, like instant-runoff voting, and is designed for single-winner elections. But instead of proceeding by rounds, it uses a point system to choose the winner. A candidate gets more points for appearing higher on a voter's ballot. The number of points earned, per ballot, for being ranked first is equal to the number of candidates running; for each step lower in rank, the number of points decreases by one. For example, if five candidates are running, the voter's top choice receives five points, the second choice receives four points, and so on, with the fifth-ranked choice (and unranked choices, if any) receiving one point. Points are summed across all ballots, and the winner is the candidate with the most points.

The Borda count works great for a small group of people picking one alternative from a set. For example, say you have a movie night at home with three friends, and you have a list of six movies you could watch. If everyone ranks the options from first to sixth (or maybe just the top three, as that will often be sufficient), it's fairly easy with a pen and paper to compute the winner using the Borda count method.

Cumulative voting is a multi-winner election method similar to block voting in that each voter can cast multiple votes, usually equal to the number of seats being filled. Unlike block voting, it allows voters to concentrate their vote by *plumping* — which means giving more than one vote to the same candidate — or by choosing fewer candidates than allowed, which effectively accomplishes the same thing. Sometimes voters are given a certain number of points to allocate as they wish to whichever candidates they like. This "points method" is essentially a type of cumulative voting.

Under cumulative voting, a politically cohesive minority can plump to achieve greater representation. So it's considered somewhat proportional — certainly better than at-large voting in its typical forms. It has been instituted as a way to address concerns about diluting the votes of racial minorities. For instance, Amarillo, Texas adopted it in 2000 for its school board, to respond to a lawsuit brought by blacks and Latinos under the Voting Rights Act.[24] The state of Illinois used cumulative voting with three-member districts for its

---

[24] ILSR 2008.

House of Representatives for more than a century — from 1870 to 1980.

Range voting, or score voting, is a single-winner method in which voters *rate*, rather than *rank*, their choices, on a prescribed range of say, 0 to 10, or 0 to 100. The voter may rate as many candidates as they like, independently. This is the system used in judging Olympic games (on a scale of 0 to 10) — or at least in some of them, such as diving. The winner is the candidate with the highest average rating.

Imagine a range voting system with a range of 0 to 1, with no fractions — in other words, 0 and 1 are the only two ratings allowed. That's equivalent to marking each candidate "yes" (approve) or "no" (disapprove). This is called **approval voting**. Voters simply put a check-mark (or equivalent) next to the names of every candidate that meets with their approval. The winner is the candidate with the most approvals. It sounds too simple to be an effective voting system, yet advocates tout its desirable features for single-winner elections. It was used in papal conclaves from 1294 to 1621[25] and apparently in Greece from 1864 to 1926.[26] In November 2018, the city of Fargo, North Dakota adopted it for local elections, after a coordinated effort organized by the Center for Election Science.

Mathematical criteria for evaluating voting systems

Which voting method is the best one to use? Unfortunately, there is no simple answer to this question. In addition to measures like proportionality, experts evaluate voting methods on a variety of mathematical "fairness" criteria. Let's take a few moments to understand some of them.

The **majority criterion** (defined for single-winner voting systems) states that whenever there is one candidate who is preferred by more than 50 percent of voters, that candidate must be elected. Any voting system that guarantees this satisfies the criterion. For example, instant-runoff voting does so because if one candidate gets a majority of first-choice votes, he wins in the first round.

---

[25] Colomer and McLean 1998.
[26] Smith 2015.

It may seem strange that any established voting system could fail to satisfy the majority criterion. But both range voting and approval voting do. The issue is that the criterion does not account for the intensity of preferences between candidates. In fact, strictly speaking, the majority criterion is defined only for *ranked* voting methods, not for rating methods such as range and approval. But we can construct an example of approval voting in which the votes reflect an apparent preference for one candidate over another, held by a majority of voters, yet that candidate does not win.

Suppose there's an election with ten voters and three candidates, A, B, and C, where A is preferred by six of the ten voters, but B meets with the approval of nine of them. Six ballots approve both A and B but not C, three ballots approve both B and C but not A, and one ballot approves C and A but not B. To satisfy the majority criterion, the voting method would need to make A the winner. But by the rules of approval voting, B is the winner because she has a total of nine approvals vs. A's seven and C's four.

Is this a defect, then, of approval voting? It depends on your perspective. It can be argued that B should be the winner because she is more of a consensus candidate — more voters approve of her than A, even though she is the first choice of fewer.

The Borda count also fails the majority criterion, because of the weight it gives to second, third, and lower-ranked choices. Consider the following election with ten voters and three candidates, A, B, and C:

Number of voters	Preference ordering	Points for each candidate
6	A>B>C	A: 18, B: 12, C: 6
3	B>C>A	A: 3, B: 9, C: 6
1	C>B>A	A: 1, B: 2, C: 3
Candidate	**Total points**	
A	22	
B	23 (winner)	
C	15	

Table 1.4. Example of the Borda count failing the majority criterion

As you can see, B wins with 23 points, even though 6 of the 10 voters rank A highest. The problem for A is that they are ranked last by everyone who doesn't rank them first, whereas B is at least second-best on every ballot.

Let's consider a few more fairness criteria, beginning with some very basic ones:

Non-dictatorship is fairly obvious: It's the property that no one individual has the power to decide the election on their own. We certainly don't want to use a voting method that fails this one.

Unanimity, or what Kenneth J. Arrow called the Pareto principle (also known as weak Pareto efficiency or Pareto consistency) is that if everyone agrees on one candidate or electoral option over all others — that is, if the choice is unanimous — then the voting system must select that choice. This is clearly another essential property.

Universality (or universal domain) is the principle that all voter preference-orderings are allowed — or as Arrow[27] states it: "All logically possible orderings of the alternative social states are admissible." This one seems very natural and desirable too. Surely we don't want the system to disallow certain combinations of voter preferences, do we?

Actually, it has been shown that if we abandon universality and insist on *single-peaked* preferences, then it becomes possible for a voting method to satisfy other fairness criteria. By "single-peaked" I mean that every voter, positioned somewhere on a left-right axis according to their views, would prefer the candidate closest to the same position on this axis. The voter's position on the left-right axis defines where their "peak" preference is located — and the closer to this position, the more preferred a candidate is. We can think of insisting on single-peaked preferences as a kind of consistency requirement, ruling out certain preference-orderings. For example, imagine a voter who ranks a far-left candidate (e.g. Bernie Sanders) highest, followed by a far-right candidate (e.g. Barry Goldwater), then a moderate (e.g. George H.W. Bush). Such a voter cannot be said to have single-peaked preferences, at least by the standard model of left vs. right.

Nonetheless, it's not very realistic to impose a requirement of single-peaked preferences upon voters — for one thing, we don't want the government deciding what would count as single-peaked. So let's take universality as essential, at least for any voting system we might reasonably wish to adopt.

In 1951, the economist Kenneth J. Arrow published a striking discovery: that no reasonable voting system can satisfy all of the fairness properties that one might reasonably consider essential — a result known as **Arrow's impossibility theorem**. The first edition of Arrow's book, *Social Choice and Individual Values*, contained a flawed proof of the theorem, which he corrected in the second edition, published in 1963. The theorem provoked a huge discussion concerning what it means — including some confusion. As decision

---

[27] Arrow 1963, p. 96.

theorists Georges Bordes and Nicolaus Tideman[28] explain, much of the confusion stems from the fact that Arrow's theorem concerns *social choice functions*, which are similar to, but not exactly the same as, voting methods. I rely on their analysis, and on that of political scientist William H. Riker[29], in the following discussion.

Given a collection of individual voters who each have a preference-ordering over a set of alternatives (i.e. a list of alternatives in order of preference), a *profile* is defined as the set of all voters' preference-orderings. A social choice function takes as input a set of alternatives and a profile, and produces as output a choice from the alternatives. In these terms, Arrow defines **independence of irrelevant alternatives (IIA)** as the following condition:

> Let S be a set of alternatives. Two profiles which have the same ordering of the alternatives in S for every individual determine the same social choice from S.[30]

In the words of Bordes and Tideman, this means that "if the voters' preferences over the potential-but-not-actual candidates change while their preferences over the actual candidates stay the same, then the choice among the actual candidates stays the same." (By "potential-but-not-actual candidates", they mean people who are eligible to run for office but are not running.) They point out that voters only give information about *actual* candidates; they don't specify a complete set of preferences over all conceivable candidates or alternatives. So all "real-world" voting methods satisfy IIA.

Arrow's theorem says that no voting system can satisfy all of these properties at once:

- Non-dictatorship
- Unanimity
- Universality
- Independence of irrelevant alternatives (IIA)
- Choice consistency

---

[28] Bordes and Tideman 1991.
[29] Riker 1982a.
[30] Arrow 2008.

Having explained the first four of these, the only one I haven't explained is **choice consistency**. This says that if a ranked voting method elects candidate A from a set of three choices, A, B, and C, then from the subset of two choices, A and B, it cannot elect B. In other words, excluding a non-winning alternative should not change the outcome.

For example, suppose you're at a restaurant and want to order dessert. The waiter informs you that the two available choices are apple pie and blueberry pie. You order the apple pie. A minute later, the waiter returns and informs you that they also have cherry pie. You tell him, "In that case, I'll have the blueberry." The waiter stoically ignores the inconsistency — if blueberry is your true preference among all three alternatives, then why didn't you select it from the original two?[31] You have failed to exhibit the property of choice consistency.

Instant-runoff voting does not have this property. To see this, consider an election involving two candidates, A and B, with eleven voters who cast the following ballots:

- 6 votes: A>B
- 5 votes: B>A

A wins in the first round with six votes to five.

Now suppose that if another candidate C had been in the race, the ballots would be:

- 2 votes: A>B>C
- 1 vote: A>C>B
- 3 votes: B>A>C
- 1 vote: B>C>A
- 3 votes: C>A>B
- 1 vote: C>B>A

Notice that the relative orderings of A and B have not changed on any ballot. We still have six voters ranking A higher than B, and five ranking B higher than A. In this election, A is eliminated in the first

---

[31] Poundstone 2008, p. 50.

round, with three first-choice votes versus four each for B and C. Two of A's votes transfer to B, so that B wins in the second round with six votes.

C's presence changed the outcome of the election from A to B. This shows that instant-runoff voting fails the criterion of choice consistency.

(Note: There seems to be some confusion about whether this property should be called "independence of irrelevant alternatives", instead of reserving that name for another condition, described above. In this confusing interpretation, C, in the above example, is considered "irrelevant" because it was not chosen in either case. In the pie example, cherry pie is considered irrelevant for the same reason. For more information see Bordes and Tideman 1991.)

Taking non-dictatorship, the Pareto principle, universality, and IIA as essential (and held by all real-world voting systems), Bordes and Tideman conclude that the gist of Arrow's theorem is that no real-world voting system satisfies the condition of choice consistency. So what exactly does this mean? And how concerned should we be about it?

For individuals, it's safe to assume that preferences are *transitive* — if you prefer option A to option B, and you prefer B to C, then you prefer A to C. If you say you actually prefer C to A, we'd wonder how you could possibly think something so nonsensical. However, it is *not* generally true that social orderings — or collective preferences — are transitive. Consider a simple case of three voters and three candidates, A, B, and C, where voter 1 ranks them A>B>C, voter 2 ranks them B>C>A, and voter 3 ranks them C>A>B. Given these preference-orderings, if we look at head-to-head (or pairwise) match-ups between candidates, we can see that two voters (a majority) prefer A to B, two prefer B to C, and two prefer C to A. Thus, the social ordering is not transitive. We say that a *cycle* exists among the options A, B and C.

In fact, it's not even clear that we can speak meaningfully of "collective preferences", except in special cases (if all voters agree that A>B>C, for example). In many cases, cyclical majorities will appear — collectively, A is preferred over B, which is preferred over C, which is preferred over A. So although individuals are generally rational (at least insofar as their preferences are transitive), social or collective rationality appears to be an illusion. This is known as the *Condorcet paradox*, or also sometimes as the *paradox of voting*. And this social irrationality is closely related to the difficulty of a voting system satisfying the condition of choice consistency. This means that all reasonable voting systems are "manipulable through strategic candidacies and similar maneuvers".[32] But, although this is bad news, it's not as bad as it may seem. Tideman explains:

> [T]he role of the Arrow theorem ... is to warn that there is a limit to what can be expected of any voting procedure. If an RBVPR [ranking-based vote-processing rule] is to satisfy the conditions of universal domain, independence of irrelevant alternatives, Pareto consistency, and non-dictatorship (all of which are essential), then choice consistency cannot be achieved. The outcomes chosen from different sets of available options, on the basis of any given RBVPR and given sequence of rankings of all of the options, will not necessarily be consistent with one another. But this should not be surprising. It should be expected that voting will entail making choices over pairs of options on the basis of majority rule. And when there is a cycle, any way of identifying a winning option will be inconsistent with majority rule for some pair.[33]

Considering the case of a voting method's choice changing, from A when choosing between A and B, to B when choosing from A, B, and C, he expands on why violation of choice consistency shouldn't be too surprising:

> With the third option present, more information is generated. To assume that this additional information could not possibly reverse the estimate of which of the first two options was the better of the two would be like assuming in a statistical undertaking that no estimate made on the basis of a given body of data will be inconsistent with an estimate based on an augmentation of the initial data with additional data. When the

---

[32] Bordes and Tideman 1991, p. 183-184.
[33] Tideman 2006, p. 140.

outcomes of RBVPRs are viewed as estimates rather than pronouncements of truth, choice consistency loses its appeal as a condition that RBVPRs must satisfy.[34]

Arrow's theorem tells us that no voting method is perfect or infallible. But we shouldn't expect infallibility anyway. We shouldn't expect any collective decision-making process to identify what is indisputably the best option; instead, we should view it as producing an *estimate* of what the best option is.

The Condorcet criterion

Before leaving the subject of voting system criteria, I want to explain one last one: the **Condorcet criterion**, named for the Marquis de Condorcet (1743-1794; pronounced "con-dor-say"), a prominent French philosopher, mathematician, and political scientist, who outlined in a 1785 essay what would become known as a Condorcet method.

Condorcet, incidentally, was well known to Thomas Jefferson, who served as Minister to France from 1785 to 1789. Madison also owned copies of his writing. It was Condorcet's work in "social mathematics" that led to the idea, suggested in a September 1789 letter from Jefferson to Madison, that contracts should expire after 19 years. However, it appears Jefferson and Madison weren't familiar with Condorcet's theories about voting.[35]

The basic idea of Condorcet's method is to compare all alternatives (or candidates) *pairwise* — in other words, one-on-one, using the voter preferences expressed in a set of rank-ordered ballots. If there is an alternative that beats all others in such match-ups, it is known as the *Condorcet winner*, and the method elects it. Such an alternative does not always exist; when there is a cycle, as in the example given above, it doesn't. In such cases, another method must be used to choose the winner. Thus the Condorcet method is really a family of methods, which all elect the Condorcet winner when it exists.

---

[34] Tideman 2006, p. 141.
[35] McLean and Urken 1992.

The Condorcet criterion is that whenever a Condorcet winner exists, the voting method must elect it. Instant-runoff voting fails this criterion. To see why, consider the same ballots listed above, in the discussion of choice consistency:

- 2 votes: A>B>C
- 1 vote: A>C>B
- 3 votes: B>A>C
- 1 vote: B>C>A
- 3 votes: C>A>B
- 1 vote: C>B>A

As noted above, B wins this election by the rules of IRV because A is knocked out of contention in the first round. But A is actually the Condorcet winner, because six of the 11 voters prefer A over B, and six of 11 prefer A over C — thus A wins all pairwise match-ups.

In a 1976 article in *Scientific American* on voting methods, Richard G. Niemi and William H. Riker discuss Condorcet methods along with the Borda count. "In our judgment," they write, "the Condorcet standard is more likely than the Borda one to give rise to a consensus, since the Borda standard can easily leave a majority of the voters dissatisfied with the outcome."

The Condorcet criterion promotes consensus by helping moderate candidates. To see why, imagine a bell curve representing the ideological views of an electorate, with most people being in the middle, tapering off towards the left and right extremes. Consider three candidates, *A*, *B*, and *C*, whose ideological positions on the left-right spectrum are as shown in figure 1.5:

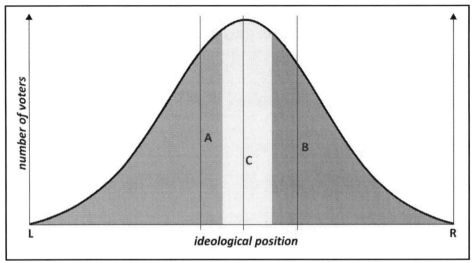

Figure 1.5. Example ideological distribution, with three candidates *A*, *B*, and *C*
(Full-color version: daneckam.com/book/btp/figures.)

Assuming that voters vote for the candidate nearest to their position on the left-right axis, candidate *A* will get a number of votes proportional to the blue area, *B* proportional to the red, and *C* proportional to the yellow. *C* has the fewest votes since the yellow area is smaller than the red and the blue. So under the standard rules of IRV, *C* would be eliminated in the first round, leading to a face-off between *A* and *B* in the second. However, *C* is the Condorcet winner because in all pairwise match-ups, he wins. In a contest between *A* and *C*, *C* would have both the red and the yellow areas (against blue), and in a contest between *B* and *C*, *C* would have both blue and yellow (against red); he would win both contests.

It may be argued that this single-peaked picture doesn't accurately depict the polarized American electorate, which looks more "double-humped", with peaks on the left and on the right. That may be true, but even if so, a Condorcet winner may exist in the center. And over the long run, giving such moderates a better chance may promote moderation in the electorate. The point is that when we're deciding on a voting system, compliance with the Condorcet criterion is a desirable feature to have, regardless of the shape of the electorate. A

Condorcet candidate is someone that more voters can live with, even if he's not the top choice of that many.

The failure of instant-runoff voting to guarantee a Condorcet winner's election is more than just a theoretical problem. Burlington, Vermont first used IRV in their 2006 mayoral elections, when Bob Kiss was elected as a member of the (leftist) Vermont Progressive Party. In 2009, Kiss faced two main opponents, Democrat Andy Montroll and Republican Kurt Wright, along with two other minor candidates. Wright led in the first round, with 33 percent of the vote to Kiss's 29 percent and Montroll's 23 percent. After the elimination of the minor candidates, Wright increased his lead to 37 percent of unexhausted ballots. Kiss had 34 percent, while Montroll was eliminated with 29 percent. More Montroll votes transferred to Kiss than to Wright, giving Kiss the win with 51.5 percent to Wright's 48.5 percent.[36]

Montroll, in the ideological "center" relative to his opponents, was a Condorcet winner, but fell victim to what's sometimes called the "center squeeze" pathology of IRV. And Wright was not elected either, despite being the plurality winner — a fact which soured many of his fans on IRV, and led to Burlington repealing it in 2010.

It's a sad reflection of Americans' lack of political sophistication that the plurality standard is so well-accepted. Electoral reformers must be ready to point out the inadequacy of plurality voting — and I believe that's not too difficult. Defending failure to elect a Condorcet winner seems more difficult.

Luckily, it turns out that it's possible to add Condorcet compliance to the instant-runoff voting method. In IRV, in each round we look for a candidate who has an absolute majority, that is, more than 50 percent. In the modified version, called "Condorcet IRV", we look instead for a Condorcet winner, and if we find one, that candidate is elected. If not, then just as in standard IRV when there's no one with a majority, we eliminate the worst-performing candidate, transfer votes according to that candidate's voters' preferences, then re-tally.[37]

---

[36] Gierzynski, Hamilton, and Smith 2009.

[37] This has also been called "Woodall's Smith+IRV method" and "Benham's method" — see Benham and Smith [date unknown] and Green-Armytage 2011.

Another way to describe this method is simply to say that a Condorcet winner must never be eliminated: If such a candidate exists and places last, and therefore would be eliminated under standard IRV, eliminate the second-to-last-place candidate instead. This makes for a better "story", I think, in that describing the vote-tallying will be focused on rounds, rather than a pairwise comparison matrix.

(Variations of Condorcet IRV might also be considered. For example, if we're concerned that a candidate who is nobody's favorite could be too wishy-washy to be automatically elected, then the rule could be modified as follows: Never eliminate a Condorcet winner **unless** she has fewer than half, or some other proportion, of the votes of the next-to-last-place candidate. This would establish a threshold for highest-preference votes and essentially make the method a hybrid that could be placed on a conceptual "spectrum" between IRV and Condorcet IRV.)

The Condorcet criterion is a good one to follow, in my view, because of its consensus-promoting tendency. Condorcet IRV is an excellent method for single-winner elections.

(It's also possible to combine Condorcet with STV for multi-winner elections — see Hill 1988. Note, from the same paper, that "worst-performing" candidate can be defined in various ways, the simplest probably being the one with fewest votes, but we could also use other metrics, such as a score based on paired comparisons.)

Which voting method is best?

We've been considering these fairness criteria in hopes of figuring out which voting method would be best to use. As I mentioned, there's no simple answer. No voting method has all the features we should want. Arrow's theorem, and related findings such as the Gibbard-Satterthwaite theorem, show that all ranking-based voting methods are subject to tactical voting and manipulation. Ironically, as Niemi and Riker write, a consequence of this is:

> [...] that manipulability is partly diminished as an issue. If all systems can be manipulated, then systems cannot be

---

According to the Condorcet Internet Voting Service, it was invented by Thomas Hill in the 19th century.

distinguished by the property of manipulability. One might want to rule out the most easily manipulated systems, but among the less manipulable systems one should probably try to find some other standard for judging among them. That other standard must be the joint consideration of what we want voting to accomplish and how well the system under consideration is likely to accomplish it.[38]

The choice of voting method involves prioritizing some criteria over others. How they should be prioritized is highly debatable. I've explained why I think the Condorcet criterion is important. Others may disagree. Some will argue for approval or range voting, which, being based on ratings rather than rankings, lie outside the scope of Arrow's theorem. However, they have not been used very much for elections to public office, and their failure to satisfy the majority criterion seems problematic to me.

There are many intriguing ideas on combining methods. A method known as *preference approval voting* (PAV) combines features of ranked-choice and approval: It involves considering the relative rankings of all candidates with majority approval.[39] In another recently devised system, known as *STAR* (for Score Then Automatic Runoff), voters rate each candidate, say with zero to five stars, and the top two scorers go to a final round in which each voter's full vote goes to whichever of those two she rated higher. There are also multi-winner, proportional rating-based voting methods, such as reweighted range voting.[40]

Fortunately, we can try out a lot of different options. There are 50 states and one district within the United States. That's 51 potentially different systems that can be tried (at the "state" level — not to mention local levels). Supreme Court Justice Louis Brandeis wrote of these "laboratories of democracy" in a 1932 dissenting opinion in the case of *New State Ice Co. v. Liebmann*:

> It is one of the happy incidents of the federal system that a single courageous State may, if its citizens choose, serve as a

---

[38] Niemi and Riker 1976.
[39] Brams and Sanver 2006.
[40] See Ryan d.u., Smith 2005.

laboratory; and try novel social and economic experiments
without risk to the rest of the country.

When an experiment fails, it can be abandoned; when it succeeds, it can be emulated by other jurisdictions. In this way, our states and other local jurisdictions can lead the way to a better electoral system for the country. Maine is in the vanguard: In 2016, it adopted instant-runoff voting for all state and federal legislative seats and for governor,[41] and in 2020 it will also use IRV in the presidential election. I hope other states will follow suit.

One thing we know is that almost anything would work better than plurality voting. In case it's still not clear why, let me offer an example. Suppose you and nine of your friends are planning a small get-together and you've decided on getting just one food item. The question is what it should be. Suppose you decide to make the choice democratically, and to use the plurality rule. Your friend Bill proposes ice cream; you prefer something saltier and nominate pretzels. The group discusses these two options. It looks like four out of ten would prefer ice cream, and the other six would rather have pretzels. Bill is unhappy about this, so he nominates a third option: peanuts. Three of the six people who were leaning towards pretzels think that peanuts sound even better. Now you vote, and ice cream wins with four votes, versus three each for pretzels and peanuts.

You see what Bill did there, right? He manipulated the outcome by introducing a third option that he had no interest in voting for. He divided the opposition to ice cream and thereby assured its victory. And he was able to do it because you picked the plurality rule for this election. Why would you do that? Do you see what Hamilton meant when he said it might be "unsafe to permit less than a majority to be conclusive"? (By the way, if it *might* be unsafe, then it *is* unsafe, because safety from something means being able to *rely* on avoiding it.)

Many of the fairness criteria I've discussed are single-winner criteria; they apply to single-member-district elections. They seem to have received more study in that context, perhaps because it's easier

---

[41] Seelye 2016.

to prove theorems under simpler conditions. Also, I suspect that meeting or not meeting certain fairness criteria makes more difference in a single-winner setting, because it's an all-or-nothing contest for the candidates. When electing multiple winners proportionally, the competing parties aren't fighting for all or nothing, they're fighting for more or less. In other words, proportionality builds in a lot of fairness on its own, and lowers the stakes for the kinds of fairness measured by some of these mathematical criteria.

The best way to achieve more fairness in representation, and to allow multiple parties to compete viably, is to use multi-member districts with proportional representation, as I outlined above. (The Fair Representation Act, introduced in 2017 by Rep. Don Beyer [D-VA], would implement this change.) However, if the U.S. polity isn't ready to accept MMDs, a reasonable first step would be to adopt instant-runoff voting or, even better, Condorcet IRV. This would give the electorate a chance to become more familiar with ranking choices, something that's also required for the single transferable vote.

There's one kind of election, though, that can't be converted to multi-winner — the election of a chief executive, or other singular office that covers an entire jurisdiction. For such elections, Condorcet IRV makes a lot of sense, and not just as a stepping stone. At the national level, there is only one such election: the one for president and vice president.

Presidential elections

I said in the Introduction that we don't need to amend the Constitution to have a multiparty system in America. And that is true: Even if the presidency remained out of reach for all but the two largest parties, if the Congress had a multiparty complexion we'd be able to say we had moved beyond the two-party system. After all, there are 537 elected officials at the federal level (plus a few elected delegates who don't get a vote), and all but two are in Congress. But it would be nice to have more robust multiparty competition for the presidency, too.

The problem, of course, is the electoral college, whose workings the Constitution does specify to a certain extent. It's the Constitution that gives a "federal bonus" of two electors to every state without regard to population, and thus ensures that small states are over-represented in the college. The voting power of a Wyoming voter is much greater than that of a voter in California, Texas, or New York.

It's the Constitution that fixes the number of electors given to each state after every ten-year census. That means a state's voting power doesn't depend on how many of its voters turn out to vote. Suppose that in one state with ten electors, 50 percent of eligible voters vote in a presidential election, while in another state, also with ten electors, only 25 percent do. Both groups will be represented by the same number of electors at the electoral college, even if twice the number of people voted in the first state as in the second. Furthermore, populations may have shifted since the most recent census. Imagine that the first state has grown in population from six million to eight million, whereas the population of the second state has declined from six million to four million. If we assume that 75 percent of both states' populations are eligible to vote, then we'd have three million voters in the first state and only 750,000 in the second — both groups represented equally in the electoral college.

One of the biggest problems with the electoral college as it currently operates is the fact that most states allocate electors on a *winner-take-all* basis — whoever gets the most votes, even if it's not a majority, gets *all* of the state's electoral votes. For example, in 1992, George H.W. Bush won all of Texas's 32 electors with just 41 percent of the vote. Bill Clinton won all of Nevada's electors with only 37 percent.

The winner-take-all rule means that candidates have no incentive to campaign in states where they are already likely to win, or likely to lose. Without the winner-take-all rule, candidates would value every vote — even in states they are sure to lose, votes could be combined with votes in other states and have a chance of affecting the national outcome. With winner-take-all, why bother? If you lose the state by a smaller margin, it doesn't matter. And if you're sure you're going to win the state, there is no benefit to increasing your margin of victory. This means that only a few states, the ones that could go in either direction, make up the battleground that presidential elections are fought on. And that means for the majority of Americans who don't live in one of the dozen-or-so battleground (or "swing", or "purple") states, their vote will likely mean nothing, at least with respect to the electoral decision. Their preference will be given no representation from their state in the electoral college. It's only because of differing regional strengths of the two parties, and some degree of balance between them — and the two-party system itself, which this electoral method supports — that their votes are represented at all, via the electors of other states.

How does the winner-take-all rule support the two-party system? Mainly because each state is contested by plurality rule. Whoever gets the most votes in the state — or, in the two states that use the district system, in the district — wins all of the electors for that state or district. That brings in the spoiler effect, which makes minor parties much less attractive to voters.

This isn't actually enough to suppress candidacies that have strong support in a certain region — such as George Wallace's in 1968. He won 13.5 percent of the popular vote nationwide, and based on wins in five southern states (Arkansas, Louisiana, Mississippi, Alabama, and Georgia), 46 electoral votes, on a segregationist platform. Contrast that with Ross Perot's performance in his first run for the presidency in 1992: With 18.9 percent of the popular vote, he won no states, thus no electors. The difference is that Perot's was not a regional candidacy; his support was spread across the entire nation.

It's easy to imagine a proportional way of allocating electors at the state level — although, somewhat oddly, it has never been used. Suppose a candidate wins 20 percent of the popular vote in a state that has 10 electors. Then he would be given two of them. Every candidate would get the same proportion of a state's electors as their proportion of the popular vote in that state, subject to rounding. (In a state with just three electors, for example, winning 20 percent of the vote might not be enough to win any electors, depending on the details of the formula used.) If every state had used this method in 1992, Perot might've gotten nearly 20 percent of the electoral college. And that probably would've meant that nobody had a majority of electors, which would've sent the election to the House of Representatives, something that hasn't happened since the election of 1824.

In such a "contingency" election, as it's known when the House decides, state delegations vote as a unit — that is, each state getting one vote — on the top three candidates. (Originally, it was top five, but that changed in 1804 with the Twelfth Amendment.) That's so profoundly disproportional to population that it makes a mockery of any claim one might wish to make that we elect our presidents democratically. In the election of 1824, the party system (such as it was) had faded and four candidates ran for the presidency, all nominally Democratic-Republicans: John Quincy Adams, Andrew Jackson, Henry Clay, and William Crawford. Clay placed fourth in electoral votes, so was out of the running; but he was Speaker of the House, and threw his influential support to Adams. When Adams won, with 13 states to 7 for Jackson and 4 for Crawford, Jackson and his supporters felt cheated, as he had won a plurality both of electors and of popular votes (although it should be noted that several states did not hold a popular vote at the time). The hard feelings, and accusations of a "corrupt bargain" between Adams and Clay, persisted through 1828, when Jackson won in a rematch against Adams.

Perhaps to avoid such an unsightly spectacle, most presidential campaigns have been built on broad national coalitions. The winner-take-all rule makes it much easier for a major-party candidate to assemble a majority in the electoral college. It punishes third-party candidates by depriving them of any electors — unless they run a regional campaign like Wallace's.

It's right that we don't declare an election ended before any candidate has won a majority. But the winner-take-all rule, which takes power away from most Americans, giving it to those in a handful of swing states, and the extremely disproportional House "runoff" (the contingency election), are the wrong way to run an election that purports to have democratic legitimacy. There's a very simple principle that democratic governments usually follow: "one person, one vote". In other words, everyone's vote should matter just as much as everyone else's. Our presidential electoral system fails miserably to embody this basic principle. The failure is partly built into the design of the electoral college, but it's made far worse by the winner-take-all rule.

Winner-take-all is nowhere in the Constitution — it was not part of the Founders' design. They expected electors to meet and deliberate before casting their votes — something that doesn't happen. They seem to have believed that the final decision would usually be made in the House, since it would be rare for a candidate to win an outright majority. As for the method of choosing electors, it was left entirely up to the states. In the early days of the republic, many states let their legislators appoint presidential electors. A few used a district system in which the state divided itself into a number of districts equal to its number of electors, with the (plurality) winner of each district getting one elector. Perhaps ironically, it seems that Thomas Jefferson played a major role in pushing the adoption of the *general ticket* method, an early form of winner-take-all. (The difference is that they used the so-called "long ballot" in which voters cast votes for individual electors. Nowadays, we cast just one vote for the presidential candidate, and it's understood that this is shorthand for voting for the slate of electors pledged to that candidate. This is known as the "short ballot".) In 1800, only two of 16 states chose electors this way; by 1832, 22 out of 24 did.

The election of 1796 was the first one which was contested, as George Washington, a consensus candidate, had served as president for the first eight years of the republic. The choice was between John Adams and Thomas Jefferson, the "North and South Poles of the American Revolution" in the words of their colleague Dr. Benjamin Rush. The election was very close: 71 electors for Adams vs. 68 for Jefferson. At the time, Virginia, Jefferson's home state, used the district method of choosing electors. Adams managed to win one of the state's 21 electors. In North Carolina, which used the same method, Adams won a single elector. Had both these states used the general ticket, Jefferson would have won. This must have irked him; he wrote in January 1800:

> All agree that an election by districts would be best if it could
> be general; but while 10 states chuse either by their legislatures

or by a general ticket, it is folly & worse than folly for the other
6 not to do it.

"Folly" because this is essentially an arms race: When one state
adopts winner-take-all, others need to follow suit or lose relative
influence. In 1800, Virginia adopted the general ticket method.
Massachusetts (Adams's home state) responded by switching to
legislative appointment of electors.[42] Jefferson won the election 73 to
65.

Incidentally, I don't know if the proportional method of allocation
was known to Jefferson; I suspect not. "Election by districts" is *not* the
best method. The drawing of district lines is vulnerable to
gerrymandering, and it's another winner-take-all method, just at a
lower level than statewide.

So winner-take-all is not a given. If every state used the proportional
method to allocate electors, our presidential elections would be a lot
more democratic. We still wouldn't count every vote equally; small
states would still count more, in proportion to population, than large
states. And we'd still have the problem of a very unfair House
contingency election in case no candidate won a majority of electors,
a more likely occurrence in this scenario. But there is very little hope
of all 50 states and the District of Columbia adopting this method,
because of the arms-race dynamic at work.

The National Popular Vote Interstate Compact (NPVIC)
So what can be done? Short of amending the Constitution, there is
one approach that would make the winner of the election the
candidate who received the most popular votes. It was outlined in
2001 by Robert Bennett, a professor of law at Northwestern
University,[43] and fleshed out in 2006 by a group of activists led by
John Koza, a professor of computer science at Stanford. It's called the
National Popular Vote Interstate Compact, or NPVIC for short. And
rather than fighting the injustice of winner-take-all, it embraces it.

---

[42] McCarthy 2012.
[43] Bennett 2001.

Here's how the NPVIC works. States enter into an interstate compact with each other that they'll appoint electors pledged for whatever candidate wins the national popular vote, regardless of whether they won in that state. But it doesn't take effect right away, that is, immediately after a state passes it. Instead, the agreement only comes into effect when enough states have joined the compact to constitute a majority of electors — 270 out of 538. How many states that is depends on which states sign up. As I write, fifteen states have joined: (in chronological order) Maryland, New Jersey, Illinois, Hawaii, Washington, Massachusetts, Vermont, California, Rhode Island, New York, Connecticut, Colorado, Delaware, New Mexico and Oregon. The District of Columbia has also joined the compact. Together these states command 196 electors, about 73 percent of the necessary 270.

If states with 270 or more electors join the compact, then their electors, all pledged to vote for the national popular vote winner, will be able to determine the election. We won't need to worry about someone again taking the presidency without having the most popular votes.

Incidentally, that's happened a few times in our history — exactly how many depends on what you are counting. Here's a quick rundown:

- **1824**: As mentioned above, no one got a majority of electors, so the decision went to the House, where the electoral-college runner-up, John Quincy Adams, was chosen as president. Andrew Jackson had won a plurality of both electors and of popular votes This election is often mentioned as the first electoral-college "misfire", the first time the winner of the popular vote was not elected. But it's hard to talk about a popular-vote "winner" when several states let their legislatures choose electors *without* a popular vote; also, the "win" was only by plurality, which should not be decisive. It should not be a surprise when a runoff yields a victor other than the first-round leader. So I don't count this as a misfire; it's just an unusual occurrence. "Works as designed" or W.A.D., as engineers say.

- **1876:** Amid a lot of counting disputes, with three states (Florida, Louisiana, and South Carolina) unable even to agree on who had won their state, Congress appointed a committee to settle the election. Along partisan lines, they awarded victory to the Republican, Rutherford B. Hayes. But the Democrat, Samuel J. Tilden, had apparently won more popular votes.

- **1888:** The incumbent president, Democrat Grover Cleveland, lost the electoral college vote despite narrowly edging out Republican Benjamin Harrison in the popular vote. Cleveland's vote is a good example of one that is "inefficiently" distributed around the nation. As I mentioned above, winning a state by a landslide is no better than winning it by a sliver, given winner-take-all. An "efficient" distribution, therefore, is for a candidate's supporters to be just numerous enough to win in enough states. Of the 18 states Cleveland won, he got more than 60 percent in six. Harrison exceeded that percentage in only one of the 20 states he won, meaning that the distribution of his votes was more efficient. (It also helped a lot than Harrison narrowly won New York, Cleveland's home state.)

- **1960:** Although it's rarely discussed, there's a convincing case that Richard M. Nixon actually got more popular votes than John F. Kennedy. It's hard to be definitive because of the unusual way Alabama's Democratic electors were chosen. At the time, the state was still using the long ballot, meaning voters were asked to vote for up to 11 electors individually, rather than simply to express which presidential candidate they supported. Long story short, while the Democrats won the state, only five of the 11 Democratic electors voted for Kennedy; the other six voted for segregationist Harry F. Byrd — even though he wasn't officially in the race. But the conventional way of reporting the Alabama popular vote has been to give Kennedy credit for the entire Democratic vote. If, instead, he is credited with only five-elevenths of the vote (which seems more reasonable, on the face of it), then Nixon's nationwide tally is higher. For the full details, see Trende 2012 and Gaines 2001.

- **2000:** The Supreme Court halted recounting in Florida, making George W. Bush the winner by a margin of 537 votes. He thus gained the state's 25 electors and won the electoral college with 271 electors, despite getting about half a million fewer votes nationwide than Al Gore.
- **2016:** Donald Trump won the electoral college 304 to 227, although Hillary Clinton won the popular vote by about 2.9 million. Many of her surplus votes came from California, where she won by 61.7 to 31.6 percent.

So, how many electoral college "misfires" have we had in our history? It depends on how you ask the question. If you ask, "How many times has the plurality winner in the popular vote not been elected president?", the answer is five or six, depending on how you count "popular votes" in Alabama in 1960. (The fundamental problem is that "popular vote" is not well defined in that situation.) But the question is misguided, because we should not take a plurality as conclusive — as our Founders understood; that's why they specified that when no candidate won a *majority* of electors, as happened in 1824, there would be a runoff of sorts, in the House. It was there, not at the electoral college, that the popular-vote runner-up was chosen as president, in a process the Founders would have accepted as normal. So, how many times has the electoral college, *per se*, elected someone who didn't get the most popular votes? Four or five.

Back to the NPVIC. What may feel strange about it is that a state's electors may all vote for someone who did not win in that state. How can that possibly be fair? In fact, California governor Arnold Schwarzenegger and Hawaii governor Linda Lingle both vetoed the bill in their state for exactly this reason. (Both states managed to successfully pass the law later.) The objection can be met quite simply: Electors would be voting for the candidate who got the most votes across the nation. The presidency and vice presidency are national offices — so their election should follow the national will, as expressed by all the voters of the nation. Given that states have full authority over how to select their electors, and that the NPVIC *complies* with "one person, one vote" whereas the system it replaces does not, I don't think we should be too worried about it being ruled unconstitutional.

Opponents of electoral-college reform may argue that the president does not just represent individual voters, he also represents (and/or acts in the interests of) states, as states. But this makes no sense. States have no consciences, no capacity for judgment or reflection; they are abstract entities, collections of individuals. To act in the interests of a state really means to act in the interests of its residents.

Many defenses of the electoral college have been made by opponents of reform. Very few of them really make sense when you examine them closely. I can't take the space here to address all of them; for that, I would recommend the book *Why the Electoral College Is Bad for America*, by George C. Edwards III (2011), which thoroughly deals with these defenses.

One oft-repeated concern is that electing the president by popular vote (also known as "direct election") would not protect the federal nature of our government. Here's an expression of this sentiment:

> By tallying votes for the highest office of the land by state, even giving each state a sort of bonus for being organized as a state, the Electoral College affirms the importance of these self-governing communities and helps secure their interest in self-government. We know this intuitively, as the whole process of presidential selection focuses national attention on the states and their distinctiveness. [...] Of course campaigns for national office ought to focus on national issues and to feature candidates of national stature, and on the whole they do. But to elect the president in a national plebiscite would either suppress what is local or, as has already been the trend, nationalize local concerns, removing their governance away from communities and into the inevitably bureaucratic machinery of a central administration.[44]

Actually, in general elections, the process focuses most attention on swing states, since the candidates usually don't campaign in safe ones. (As for primaries, they are basically intra-party affairs, about which I'll

---

[44] Stoner 2001.

have more to say later.) Federalism is well-protected by the simple fact that we have separate state and national levels of government. The existence of the Senate, where every state gets exactly two senators, also protects it. As Edwards writes,[45] "There is virtually no aspect of the constitutional system more secure against fundamental change than federalism." Directly electing presidents would not threaten federalism.

If you find yourself debating someone who supports the current system, there are two questions you might find it useful to ask. First, why should anyone's vote count more than anyone else's? You may hear something like this: "We're a republic, not a democracy." That's true, but does that imply that some people's votes should count more than others, based merely on where they live? "Republic", for practical purposes, means representative democracy — which in no way implies that the representation is supposed to be unfair or lopsided. Electing our presidents by popular vote would not change the fact that we are a republic. Second, if the electoral college is such a great system for choosing an executive, why doesn't any state use something similar — that is, a mini-electoral college — to elect its governor?[46]

If the idea of every vote being equal somehow stood in contradiction to the idea of a republic, the Founders could not have called it a "republican principle" that a majority should defeat a minority. In *Federalist* no. 10, Madison says that it is "the republican principle, which enables the majority to defeat" the views of a minority, "by regular vote." In a letter to Jefferson dated Oct. 24, 1787, Madison writes of "the republican principle which refers the ultimate decision to the will of the majority", and of "republican Government, where the majority must ultimately decide". In *Federalist* no. 22, Hamilton calls it a "fundamental maxim of republican government [...] that the sense of the majority should prevail."

The NPVIC has one big problem: It uses the plurality rule. That brings in the problem of vote-splitting, and the very real possibility

---

[45] Edwards 2011, p. 169.
[46] Illing 2016.

that the winner could be despised by a majority of voters. There are ways to deal with this problem, though.

In 1969, having witnessed George Wallace win 46 electoral votes the previous year, Congress was highly motivated to reform the system, and actually passed an amendment to the Constitution by a vote of 338 to 70. The reform they passed specified a minimum threshold of 40 percent of the popular vote to win — a sort of "plurality plus" standard. If no candidate received that many votes, a runoff between the top two candidates would be held. Unfortunately, the amendment was stopped by a filibuster in the Senate in 1970.[47] While this "plurality plus" formula would have been an easy improvement, it is obviously not the ideal.

Condorcet IRV would be a great system to use for presidential elections, in the long term. The Condorcet criterion helps moderate, consensus candidates, favoring them over candidates on the extreme left or right. Now, if you're a leftist or a rightist, that may not sound very appealing. But we need to remember that when we're electing a president, we're electing someone to represent the whole country. A centrist does that better than an extremist, almost by definition. That's why the Condorcet criterion makes perfect sense for presidential elections. (Note: I use the term "centrist" not in reference to any specific set of ideas, but instead to the "center of gravity" of political discourse in any given polity. On this account, the game of politics for leftists and rightists is to try to move the center in their direction.)

For the short term, since neither IRV nor the Condorcet criterion is well-understood among the masses, the NPVIC makes sense. It would give us a chance to stop thinking of the race for the presidency as a state-by-state contest, and start thinking of it as the national election it really should be. Once we get used to that (which won't take long), we'll want to do something to deal with the spoiler effect.

Miscellaneous provisions
Now, I've spelled out the main features of the recommended path to a robust multiparty system:

---

[47] CQ Almanac 1970.

- For legislative assemblies, proportional representation (PR) with multi-member districts (MMDs) and voting via the single transferable vote (STV);
- for singular offices, such as president and governor, Condorcet IRV (or something better — where "better" is up for debate, but we know for sure it's not the plurality rule).

A few other changes would also be very helpful. These are mostly obstacles that we need to remove from the pathway. If we decide that we need more than two parties in government, then the need to remove these obstacles will probably become fairly obvious.

Some of the most obvious are unfair laws concerning ballot access. In Georgia, for example, the law concerning ballot access for independents and minor-party candidates is so strict that since 1964, no such candidate has qualified except one (Billy McKinney in 1982), who was only excused from the petitioning requirements because the boundaries of his district were not set early enough. The law requires a petition of 5 percent of registered voters, and a filing fee of 3 percent of the annual salary of the office.[48]

In Texas, for an independent candidate to qualify for the presidential election requires a number of petition signatures equalling 1 percent of the total votes cast in the state in the previous presidential election — in 2016, that was 79,939 signatures, from voters who did not participate in either the Democratic or Republican primaries. And all these signatures must be collected within a period of 68 days.[49] Without millions of dollars to spend on a highly-organized petition drive, this is a very high hurdle.

In North Carolina, until 2017, "people seeking to form a political party had to garner signatures equal to 2 percent of the voter turnout in the most recent gubernatorial election, with at least 200 from each of four congressional districts. That would be close to 100,000 signatures based on the 2016 election."[50]

---

[48] Winger 2016, 2017.
[49] Lovegrove 2016.
[50] Browder and Burns 2017.

Ideally, in a competitive party system, parties would have the freedom to choose nominees as they see fit, without undue regulation by the state. But states restrict ballot access in primaries as well as in general elections. In New York, for example, in 1996 Bob Dole was the only presidential candidate who managed to qualify for the Republican primary ballot in every part of the state.[51] Steve Forbes, Lamar Alexander, and Pat Buchanan were among those unable to match his feat.

A telling indicator of the basic unfairness of such laws appeared in May 2016. Panicked by the prospect of Donald Trump winning the Republican nomination, a group of influential Republicans — including Mitt Romney, William Kristol, and Erick Erickson — tried to recruit an independent conservative candidate to keep him out of the White House. Ballot access laws posed an obstacle — the deadline for independents to get on the ballot in Texas had already passed, for example. But this problem was not considered insurmountable — "organizers said they think a legal challenge there could be successful", reported the *Washington Post* on May 14[52]. Why? Because the law is so obviously unfair — and justice is available to those with deep enough pockets.

In Texas, instant-runoff voting is not allowed, according to a 2001 opinion by the secretary of state, who answered "No" to the question of "whether the word majority as used in the [Texas Election] Code is broad enough to include the meaning of preferential voting, and whether the provision allowing outside law to provide different runoff procedures includes the 'instant runoffs' of preferential voting."[53] Let's break this down and see how one might respond to this interpretation.

Texas law says that "To be elected to a city office, a candidate must receive a majority of the total number of votes received by all candidates for the office." Cities may use election by place or by "another system of election that is consistent with an election by majority vote".

---

[51] Winger 2002, p. 248.
[52] Rucker and Costa 2016.
[53] Cuellar 2001.

As pointed out earlier, the idea of instant-runoff voting is to respect the principle of majority rule. It simulates a series of runoff rounds to ensure that the winner has an absolute majority. In theory it is functionally the same as holding a runoff election except that there may be more than one extra round. Surely adding rounds does not make the method inconsistent with "election by majority vote".

The secretary of state also wrote: "although preferential voting does indeed result in a mathematical majority, we cannot ignore the fact that by assigning legal weight to a voter's second, third, or fourth choice as if it were the voter's first choice in order to achieve a majority without a runoff, preferential voting changes the usual meaning of 'votes received by all candidates'".

This seems like a misunderstanding of how IRV works. It doesn't assign "legal weight" to a voter's second choice in the first round. In every round, only the voter's top uneliminated choice gets any weight. "Votes received by all candidates" should be understood in the context of a given round of voting. Isn't that how we understand it when we hold a standard runoff election? If "assigning legal weight" includes voting for your second choice in a runoff, how is that different from the weight given to a second preference under IRV?

These few examples only begin to scratch the surface of hinting at the tip of the iceberg of how many unfairly restrictive ballot access laws have existed, and continue to exist, in the United States. A complete rundown would fill a whole book. For anyone who wants to dig into this area further, I would recommend *Ballot Access News* (at ballot-access.org), a monthly newsletter edited and published by Richard Winger since 1985.

Here's another example of unfair rules that impede a competitive party system. In some states, having a felony conviction on your record means you cannot vote, even after you've served your sentence. For the 2000 election, Florida officials added the names of supposed felons to a list of voters to be purged from the rolls, requiring only a 70 percent match between the voter rolls and the felon database, which meant that "false positive" matches were likely if, say, a voter's middle initial didn't match that of a felon.[54] Was this done out of a misguided sense of justice, a belief that ex-felons don't deserve the vote? Maybe, for a few. But when you consider the partisan implications of such an act, a more powerful incentive becomes clear: African-Americans, who made up about 11 percent of Florida's registered voters at the time, "accounted for 44 percent of those removed from the rolls".[55] And African-Americans overwhelmingly vote for a certain one of the two major parties.

Electoral fusion would also be useful to minor parties. In electoral fusion, two or more parties nominate the same person for a given office. Each party gets a separate line on the ballot, even though the candidate is the same. By choosing one party line over another, voters for that candidate also express their party preference. Candidates thus know from which parties their support comes, and if they win, better understand their mandate.

Fusion can be a good way to avoid splitting the vote — though if we adopt a better voting system, that's not as much of a worry as it is under single-member plurality. It was widely used in our past; for instance, in the 1872 presidential election, the Democrats fused with the Liberal Republican Party in endorsing the latter's nominee, Horace Greeley. They knew that nominating someone else would only split the opposition to incumbent Ulysses S. Grant (who won decisively anyway). Greeley was the first presidential candidate to be nominated by two parties.[56]

In 1896, the Democrats and Populists fused in nominating William Jennings Bryan for the presidency. They nominated different vice-presidential candidates, though: The Democrats chose Arthur Sewall of Maine, while the Populists picked Thomas E. Watson of Georgia.

Unfortunately, most states banned fusion by the early 20th century. The first anti-fusion legislation was passed in 1893 in the state of South Dakota, where Republicans were concerned about fusion between Democrats and Populists. In large part, such legislation was a power grab enabled by the adoption around 1890 of the "Australian",

---

[54] Berman 2015, pp. 208-210.
[55] Hiaasen et al 2001.
[56] Snay 2011, p. 178.

or secret, ballot, printed by the government. (Previously, in most states, ballots were supplied by the parties.) As Peter H. Argersinger explains:

> By providing for public rather than partisan control over the ballots and by featuring a blanket ballot, the Australian system opened to Republicans, given their dominance in state governments, the opportunity to use the power of the state to eliminate fusion politics and thereby alter political behavior.[57]

Today, fusion is legal in only eight states, and is commonly practiced only in New York. There, minor parties are well-established and play an important role in state elections. In the gubernatorial election of 2010, for example, the Working Families and Independence parties each contributed more than 3 percent of Democrat Andrew Cuomo's winning 63 percent of the vote. The Conservative Party contributed 5 percent of the vote to his opponent, Republican Carl Paladino.

The most thorough examination of fusion I know is *The Tyranny of the Two-Party System* by Lisa Jane Disch (2002). I would highly recommend this illuminating book for those who want to know more about the history of fusion in America, as well as of the idea of the two-party system. Fusion was a common feature of 19th century politics, as Disch explains:

> Nowadays it may seem quite obvious why candidates ought not to run on more than one ballot line at a time; in the nineteenth century it was equally obvious why they should do so. Fusion flourished in the nineteenth century not because it was permitted but because it was possible and not prohibited. It was, in other words, the default setting of an electoral system where citizens voted by party ticket. Antifusion legislation changed this default setting.[58]

The Commission on Presidential Debates (CPD) should be reformed or replaced as the sponsor and producer of televised presidential debates. This commission was founded in 1987 by the two major

---

[57] Argersinger 1980, p. 291.
[58] Disch 2002, p. 56.

parties to take over management of these debates. In 1988, the Republican and Democratic campaigns jointly presented a list of demands for how the debates should be run to the League of Women Voters, which had sponsored them since 1976. The League balked, saying the demands would "perpetrate a fraud on the American voter".

> Most objectionable to the League, [League President Nancy M.] Neuman said, were conditions in the agreement that gave the campaigns unprecedented control over the proceedings. Neuman called "outrageous" the campaigns' demands that they control the selection of questioners, the composition of the audience, hall access for the press and other issues.[59]

Presidential debates should be supervised by a non-partisan (not bi-partisan) group, whose only goal is to serve the interests of voters. The League of Women Voters seems like a good choice (among many good options).

In general, parties in power have an incentive to maintain their dominance by making things harder for other parties. Another example of this is straight-ticket voting — providing, on voters' ballots, a "shortcut" option to vote for all the candidates of a certain party. This makes things a lot easier for supporters of that party, since often ballots include a lot of races, meaning it's time-consuming to cast votes in all of them. But not all parties get a checkbox in the "straight ticket" section of the ballot. Often, it's only the Democrats and Republicans. This is unfair to new and small parties. A healthy multiparty system would avoid giving an unfair advantage to any side.

It's human nature to want to hold on to what has been gained. Parties, as institutions, want that too. Powerful parties tend to abuse their power to prevent challenges from newcomers. It's in their interests, as part of government, to maximize their influence, to try to pass their policy agenda. But these interests conflict with the interests of voters when they run roughshod over the representation of alternative viewpoints. As I'll develop in the next chapter, parties in

---

[59] LWV 1988.

government have different aims than parties in the electorate. A strong democracy requires balancing these dynamics.

Competition is essential for the pursuit of accountability. As we come to understand this, and that two parties are not enough, it will become ever more clear at what points major parties are abusing their power to reduce competition and feather their own nests. Ballot access laws, felony disenfranchisement, anti-fusion laws, and straight-ticket voting are just a few examples of this general tendency.

Conclusion

This chapter has laid out where we need to go, and how to get there in terms of the laws and structures that need to be changed. As I've explained, no constitutional amendments are needed — although we will eventually want to replace the electoral college. In that sense, the path to a multiparty system is straightforward. If we just change our voting systems and our methods of districting, it will happen — and this is not just my conclusion. There is general consensus in political science that proportional representation and multi-member districts tend to lead to a multiparty system. Essentially, despite a few apparent exceptions, and some vagueness in formulation, Duverger's laws work. It's not that proportional representation automatically increases the number of parties, but that it removes obstacles to the establishment of new parties.[60] There is little question that in a polity as large as the United States, removing such obstacles would lead to more parties.

However, getting it done will require political will. The difficult problem is not so much how to change the system to multiparty, but how to generate enough political will to make the change. We've got to want it, and demand it. That's why much of this book will be devoted to explaining the importance of change, and how voters can exert influence on their elected representatives.

First, though, we need to get a bit more historical and comparative perspective, to understand how party systems fit into the theory of democracy. That's what the next chapter is about.

---

[60] See Sartori 1997, chapter 3, pp. 27-52 for a fuller account, including of the exceptions.

2. Party System Function and Malfunction

"How about a *no-party* system?" That's something I heard more than once while writing this book. Why have political parties at all? Indeed, the Founding Fathers had a deep mistrust of them, and didn't want or expect them to be part of the American system. In his farewell address of 1796, George Washington said, of the "spirit of party":

> It serves always to distract the public councils and enfeeble the public administration. It agitates the community with ill-founded jealousies and false alarms, kindles the animosity of one part against another, foments occasionally riot and insurrection. It opens the door to foreign influence and corruption, which finds a facilitated access to the government itself through the channels of party passions. Thus the policy and the will of one country are subjected to the policy and will of another.

Other Founders also took a dim view of political parties. Alexander Hamilton wrote, in *Federalist* no. 1 (1787), "Nothing could be more ill-judged than that intolerant spirit which has, at all times, characterized political parties." John Adams wrote, "There is nothing which I dread so much as a division of the republic into two great parties, each arranged under its leader, and concerting measures in opposition to each other. This, in my humble apprehension, is to be dreaded as the greatest political evil under our Constitution." *Federalist* no. 10 (written by James Madison in 1787) is frequently invoked as an expression of the Founders' hostility to political parties, although Madison used the word "faction" instead of "party". "Parties," wrote Supreme Court Justice John Paul Stevens in a 2000 dissent[61] "ranked high on the list of evils that the Constitution was designed to check".

---

[61] *California Democratic Party v. Jones*.

Yet political parties are inevitable in representative democracy. They are an important bridge between the people and their elected representatives. "Modern democracy is unthinkable save in terms of parties," wrote the prominent political scientist E.E. Schattschneider in his 1942 book *Party Government*; far from being "merely appendages of modern government," he said, parties are "at the center of it and play a determinative and creative role in it."[62] Explaining why we need them, what they are for, how they should function, and how they may fail to function properly are the subjects of this chapter.

We need to be clear in our terminology. What is a party? What is a *system* of parties? And what is the relationship between a party system and the larger system of democratic government it's a part of? For that matter, what is this thing we're calling "democracy"? In this chapter, I'll aim to answer all of those questions, and also provide some context for understanding our system, both historically and with reference to other party systems around the world.

Such questions are longstanding, yet a continuing source of controversy. In answering them, since I don't have much authority of my own, I will (a) stick mostly to well-accepted theories, and (b) make clear where the ideas come from, so you can check my work. When it comes to party system function, a lot of what I'm going to lay out comes from Giovanni Sartori (1924-2017), an Italian political scientist who taught in the U.S. for many years from the 1970s to '90s, specializing in comparative politics and democratic theory. His book *Parties and Party Systems* (1976) is widely recognized as a major milestone in the study of political parties. It and two later books, *The Theory of Democracy Revisited* (1987) and *Comparative Constitutional Engineering* (1994; second edition 1997), I've found to be very enlightening. One thing I like about Sartori is his emphasis on qualitative analysis. In a famous 1970 paper titled "Concept Misformation in Comparative Politics", he pushed back against a growing movement for quantitative analysis, in political science as well as other social sciences. The problem was not with wanting to quantify things, but that too often, scientists were taking

---

[62] Schattschneider 1942.

measurements before fully working out the nature of the variables being measured.

If we are to understand clearly the objects of study — party systems — then the qualitative must precede the quantitative. So this chapter begins by defining a few terms.

Democracy

A party system is a *sub-system*: part of a larger system of democracy. In particular, it fits into a system of *representative* democracy (in the case of the U.S. and other countries with no monarch, also known as a *republic*). I know that some people think the American system has very little to do with real democracy, because it's not direct democracy, or because our choices are so constrained, or for other reasons. But despite the glaring imperfections of the system, voting does matter. The people are the ultimate authority.

The Oxford English Dictionary defines *democracy*, in the context of government, as:

> Government by the people; esp. a system of government in which all the people of a state or polity (or, esp. formerly, a subset of them meeting particular conditions) are involved in making decisions about its affairs, typically by voting to elect representatives to a parliament or similar assembly.

The word shouldn't be taken too literally. It comes from the Greek "demos", meaning people, and "kratos", meaning power. So, literally it means "power of the people". In ancient Athens, this meant the citizens making decisions for their city directly. But this kind of direct democracy doesn't work so well on a national scale. If we followed this literal definition, we'd have to conclude that there are no democratic nations in the modern world. That wouldn't leave much scope for using the word.

The democracy of ancient Athens differs in another important way from modern democratic nation-states, as Sartori illuminates in *The Theory of Democracy Revisited*. Most modern democracies are actually a combination of liberalism and democracy: *liberal democracy*. I don't mean the American version of "liberal", which is close to "progressive" or "left-of-center", but rather the historical, classic version of liberalism that aims to guarantee the liberty of individuals through such things as rights and the rule of law — the liberalism that began (in Sartori's view) with John Locke (1632-1704). William Blackstone, Montesquieu, James Madison, and Benjamin Constant are also considered important early theorists of this liberalism, further developed later by the likes of John Stuart Mill.[63] This liberalism has continued to evolve over the many years since their lifetimes.

I'm especially speaking of *political* liberalism, not *economic* liberalism, which contains the doctrines of *laissez-faire* — the basis for what has more recently become known as *neoliberalism*. Sartori traces the historical confluence of these two sets of ideas, which overlap but are more distinct than is sometimes appreciated. The emphasis of political liberalism is on civil liberties, which are deeply ingrained in our modern conception of democracy.

There was no constitution in the democracy of ancient Athens. People were subject to the whims of the majority. It was a major concern for Madison and the other Founders to avoid such a problem. Under liberal democracy, we have the important additions of the rule of law and of due process, designed to protect individuals from the abuse of state power.

"Democracy", Sartori writes, "is the by-product of a competitive method of leadership recruitment."[64] He elaborates:

> Democracy is a system in which *no one can choose himself, no one can invest himself with the power to rule, and, therefore, no one can arrogate to himself unconditional and unlimited power.* To be sure, this is a definition that states the characteristics of democracy in the negative. It cannot be, in any sense, an exhaustive definition. Within this limitation, however, it displays a peculiar strength. For one thing, it sets forth defining properties (not contingent or accompanying properties). That is to say that any social or political system based on different principles is not, *by definition*, a democracy. In the second place, our definition seems to lie at the intersection at which,

---

[63] Sartori 1987, pp. 374-375.
[64] Sartori 1987, p. 152.

and indeed before which, the description and the prescription depart from one another. When we say that only *others* can empower *you*, this is both a descriptive statement (democracies are in fact constructed on this principle) and a prescriptive declaration (democracies should be so constructed).[65]

This seems like the sort of broad and inclusive definition we need for the purposes of this book. It clearly includes representative democracy, which is the system we have. The focus of this book is on liberal, representative democracy, meaning that our government is elected, and that its scope of action is limited by inviolable rights. There's a lot more to the story, but I don't have the space here to cover it all — for a more complete understanding, I recommend Sartori's book.

Alongside the theoretical view of democracy, we can also take a more empirical view. We can ask, Which countries in the world are (reasonably) called democracies? The Economist Intelligence Unit publishes an annual Democracy Index, based on 60 indicators and grouping 167 countries into five categories: full democracy (scoring between 8 and 10 points), flawed democracy (6 to 8 points), hybrid regime (4 to 6), and authoritarian regime (0 to 4). In 2018, 75 countries qualified as either full or flawed democracies. Here are the top 25:

Rank	Country	Score	Democracy category	Effective number of parties[*] (as of)
1	Norway	9.87	Full	4.39 (2013)
2	Iceland	9.58	Full	5.09 (2016)
3	Sweden	9.39	Full	4.99 (2014)
4	New Zealand	9.26	Full	2.96 (2014)
5	Denmark	9.22	Full	5.75 (2015)
6=	Canada	9.15	Full	2.50 (2015)
6=	Ireland	9.15	Full	3.80 (2016)

---

65 Sartori 1987, pp. 206-207; emphasis in the original.

8	Finland	9.14	Full	5.84 (2015)
9	Australia	9.09	Full	2.44 (2016)
10	Switzerland	9.03	Full	4.92 (2015)
11	Netherlands	8.89	Full	8.17 (2017)
12	Luxembourg	8.81	Full	3.93 (2013)
13	Germany	8.68	Full	2.80 (2013)
14	United Kingdom	8.53	Full	2.48 (2017)
15	Uruguay	8.38	Full	2.64 (2014)
16	Austria	8.29	Full	4.59 (2013)
17	Mauritius	8.22	Full	1.66 (2014)
18	Malta	8.21	Full	1.98 (2017)
19	Spain	8.08	Full	3.80 (2016)
20	Costa Rica	8.07	Full	4.73 (2018)
21	South Korea	8.00	Flawed	2.65 (2016)
22	Japan	7.99	Flawed	2.34 (2014)
23=	Chile	7.97	Flawed	7.48 (2017)
23=	Estonia	7.97	Flawed	4.19 (2019)
25	**United States**	**7.96**	**Flawed**	**1.99 (2018)**

Table 2.1. Top 25 countries according to the Democracy Index
* Laakso and Taagepera's (1979) "effective number of parties" (ENP) measure.
Source: The Economist Intelligence Unit (EIU 2019). My ENP calculations.

The United States fell below 8.0 for the first time (since the index began) in 2016, making the transition from "full democracy" to "flawed democracy". (Of course, these are just labels: We've never been without flaws.) While it's no surprise to see Nordic countries at the top of the list, it's a little more disappointing to see the U.S. trailing Uruguay, a country that has only been practicing democracy continuously since 1984. Shouldn't we expect that with more practice of democracy comes higher quality? And if we find cases where this isn't so, doesn't it occasion a search for where the malfunction lies? I would submit that in the case of the United States, to a large extent, it's in our party system.

Along with Democracy Index scores, I've included each country's "effective number of parties", calculated for the most recent national legislative elections available at the time of writing. This measure was designed to deal with the question of how to count the number of parties while weighting their share of seats. Suppose you're studying a party system with two large parties and one small one. Do you say it's a three-party system, even though one of the three is much smaller than the other two? Or do you call it a "two-and-a-half"-party system? The *effective number of parties* measure, or ENP, published in 1979 by Markku Laakso and Rein Taagepera, gives us a way to answer this precisely, based on the seat shares of each party.

In this case, let's say the biggest party has 48 percent of the seats in the national legislature, or a seat share of 0.48. Let's say the other two parties have seat shares of 0.40 and 0.12 respectively. By the Laakso-Taagepera formula, we square each of these shares, then add them all up, then take the inverse: $(0.48)^2 + (0.40)^2 + (0.12)^2 = 0.2304 + 0.16 + 0.0144 = 0.4048$, the inverse of which is about 2.47. So yes, in this case we have, roughly, a "two-and-a-half" party system. (If all three parties were the same size, the effective number of parties would be exactly 3.)

ENP collapses a lot of differences into a single number; it's important not to read too much into it. But I included it in the table because I think there is a connection between party systems (especially in their ability to promote accountability) and quality of democratic governance. Of the top ten countries, six have an ENP of between 4 and 6. One has about 3, one has a bit less than 4, and two have about 2.5. (By the way, in Australia's case [ENP: 2.44] I am treating the Liberals and Nationals as one party, as is conventional because of their longstanding alliance.)

The United States is the only country in the top 25 that has an ENP less than 2, aside from Mauritius and Malta — which have populations of about 1.35 million and 415,000 respectively (according to the CIA World Factbook). In the case of those two countries, their minuscule size probably leaves less scope for minor parties, and also it may be relevant that both countries were British colonies — Mauritius from 1810 to 1968, Malta from 1814 to 1964. Their experience of a party system has probably been strongly shaped by the British example. Note that the U.K. has a fairly low ENP by the standards of "full democracy" countries, and that historically, though less so in recent times, the British parliament has often been a canonical example of two-partyism.

I introduced ENP here to show how the two numbers line up. But the empirical question was, How many democracies are there in the world? And the answer, relying on the Democracy Index and including both "full" and "flawed" categories, is 75. How many of those are *representative* democracies, with political parties? All of them — because, as Schattschneider noted, modern democracy without parties is "unthinkable".

The term "representative democracy" essentially equates (when combined with the lack of a monarch) to a *republic* — which is, of course, what we have, within a constitutional framework including the separation of powers, levels of government from local to federal, civil rights, and more. When people complain that we aren't a democracy, but rather a republic, I think they are missing the point. The principle that everyone should have an equal vote is not anti-republican. Nor does democracy, as I understand it in connection to liberalism, pose a threat to the constitutional framework or the idea of limited government. But here is where many people get the wrong idea:

> Think of a democracy like this: If the majority of your neighbors voted to paint all houses bright purple you would be forced to follow suit. Okay with you?[66]

We need to understand "democracy" not in its literal but in its modern sense, which is *liberal* democracy. Liberalism adds the concept of *rights* to the mix, which limits the scope of government control. That is, the Constitution protects individuals from the violation of rights that majorities might otherwise impose on them. This concerns the idea of the *tyranny of the majority*, about which I'll have more to say later in the book.

---

[66] Dimond 2014.

Representation

With representative democracy as a given, we next have to
understand what we mean by *representation*. There are several
different ways of understanding the concept — or what might even be
called *theories*. Sartori[67] identifies seven theories, including two that he
considers essential for real political representation:

1. The **electoral** theory — the people freely and periodically elect
    a body of representatives.
2. The **responsibility** theory — the governors are accountable or
    responsible to the governed.

As a condition (of democratic representation), the first of these is
necessary but not sufficient: "The mere occurrence of elections does
not indicate, in itself, a representational system". On the other hand,
with regard to the second, "accountability to the people is a mere
phrase if it cannot be enforced by the sanction of electoral removal"
— so this second condition is likewise necessary.

There are other theories he finds less appealing:

3. The **mandate** theory — the governors are agents or delegates
    who carry out the instructions received from their electors.
4. The *idem sentire*, or syntony, theory — the people feel the
    same as the state.
5. The **consent** theory — the people consent to the decisions of
    their governors.
6. The **participation** theory — the people share, in some
    significant way, in the making of relevant political decisions.

The mandate theory has been widely discredited as a mechanism
for representative democracy. (For example, see Edmund Burke's 1774
Bristol speech.) The next three, numbers 4, 5, and 6, Sartori describes
as too vague, and more like a consequence of, rather than a "founding
condition" of, a system of representation. They may be good qualities

---

[67] Sartori 1968.

for a representational system to possess, and may frequently coincide with such systems, but are not defining features of them.

Finally, there is also a "resemblance" theory which he deems desirable, but not strictly necessary:

7. The **resemblance**, or mirroring, theory — the governors are a representative sample of the governed.

Resemblance, Sartori points out, does not assure us that the government will act in the interests of those it resembles. However, it may make it easier for parts of the public to have confidence in government. And meeting a minimum standard of resemblance may be a good indicator of effective political representation.

The reason Sartori emphasizes the first two theories as crucial is to stay within the context of democracy. After all, to "represent", by itself, doesn't necessarily mean that much. Many kings and queens have claimed to "represent" their people. But that was by divine right, or some other unaccountable theory — it's of no value in a working theory of democracy. What we're primarily interested in is how to form a representative body, in order to transfer power from a theoretically sovereign people to a much smaller group capable of actually exercising it. And how to ensure that this small group is, and remains, *answerable* to the people. The emphasis is on the electoral theory of representation because it, Sartori writes, "is the theory of responsible and responsive representation; it is not concerned with satisfying the requirement of similarity but with securing the obligation to respond."

This "obligation to respond", and to do so responsibly, amounts to *accountability*. We need our government to be accountable to us, the people who elected it. *Responsible and responsive representation* is, in a nutshell, what we need more of. Our system is neither very responsible, nor very responsive. Could this be because our "representative democracy" is not actually very representative?

Parties and party systems

The next definition we need is of the word *party*. One of the early (1770), classic definitions is Edmund Burke's: "Party is a body of men united for promoting by their joint endeavours the national interest upon some particular principle in which they are all agreed."

However, this has come to be seen as a bit too narrow, and too normative. Schattschneider proposed a broader, more functional approach in his 1942 classic *Party Government*:

> A political party is first of all an organized attempt to get power. Power is here defined as control of the government. That is the objective of party organization. The fact that the party aims at control of the government as a whole distinguishes it from pressure groups.[68]

Sartori defines the word more concisely as follows:

> A party is any political group identified by an official label that presents at elections, and is capable of placing through elections (free or nonfree), candidates for public office.[69]

While Schattschneider's definition separates "party" from "pressure group", Sartori's also separates it from "faction", by insisting on an "official label" for the party. Furthermore, he deliberately leaves out a requirement of fair competition from the definition (with the phrase "free or nonfree"), accounting for the word's application to one-party states such as China. By this exclusion, he doesn't mean to legitimize the democratic character of such states, but simply to understand the word "party" at the proper level of precision — which must be pre-normative if we wish to use a phrase like "one-party state" with any accuracy. And in fact, there are some functions performed in a one-party state that are not in a partyless state.

Some of the main functions of party are embodied in what Sartori terms *channelment* (which he also calls "canalization" — also known simply as *channeling*): providing channels for people to enter politics, for power to be acquired, and for it to be exercised. One-party states take advantage of this form of channelment. But competitive party

---

[68] Schattschneider 1942, p.35.
[69] Sartori 1976, p. 63.

systems also provide channels for dissent to be brought within the ambit of politics. More generally, they allow for *expression* by the voters — another crucial function of a party system in democracies, which party-state systems do not allow. Sartori elaborates:

> A subsystem of parties (in the plural) allows expressive communication, that is, enables the citizens to communicate *to* the state. Conversely, a party-state system provides a communication network devised for communicating *to* the society. It is not simply that a party system allows a choice among channels while a party-state system offers a channel without choice. The critical element lies — we know — in the autonomy of the subsystem. In and by itself, a choice among channels could approximate a choice among chains. The point is whether the political communication network is shaped at the subsystem level, independently from the state system. If this is the case, then a party subsystem links a people to a government by providing an expressive system of communication that keeps the state under control. Conversely, the party-state identification links a government to the people by creating a system of authoritative communication that keeps the citizens under control. Hence a party system can be defined as a system of free (autonomous) canalization in which *expression prevails*, throughout the political system, over repression; whereas a party-state system can be defined as a system of compulsory (monopolistic) canalization in which *repression prevails*, all along the line, over expression.[70]

This paragraph neatly sums up the relationship between communication, channelment, and expression, all essential concepts for understanding the functions of party. It also takes us to the next level — the party *system*, which is this book's primary object of reference. At the most basic level, a party system is simply a system of parties. But Sartori here gives another definition: "a system of free (autonomous) canalization in which *expression prevails*, throughout the political system, over repression". A party system is a vehicle of

---

[70] Sartori 1976, pp. 57-58.

representation — "a means for reducing unmanageable numbers to a manageable size"[71] — and thus essential for the practice of democracy. To have true representation in government, the people need freedom of expression, which depends on some degree of choice.

One might ask whether the U.S. actually has a party system, by the standard that "expression prevails". Though we don't have a "monopolistic canalization", we do seem to have a *duopolistic* one, and duopoly suffers, to some extent, from many of the same problems as monopoly. I would say that a limited form of expression does prevail, in the sense that voting matters; but it's far too constrained an expression. We have a dysfunctional party system, which can be improved to perform much better in terms of promoting expression and accountability. Could the dysfunction be caused by a lack of "subsystem autonomy"? I think this is a big part of the story — in all the ways that the parties in power rig the system to their own advantage, such as by gerrymandering.

Political scientists often speak of three different aspects of parties:

1. The party in government;
2. The party in the electorate;
3. The party as an organization.

Party in government is what responds to voters' demands, by implementing policy (or trying to). It simplifies legislative negotiations by reducing large numbers to more manageable ones. And it helps shape government, constrained (to some degree) by party discipline, image (or optics), and pressures for accountability.

Party in the electorate helps give structure to a polity, by framing issues and channeling voter demands. Party images, or "brands", are defined (and refined) to appeal to the electorate, and compete with each other, providing an avenue for meaningful expression through choice.

Party as an organization helps connect society to politics, by letting like-minded citizens work together to shape and advance the interests of the party. It also helps to recruit, cultivate, and support politicians.

---

[71] Sartori 1968.

In party-state systems (that is, one-party states), it acquires additional significance as a major instrument of authority. But in democratic countries, it has less to do with accountability than the first two aspects of party, which sit at the intersection of representation and the exercise of power.

There's a conflict of the public interest between party in government and party in the electorate. It's very tempting for the party in government to make sure the rules favor themselves in the electorate — to tilt the playing field. But this works against the healthy competition that is vital for accountability. I'll return to this problem later in the book.

The party system as subsystem

To help visualize how the party system fits into the overall scheme of American democracy at the national level, I offer figure 2.1, below.

The basic structuring principle of this diagram is that government is elected from society, which includes the many shaping influences of a polity, such as identity (ethnic, religious, class, or otherwise), ideology, and the media. Voters elect, via the voting system, the members of the legislative and executive branches of the government. The actions, or performance, of government constitute *governance*, which feeds back to the top part of the diagram because it affects the sociopolitical conditions which influence the behavior of voters.

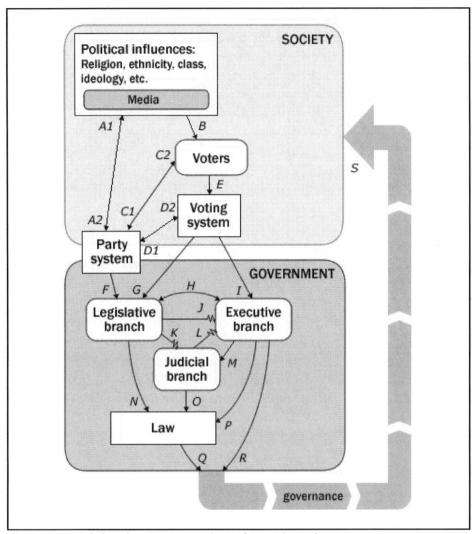

Figure 2.1. High-level system overview of American democracy

Within government, the idea of checks and balances is important, helping to ensure that none of the three branches of government has too much power. I borrow the symbol for electrical resistance, an angular squiggle, to show a "check" of one institution upon another. The more common connector is an arrowhead, indicating either influence or definition — for example, the law is defined jointly by the three branches of government, primarily by the legislative branch but with important contributions by the other two branches.

I've labeled the connections, or arcs, to facilitate discussion of the system's dynamics. Here are descriptions of each connection:

A1: The party system's influence on society. How our partisan attitudes affect how we think about ourselves and society.

A2: The influence of sociopolitical constructs on our party system.

B: The influence of sociopolitical constructs on voters (and especially how they behave).

C1: The influence of voters on the party system — through membership, political and financial support, etc.

C2: The party system's influence on voters (similar to *B* but structured in a partisan way).

D1: The influence of the voting system on the party system.

D2: The party system's influence on the voting system.

E: The starting point of democracy: The voters express themselves via the voting system.

F: The party system's influence on government (in general). Primarily manifest in the collaboration between the legislative and executive branches (arc *H*).

G: The formation (or constitution) of the legislative branch based on the voting system's processing of votes.

H: The partisan connection(s) between the legislative and executive branches. The president and vice president are usually members of one of the major parties in Congress.

I: The formation of the executive branch based on votes processed by the voting system (which includes the electoral college).

J: Legislative checks on the executive: impeachment and confirmation of appointees (which affects arc *M* for the judiciary branch).

K: Legislative checks on the judiciary: impeachment of judges.

L: Judicial checks on executive action.

M: The executive's power to appoint members of the judiciary.

N: The power of the legislative branch to define the law, subject to the Constitution.

O: The power of the courts to interpret, overrule, and sometimes modify the law.

P: The influence of the executive branch on defining the law, mainly through the veto power and the VP's tie-breaking vote in the Senate. (The veto power could also have been represented by a check on the legislative branch, but drawing it this way is simpler.)

Q: The influence of the law on governance.

R: The influence of executive decisions and administration on governance.

S: The effects of governance on society.

Party in government, connected via arc *F* to the "party system" block, mainly appears in arc *H*, which connects the legislative and executive branches. In the context of a two-party system, the President either "has a majority" in the House and/or Senate, meaning he belongs to the same party as the majority congressional party, or he doesn't. It's easy to imagine that in a multiparty system, the President would never, or rarely, have an actual majority in either chamber of Congress. This would reduce the power of the President in shaping legislation — which many would consider a good thing. For example, did the Founders ever imagine that the President would customarily write the budget that Congress then considers passing into law? I seriously doubt it: passing a budget is one of the prime functions of a legislature. Similarly, the Founders gave the power of declaring war to Congress. But that hasn't seemed to matter to a lot of presidents.

Arc *H* also represents a diminishment of accountability within the design of the checks and balances between the branches of government, by modifying the function carried out along arc *J*. Partisan loyalties between Congress and the presidency mean that some members of Congress tend to give the executive a free pass when it comes to confirming appointees or considering impeachment when necessary. Conversely, partisan enmities sometimes lead to "witch hunts", such as impeachments that aren't so well-founded, or unfair blocking of qualified appointees. Both effects are dysfunctional — so arc *H* is problematic. I'll have more to say about this later in the book.

At the same time, many political scientists have pointed out that an important role of parties in the American system is to break through the gridlock that can result from the separation of powers and from the multitude of checks and balances designed by the Founders. So arc *H* can also help the executive branch cooperate with the legislative branch to act in the interests of the people. Party ties can also improve cooperation between the House and Senate. For simplicity, the diagram omits the bicameral nature of the legislative branch, a significant check built into our government.

Most of the connections of the "party system" block in this diagram are outside of government: They concern the party in the electorate. That's because (a) our party system is extra-constitutional — it's not built into the Constitution; and (b) I have more to say about the party in the electorate. That's where freedom of choice is lacking, so I think that's where the system failure begins.

Arc *D1*, the voting system's effects on the party system, was the main subject of chapter 1. Arc *D2*, the party system's effects on the voting system, mostly represents a negative influence, the abuse of power to arrange the system to one's own advantage as a partisan. This was also discussed at the end of chapter 1. Because changing the voting system is a matter of law, arc *D2* has a lot to do with party in government — so *D2* can be seen as a "shortcut" path for *F-N-Q-S*.

Arcs *C1* and *C2* are pretty straightforward — *C1* representing how voters not only make up the membership of parties, and support them in other ways (including financial), but also make demands on their parties through voting (especially in primaries), polling, and direct contact with politicians. *C2* represents the influence of parties on their members, and in fact even on independents, who have to cope with the options presented by the party system. Many partisan voters take cues from their party leadership.

Arc *B* is essentially the many-faceted influence of culture on voters and voter behavior, much of it filtered and shaped by the media, who are a major influence on how political questions are framed. Arcs *A1* and *A2* show that the party system both influences and is influenced by sociopolitical constructs, such as ideology and identity. Influences (*A1*) because partisan interests help shape ideological questions, as well as how people think of themselves. This is perhaps especially true in a polarized two-party system where hatred of the other side has become a key principle of politics. How the party system is influenced by sociopolitical constructs (*A2*) probably seems rather obvious — in the "common-sense" theory of how political parties form, like-minded individuals come together on the basis of their shared identity or outlook.

But how do such people decide which political questions should be priorities for them, for basing a party on? If you put three people in a room, they'll have about eight different opinions, right? Answering this question is what the concept of *cleavage* is all about.

Cleavages, alignments, and realignments
A *cleavage*, in political science, is a division of the electorate into distinct camps. On an issue like abortion, for example, there's a deep cleavage between the pro-life and pro-choice camps. The same is true of issues like nationalized healthcare, foreign trade, environmental protection, and many others. Party cleavage is the sorting of the electorate into different parties. For a long time, the basic cleavage dividing the Democratic and Republican parties was big government versus small. An active role for government, including wealth redistribution and a strong social safety net, versus minimal government with taxes as low as possible.

A *cross-cutting* cleavage is a division on some issue that cuts across party cleavages. Sometimes a new issue arises, or an existing issue becomes more salient, which doesn't sort out along party lines — in each party, some take one position, others an opposing position. In such cases, the parties either adapt to the cross-cutting cleavage, or a new party emerges. One classic example of this dynamic is the issue of slavery in the 1850s. The Democrats and Whigs, the two major parties at the beginning of the decade, did not take an explicit stand on the issue; in fact they had worked hard over several decades to keep it from becoming a central issue. But eventually it became a strong, cross-cutting cleavage that couldn't be ignored. The Republican Party was founded in 1854 to advocate for abolition of slavery, and this led to the almost immediate demise of the Whig Party.

In his book *Dynamics of the Party System*, James L. Sundquist proposes a model of how parties form around cleavages, and how they respond to changes. He presents something similar to figure 2.2, below, to illustrate the realignment of the 1850s:

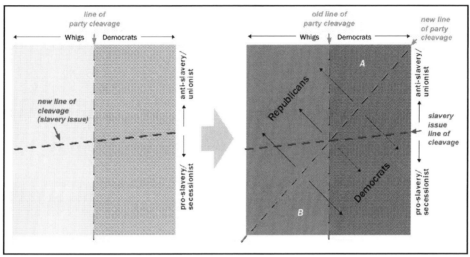

Figure 2.2. Partisan realignment of the 1850s (adapted from Sundquist 1983).
(Full-color version: daneckam.com/book/btp/figures.)

The left side of this diagram shows the old party cleavage between Whigs, on the left, and Democrats, on the right. The issue of slavery (combined with the question of secession) is the cross-cutting cleavage, shown as a close-to-horizontal, dotted line cutting across both parties. As the issue becomes more salient, the old party cleavage gives way to a new one (shown on the right side) between Democrats and the new Republican Party, which is aligned with the anti-slavery pole, at the top edge. The triangular area labeled "A" represents those anti-slavery Democrats who left their party to join the Republicans. For them, the issue of slavery dominated other issues that bound them to the Democratic Party. For other Democrats (shown in the bluish area to the right of *A*), although they were anti-slavery, the issue was not important enough to compel them to jump ship.

Conversely, while most Whigs went with the Republican Party, some, especially in the South, became Democrats (shown in area "B").

The realignment of the 1850s was the last time the U.S. saw a change in the identities of the two leading parties. But realignments also happen without one party replacing another. FDR's New Deal of the 1930s triggered a party realignment. The Democratic Party became the party of more active government, of what we now call the "safety net" of government-backed pensions (Social Security) and welfare programs, while the Republican Party became the party for those who thought such programs should be outside the scope of government.

Sundquist lists four possible responses of the two-party system to a cross-cutting cleavage:

1. No realignment. The issue either fades away or is somehow rationalized within the current party cleavage structure.
2. Realignment by the existing parties. The parties adjust their stances to take account of the new issue — possibly by absorbing a third party. (Sundquist provides two scenarios for this type of response, one with a third party playing a role and one without.)
3. Realignment by replacing one of the two parties. One of the parties falls by the wayside, making way for a third party — as happened in the 1850s, when the Republicans replaced the Whigs.
4. Realignment by replacing both parties. Although this hasn't happened in the U.S., it is possible.[72]

Realignments don't always happen all at once. In many respects, the realignment of the 1930s extended far beyond that decade. The New Deal, and especially the later anti-segregationist direction of the national Democratic Party, did not sit too well with Southern Democrats, who were a faction distinct from the national party. The coherence of the Southern Democrats as a voting bloc gave the U.S. what some have called a *de facto* "three-party" system during the

---

[72] Sundquist 1983, pp. 24-34.

middle part of the 20th century.[73] It wasn't until the Reagan revolution of the 1980s that conservative southerners fully switched to the Republican Party, finally bringing to an end the realignment that began (or accelerated) with the New Deal. Sundquist refers[74] to "transparent overlays" as the best way to understand new lines of party cleavage — each division layered on top of older ones, which continue to figure in the loyalties of some voters, in a less defined or "blurred" way. The accumulation over time of cleavage overlays causes intra-party tensions, and contributes to ideological incoherency.

In his book, Sundquist focuses on three major party realignments — the third, in addition to those of the 1850s and 1930s, is the realignment of the 1890s triggered by the rise of populism with the People's Party. The cross-cutting cleavage in this case was the question of allowing silver to be used as currency, and the critical election occurred in 1896, when William Jennings Bryan ran unsuccessfully for president as the nominee of both the Populists and the Democrats (along with the Silver Party and Silver Republicans, two minor parties). Sundquist analyzes this as a realignment of the existing parties through the absorption of a third party, ushering in a new era with much improved fortunes for the Republicans.[75]

Party realignments of this sort would happen much more smoothly in a multiparty system where parties could rise or fall organically, where a shift of partisan loyalties would not necessarily cause such disruption to the overall system, as it does when just two parties lay claim to almost the entire electorate.

Ideological permutations

A multiparty system allows for greater variation in the policy positions adopted by each political party. It alleviates the need for issues to be prioritized in terms of defining what the party stands for. To illustrate, let's build a simplified model of issue cleavages, in which all of politics breaks down into just three "issue areas": social issues,

---

[73] See, e.g., Montgomery 1954; he dates this three-partyism to 1876.
[74] Sundquist 1983, p. 17.
[75] Sundquist 1983, pp. 160-161.

economic issues, and foreign policy. And let's further suppose that for each of these issue areas there are just two positions, as shown in the following table:

Issue area	Position 1	Position 2
Social issues	Conservative	Liberal
Economic issues	Conservative	Liberal
Foreign policy	Hawkish	Dovish

Table 2.2. Simplified example of issue cleavages

How could a party system allow for these different viewpoints to be represented? The quick answer might be that one party is conservative/hawkish, and the other is liberal/dovish. But for some voters this would not be a good solution. Suppose you're liberal on social issues, but conservative on economic issues and hawkish on foreign policy. If you join the "conservative" party, your views on social issues are not represented by that party; and if you join the "liberal" party, your views on economic issues and foreign policy are not represented. Two parties are not enough to represent all the permutations of views on these three issue areas.

Each of these issue areas can be thought of as a dimension. With three issues, we're looking at a three-dimensional space, with eight defined regions making up the full range of ways to combine positions. These can be listed as follows, where we use "C" to mean the conservative position, "L" to mean the liberal one, "H" to mean hawkish, and "D" to mean dovish; and we list them in the same order as they appear in the table above:

1. CCH (that is, conservative on social and economic issues, hawkish on foreign policy)
2. CCD
3. CLH
4. CLD

5. LCH
6. LCD
7. LLH
8. LLD

Suppose a two-party system with one party being "conservative" (including hawkish on foreign policy) and the other "liberal" (including dovish). For anyone whose views match permutations #1 (CCH) or #8 (LLD) above, the choice of which party to support is an easy one. But for anyone whose views match permutations #2 through #7, to support either party means compromising some of their views. That's assuming that the conservative party consistently takes conservative positions, and the liberal party consistently takes liberal ones. On the other hand, we could just define "conservative" as any of the permutations #1 through #4, and "liberal" as any of the other permutations. But then, what policies will the parties pursue?

Our two parties often fudge (and dodge) on issues; they obscure and misdirect; they try to paper over distinctions. They also often claim support for their positions which is not fully justified by the views of the voters. For example, suppose every voter with views matching permutations #1 through #4 votes conservative, and everyone with views matching #5 through #8 votes liberal. Suppose the conservatives win with 52 percent of the vote, and that the leadership of the party in government holds the ideology CCH (regardless of how many of the party's voters hold those views). They are likely to claim that they have a mandate for CCH, even though many of their voters partly disagree.

And again, this three-dimensional analysis is actually extremely simplified. A more realistic list of issue dimensions would look something like this:
1. Economic issues — including budget balance and trade policy
2. Social issues — formed around religious and cultural beliefs
3. Education policy
4. Environmental policy
5. Healthcare policy
6. Defense and foreign policy

7. Gun policy
8. Welfare policy

With eight dimensions, supposing (perhaps simplistically) two possible positions for each, we have 2^8 (two to the power of eight), or 256 different permutations of positions that a voter can adopt. And even this doesn't exhaust the number of issue dimensions that actually exist — for example, affirmative action could be another one, as could space exploration (or science policy, more generally).

Some of these dimensions go together, however, leading to a kind of "clumping" effect. For example, if a particular voter believes in single-payer, government-funded healthcare and a generous welfare policy, it's likely she will also believe in a generous education policy. Some permutations are more consistent, coherent, and compelling than others. That's good news because it means we don't need 256 parties to represent all the coherent ideologies that Americans hold. But it seems quite clear that we need more than two, if we are to take seriously the idea that voters should be able to pick a party whose positions they agree with.

Ask yourself this: Which of the two dominant parties is in favor of free trade? Not long ago, it would've been easy to answer this question: It was the Republicans. And the Democrats were against free trade, because they were on the side of labor unions. But then, President Bill Clinton signed the North American Free Trade Agreement (NAFTA), which came into effect in 1994. Then, in 2016, Donald Trump campaigned on a platform of *opposing* free-trade agreements. So now, the issue is essentially a cross-cutting cleavage, with parts of both parties in favor and other parts opposed. Are the two parties actually in the process of swapping positions? We can probably only know with hindsight, years from now.

A voter who feels strongly about trade policy (such as a union leader or someone in the import/export business) has no clear, partisan way to express his preferences at election time. On the one hand, neither party can be relied upon to support free trade, and on the other, while the current political winds seem to favor the anti-trade position in both parties, who can say where they'll be in the future? By contrast, in many countries people can vote for parties with names like the "Liberal Democrats", which makes their stance on the issue clearer (at least for those who understand the connection between liberalism in its economic dimension and free markets). Or, they can vote for a labor party, something that has very rarely had any real representation in the United States.

Ideology isn't the only factor for voters in choosing a party. There are also social considerations: Many people, for example, identify as Democrat or Republican because that's how they were brought up. Or it's the party of their church or other social group. These can be thought of as "tribal" considerations.

Competence and credibility are other important considerations — despite frequent diatribes against "professional politicians" in American politics. Politicians, like members of other professions, benefit from having specific skills, such as rhetoric and negotiation. Politics is "the art of the possible". To be effective, politicians need to be able to judge what's possible, explain it to voters, and figure out how to achieve it.

But these considerations don't change the fact that partisan differences make the most sense when organized around ideological differences. Yes, one's family's political preferences carry a lot of weight. But how are those preferences formed in the first place? And when a son or daughter grows up and begins to think independently about politics, doesn't it make sense for their choices to be based on ideology, rather than merely reacting to their parents' views? Similarly, competence is important, but competence to do what? To steer effectively, you need to know where you want to go. Ideology is, or should be, the main foundation of party politics.

Cybernetics and variety

The "rule of anticipated reactions"[76] describes a major source of accountability in representative democracies. It says that elected officials will, when deciding how to act (especially on sensitive issues), try to anticipate how voters will react — and this can be seen as a sort

---

[76] Friedrich 1937.

of "feedback" mechanism, a rule that "connects and keeps in tune the voting act with the representative process".[77]

The idea of a feedback mechanism calls to my mind the discipline of *cybernetics*, the study of the control of systems. The field was pioneered soon after WWII by Norbert Wiener, Ross Ashby, and others. It has been applied mostly in business, in order to optimize efficiency, flexibility, or the like, but it has wide application in many areas. The word was imported from the Greek *kybernetes*, which means "steersman".

At a high level of description, democratic governance is a control system, a way for the people to control their own society and economy through the power of elective government. All control systems need self-monitoring in order to take account of their own performance — so the effects of governance, which are the "outputs" of the system, feed back into it as "inputs", and this feedback enables it to steer itself.

But not all feedback is created equal. Is our system getting the right sort of information, with high accuracy, from the feedback of voting? How strong is the feedback "signal" — or better yet, how valuable?

In cybernetics, the word "variety" is used to refer to the number of states (or, roughly, possible configurations) of a system. The more the variety embodied in a system, the more complicated it will be to control effectively. The "law of requisite variety" says, basically, that a mechanism for stable control of a system must include enough sophistication to account for the possible states of the system controlled.

With only two viable parties, the feedback "signal" is weak — because it lacks *requisite variety*. The meaning of the vote is not clear. Suppose, for example, that a voter casts a vote for the Republican party. How should this feedback be interpreted? How is it processed by the system? Is she expressing support for free trade, or opposition to it — in other words, for protectionism? The signal is so weak, or muddled, that we actually have no idea — because the party straddles the issue. Lacking meaningful feedback from voters, what seems

---

[77] Sartori 1987, p. 155.

likely is that the system will follow signals it gets from elsewhere — like special interests.

Voters need a greater degree of choice than just two parties to express the variety of their policy preferences. Without requisite variety, feedback cannot be as effective as it's supposed to be in monitoring the system. By adopting a multiparty system, we would increase variety and therefore improve the chances for government to work in the interests of the people.

The system diagram above (figure 2.1) is a cybernetic view of a democratic system. You can picture the lower block, "government", as a command structure sitting atop the upper block, like the bridge of a giant ship. The steering, or feedback, function is shown in arc S, labeled "governance". This basic structure of the system is designed to work effectively — there's a lot of wisdom in the checks and balances at the heart of it, for example — and it can work a lot better than it does. But without requisite variety, and thus lacking adequate feedback, it's no wonder the system performs far short of its potential.

Comparing the American party system with others

Now that we've briefly considered some of the key concepts relating to party systems and democracy, it's time to place the American system in context by considering how other democracies organize their political parties.

Our two-party system is unique among large democracies. No other country has a system that so thoroughly locks out third parties from competing for votes. Some countries have systems in which two parties are dominant — such as the United Kingdom, historically at least — but they aren't so exclusive of minor parties. The word *duopoly* — similar to monopoly, but with two dominant groups instead of one — applies to our system in a way it does not apply elsewhere.

Consider the U.K., the originator of the "Westminster model" which, thanks to the history of the British Empire, is the basis for the governing systems of several major countries. This is the standard parliamentary system, with a prime minister and cabinet chosen from among the elected officials of Parliament (the legislative assembly). Historically, the British parliament has been divided into two main groups, beginning in the late 17th century with the Tories and the Whigs. In the early 19th century this dichotomy was replaced by a new version, consisting of the Conservative Party (nicknamed "Tories") and the Liberal Party. In the 1920s the Liberals were supplanted by the Labour Party, giving us the primary oppositional dynamic that continues to this day: Labour vs. Conservative. The Liberal Party faded in strength and eventually reconstituted itself (in the 1980s) as the Liberal Democrats, which is one of the biggest "third" parties in the U.K.

Despite this history, which seems to provide the original template for two-party systems on planet Earth, there have long been a number of MPs (ministers of parliament; analogous to U.S. representatives) from parties other than the dominant two. In the election of 1979, for example, of the 635 seats in the House of Commons, 11 were won by the Liberal Democrats; 16 were won by regional parties, such as the Scottish National Party (SNP), the Welsh Plaid Cymru, and Northern Irish parties like the UUP, DUP, and SDLP. From the 1870s through the end of World War II, the number of seats claimed by third parties and independents was never less than 8.5 percent, with the norm substantially higher. In 2017, the most recent election, nine different parties won seats (not counting that of the Speaker, who is non-partisan). If the U.K. has a two-party system, it's clearly not of the same character as the American one; it is far from a duopoly.

A similar story can be told about Canada and Australia, both former colonies of the U.K. which adopted (with some modifications) its parliamentary system. In the 2015 elections to the Canadian parliament, the Liberal Party and Conservative Party won most of the seats, with 184 and 99 respectively. But the New Democrats won 44 seats, the Bloc Québécois won 10, and the Green Party won one seat — hardly a duopolistic result. (Noting that third parties have been important enough to frequently require the formation of minority governments, Sartori asked, "[W]hy on earth is Canada generally considered to be a two-party country?".[78])

---

[78] Sartori 1997, p. 38.

In the 2016 Australian elections, Labor won 69 seats in the House of Representatives, while the other major "party", the Liberal-National coalition, won 76. Three other seats were won by minor parties and two by independent candidates. In the Senate, Labor won 26 seats, the coalition won 30, and minor parties won 20 (including 9 for the Green Party). Again, this is not the sort of two-party system that we know in the U.S.

These Westminster-style systems are usually, but not always, dominated by two parties. There's intense competition between parties, and the identities of the two leading ones occasionally change. It's fair to say these party systems are *dualistic* (in tendency, and to varying degrees), but they are not *duopolistic*.

There are some minor exceptions to this rule — such as Jamaica, another Commonwealth nation, which has only two parties that win seats, the People's National Party and the Jamaica Labour Party. But this is a country with a population of fewer than three million — less than one percent of the U.S. population. Barbados is a similar but smaller example, with a population of fewer than 300,000. It's not surprising that such small countries have a small number of parties.

Standing in contrast to these systems (which use single-member districts) are the countries where at least one of the legislative assemblies is elected using proportional representation (PR) from multi-member districts. The best examples of these are in Europe — the Netherlands, Belgium, the Scandinavian countries (Denmark, Norway, and Sweden), Finland, Spain, Portugal, Poland, the Czech Republic, Italy (in modified form), Ireland, and others. These countries differ in how they divide into districts and how many parliamentarians are elected from each district. In the Netherlands, seats in the lower house are distributed on a nationwide basis, meaning the whole country is essentially one big district. Similarly, Israel elects the members of the Knesset as one giant electoral district using PR. All of these countries use party-list PR except for Ireland, which uses the single transferable vote. All have multiparty systems.

(PR is also used in many countries that don't score so well on measures of democracy, such as Turkey, Russia, Ukraine, Indonesia, Cambodia, South Africa, and Brazil. Using PR is no guarantee of a healthy democracy, but nor is it the cause of poor health; dysfunction has many sources. Most of these countries have not had continuous democratic regimes for more than a few decades.)

Germany pioneered its own type of electoral system, known as *mixed-member proportional representation* (or MMP — also known as *personalized* PR), which it began using in 1953. Each voter casts two votes, the first for a candidate in her district, the second for a national party. There are currently 299 districts, and each of the "constituency" elections (the first vote) is a simple plurality contest — so they are most often won by the biggest parties; a small party will typically win no seats, unless it is geographically concentrated. But the second vote, for an equal number of 299 seats, is nationwide, party-list PR, subject to a 5 percent threshold, and whatever disproportionality results from the constituency elections is made up for by adding seats in the Bundestag, so that all qualifying parties are represented proportionally. So it's PR by other means, and therefore it's no surprise that Germany has a multiparty system.

The MMP electoral system has served as a model for other nations: Bolivia and New Zealand adopted it in 1994, Lesotho in 2002. From 1853 through 1993, New Zealand used a plurality system, with the exception of 1908-1913, when it used a two-round system. This sudden change, which took effect in 1996, provides a good opportunity to explore its effects on the country's party system. To me, that means it's time for another chart.

In figure 2.3 (below) I've charted the effective number of parties (ENP) over New Zealand's history from the beginning of its party system in 1890 up to 2017. I've shown three different measures of ENP: the Laakso-Taagepera measure already mentioned earlier and two updated measurements, one by Dunleavy & Boucek (2003), the other by Grigorii V. Golosov (2010). The difference between these measures is not important. What's interesting is that we see a large increase in ENP starting in 1996. The Laakso-Taagepera index, for example, rose from 2.2 in 1993 to 3.8 in 1996. Such an increase is what we'd expect from switching from a plurality, first-past-the-post system to MMP. We see a subsequent decline in ENP starting around 2005, as, it would seem, a new system stabilized. (It may be true that when times are good, as they've been in New Zealand, there is less pressure, and/or less volatility, in the landscape of party competition. In that case, the decline in ENP could be the result of a natural "settling" process, and doesn't indicate a structural problem; the system presumably retains its capacity for a higher ENP when necessary.)

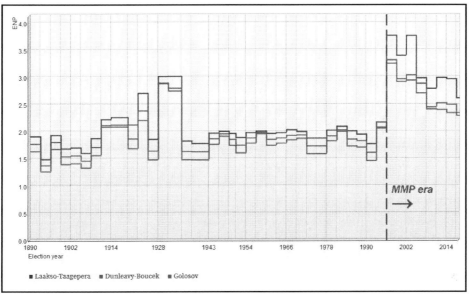

Figure 2.3. Effective number of parties in New Zealand, 1890-2017 (simplified)
(Full-color version: daneckam.com/book/btp/figures.)

That's a quantitative look at New Zealand's party history. What about a qualitative look? In fact, while the period from 1935 to 1996 looks like a classic picture of two-partyism, from 1928 to 1935 there is a surprising elevation of ENP to about 3, and significant ups and downs in the years before that as well. These things need some kind of explanation. I think the relative increase from 1911 to 1919 has a lot to do with the two-round voting system that New Zealand adopted from 1908 to 1913. But we need something more to explain the volatility of the 1920s and early 1930s.

Part of the story is that the New Zealand Labour Party, founded in 1916, rose to become the strongest party by 1935. Meanwhile, the

Liberals faded in strength, renaming themselves the United Party before merging with the conservative Reform Party to form the National Party in 1936. A similar displacement of Liberals by Labour happened at around the same time in the United Kingdom. The rise of labor-based parties seems to have been a global phenomenon in the early 20th century. So actually, maybe this is pretty much the whole story. In figure 2.4, below, I map the entire party history of New Zealand, as reflected in seats in parliament. (Obviously this leaves out a lot of parties which competed for seats but did not win them.) Each horizontal row shows the number of seats held by each party (or by independents, shown in gray at the right) as a percentage of the total. At the top is the composition of New Zealand's 11th Parliament as elected in 1890 (when political parties emerged); at the bottom, its composition at the time of writing.

We can see in this chart that what was going on in the 1920s and '30s was the rise of the Labour Party at the expense of the Liberals, followed by first a coalition, then a merging of the United and Reform parties. There does not appear to be much minor-party representation during these years outside of the parties involved in this shift. In contrast, after 1996 the system appears to become much friendlier to the sustained presence of minor parties.

The upshot of the New Zealand case: They cared enough about the health of their democracy to make changes to improve their system. So can we — if we make up our minds to do so. (See Eckam 2017 for interactive versions of the above two charts.)

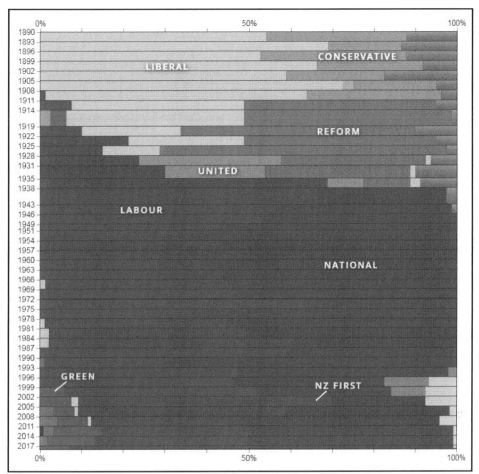

Figure 2.4. Party history of New Zealand, 1890-2017 (simplified) (Full-color version: daneckam.com/book/btp/figures.)

Let's finish up this whirlwind world tour with a visit to Latin America, home to many of the world's *presidential* democracies. The distinction between presidential and parliamentary systems is a crucial one. In the latter, including all the countries described so far in this section, there is no separate executive branch; instead, there is a prime minister, who is chosen from the legislative assembly — the parliament — and is usually the leader of the party with the most seats. The people don't vote directly for prime minister, they vote to elect members of parliament, who then choose the prime minister.

(Sometimes this position has a different name, such as "chancellor" in Germany.) Another important difference is in the length of officeholders' terms. In the U.S., federal officials serve fixed-length terms of two, four, or six years. In most parliamentary systems the duration of the term is not fixed, and elections can be called at various times, such as following a vote of "no confidence" in the prime minister's administration by the parliament.

Most of the well-functioning multiparty democracies in the world are parliamentary, not presidential, systems. The only purely presidential countries in Europe are Switzerland, the Republic of Cyprus, and Belarus. In Switzerland, the executive power is embodied in a seven-person Federal Council; the president is merely the presiding officer of the council, with no significant extra powers. Cyprus is tiny, and Belarus is not very democratic.

Turning to Latin America, we don't find a lot of clear success stories, historically, in terms of democratic function. Many parts of the region have long suffered from corruption, military coups (some supported by the CIA), extreme inequality, poverty, and crime. In terms of party systems, Brazil, as one example, has had a multiparty system since the restoration of civilian rule in the mid-1980s, but it has often suffered from fragmentation and is hard to call "successful". (On the other hand, it hasn't exactly done badly, in the economic realm at least — depending, of course, on what we compare it to.)

For many decades, Mexico was at another extreme, a "dominant-party" system in which the Institutional Revolutionary Party (PRI) reliably occupied most of the seats in the federal legislature. But the PRI has not had a majority of seats in the lower house since 1997. There are currently eight parties represented in that legislative body. So it looks like Mexico has moved well beyond its "pseudo-one-party-system" past.

How has the country performed as a democracy? Clearly there's a lot of work left to do on that score. In the 2018 Democracy Index,[79] the country ranked 71st, as a "flawed democracy", tied with Sri Lanka and just ahead of Hong Kong. It went from a score of 6.67 in 2006 to

---

[79] EIU 2019.

6.19 in 2018. So having more parties is no guarantee, in itself, of better governance. Giving voters more options should promote the interests of accountability. But there are other factors, too. In Mexico's case, there are powerful criminal syndicates at work, fighting government efforts to enforce the law. There is also the powerful legacy of colonialism, as throughout most of Latin America. In most of the region, real democracy has only been established since the 1980s, with scholars referring to the conditions in Mexico up to then as "electoral authoritarianism".[80] Latin America is widely recognized as one of the main locations for the "third wave" of democratization in the world (first identified as such by Samuel P. Huntington in a 1991 paper).

Perhaps a partial exception to this general rule is Chile, which had a vibrant multiparty democracy from 1933 to 1973. In 1970, Salvador Allende was elected president of the country, and began to nationalize industries under his socialist program. His government hired the noted cyberneticist Stafford Beer to build a control system to help manage the economy; it was dubbed Project Cybersyn.[81] Figure 2.5 is a photograph of the project's prototype operations room. It's an interesting experiment, which caught my eye as I researched possible connections between democracy and cybernetics, and it would have been interesting to see how it worked out. (I'm not sure whether so much economic nationalization was a good idea, but the general idea of applying cybernetic thinking to government is very appealing.) Unfortunately, Allende was overthrown in a CIA-led coup on September 11, 1973, and the project was abandoned before it could be put into production. The country was ruled by the dictator Augusto Pinochet until 1990, when multiparty democracy was restored. In the current Chamber of Deputies, the lower house, eleven parties are represented, most of them belonging to one of two large inter-party coalitions.

---

[80] Morse 2012.
[81] Medina 2015.

Figure 2.5. *Opsroom* of project *Cybersyn*. Design Group of the INTEC, Santiago, 1972. Photo: Gui Bonsiepe. Used by permission.

I'm not an expert in Latin American history, and of course the full story of political parties in that region is far more complex than I have the space to deal with here. Suffice it to say, for now, that democracy has taken root there over the last few decades, mostly with multiparty systems and mostly in the context of presidential (rather than parliamentary) systems, and although in some cases the combination has been problematic, in others it has worked well. We'll take a closer look at the problems later in the book.

The odd thing is, look at any large democratic country in the world today, and you find multiple parties competing in elections, and multiple parties winning seats. Countries that historically had two dominant parties, such as Uruguay, today have several parties in their national legislative assemblies. And countries that have been labeled as "two-party systems", such as Britain, Australia, and others, on closer examination have a far more dynamic system than such a label implies. The United States is truly exceptional in the extent to which third parties are effectively locked out of government. Why?

Evolution of the American party system

How did we go from having no parties to the two-party system we have today? Over nearly two and a half centuries, many changes have occurred — ones significant enough that it's fair to say there were different "systems" in place at various times, each new one supplanting its predecessor at key junctures of our history. Figure 2.6 (below) maps out the history of political parties as seen in the number of seats (in percentage terms) they had in the House of Representatives, from the first Congress up to 1981. (I stopped there for reasons of space — there's been no change in the duopolistic character since. See Eckam 2016b for a more complete, interactive version of this chart, including the ability to zoom in on the right side to see all the minor parties represented.) The main data comes from Martis's book *The Historical Atlas of Political Parties in the United States Congress: 1789-1989* (1989), while the periodization scheme on the left side is based on the work of Walter Dean Burnham, William Nisbet Chambers, V.O. Key, and others.[82] The applicability of the labels used is up for debate, but there's no question that there were major differences between different eras.

Parties in the First Party System were different from today's parties. Initially, factions emerged within Congress, growing out of an earlier division of sentiment into Federalist and anti-Federalist camps. Martis uses the labels "Pro-Administration" and "Anti-Administration" for these early congressional factions. He refers to the time of the First through Third Congresses (1789-1795) as the "no-party period", during which voting blocs formed in Congress, either around Hamilton and the Federalists or around his opponents, chief among them Thomas Jefferson, who founded the Democratic-Republican Party in the mid-1790s. Martis explains some of the ways these so-called "parties" were different than today's:

---

[82] E.g. Chambers and Burnham 1967.

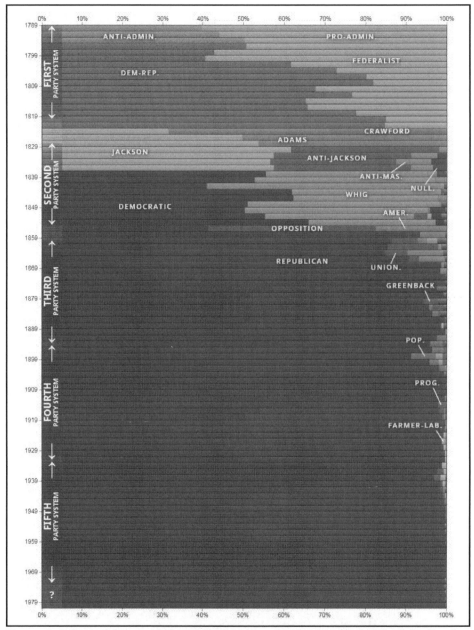

Figure 2.6. Party history of the United States, 1789-1981 (simplified) (Full-color version: daneckam.com/book/btp/figures.)

While these early blocs and parties had significant ideological differences, the formal structure of the parties was incomplete with respect to such items as a national organization and participation in elections. Although a relatively large number of individuals voted in elections, the general populace was also sheltered from influence by the legislative election of the electoral college, senators, and in many states, governors, and by the development of the congressional caucus for the nomination of presidential candidates.[83]

By the time of the Fourth Congress (1795 to 1797), partisan distinctions were sharp enough, and organized enough, that Martis feels ready to use party names. The Federalist versus Democratic-Republican split dominated the First Party System, which in its later years saw a decrease in party competition as the Federalists waned in popularity. This led to a period known as the "Era of Good Feelings" from about 1815 to 1824 in which the Democratic-Republicans were the only nationally competitive party. This breakdown in party-oriented competition was so thorough that the re-election of President James Monroe in 1820 happened without any serious opposition. The four main candidates in the 1824 presidential election were all Democratic-Republicans. John Quincy Adams's victory over Andrew Jackson set the stage for a revolution in the party system, led by a highly capable New York politician named Martin Van Buren.

In Jackson, the populist Tennessean war hero, Van Buren saw an opportunity to revive the old Jeffersonian spirit of the Democratic-Republican Party, by building an "intersectional" alliance between the North and the South. He began this effort by forging an alliance between two political machines: his own Albany Regency, and the Richmond Junto of Virginia. John Quincy Adams, son of the Federalist second president, represented a tradition of trying to rise above party, and had many Federalist supporters. Van Buren understood that defining a group in opposition to another group can be a strong unifying force, and shunned all Federalist influences in

---

[83] Martis 1989, p. 2.

forming his new coalition. He considered both President Adams and his longtime New York rival DeWitt Clinton to be Federalists in disguise.[84]

In some ways, the Regency represents a prototype for American mass political parties: While they based their political identity on certain broad principles (i.e. republicanism, as opposed to allegedly "monarchical" and nationalizing tendencies of the misnamed Federalists), they also made party unity a high priority. "The practices that tended to preserve the party became the real 'principles' of the party, for the ultimate 'principle' was self-preservation".[85] In this sense, the Regency was one of the earliest full expressions of party-as-organization. This discipline was necessary for party cohesion. But when loyalty to the group becomes so paramount that policy differences fail to get a hearing, there's a grave malfunction of democracy. And so it has become in our system. I'll take a closer look at such excessive teamsmanship in the next chapter.

The Regency also seems to represent the first time in American politics that the idea of party opposition was accepted as an institutional good. Until then, many national politicians had preferred to think of party divisions as temporary, a necessary evil interrupting a long-term unifying spirit. This was the "amalgamating" view of such men as Presidents James Monroe and his successor John Quincy Adams. But the intensity of party competition in the state of New York had revealed the value of organized opposition. As Enos Throop (governor of New York from 1829 to 1832 and a close friend of Van Buren) wrote:

> Those party divisions which are based upon conflicting opinions in regard to the constitution of the government, or the measures of the administration of it, interest every citizen, and tend, inevitably, in the spirit of emulation and proselytism, to reduce the many shades of opinion into two opposing parties.... Organized parties watch and scan each other's doings, the public mind is instructed by ample discussions of public

---

[84] Hofstadter 1969, pp. 221, 231.
[85] Wallace 1968, p. 469.

measures, and acts of violence are restrained by the convictions of the people, that the prevailing measures are the results of enlightened reason.[86]

Van Buren took the ideas he had developed during his career in New York politics and used them to build a national coalition in support of Andrew Jackson; this became the Democratic Party. The labels used in these early days are a bit confusing. Van Buren thought of what he was doing as reviving the old "Republican" spirit, by which he meant the party of Jefferson, then widely known as "Republican", but which today we usually call "Democratic-Republican". Martis calls this group, in the 1820s, "Jacksonians" because they first rallied around Jackson, who made Adams the second one-term president (his father having been the first) with his 1828 victory.

If you ask Google when the Democratic Party was founded, the answer you get is 1828. But that's debatable. Yes, Jackson was elected that year, but you wouldn't have found "Democratic Party" next to his name on any ballot. The party was not yet known by that label. In fact, when it held its first national party convention in 1832, it still didn't refer to itself that way; the 1840 national convention seems to have been the first time it did. (They usually referred to themselves as "Republicans", as Jefferson had done for his party.) Martis doesn't apply the Democratic Party label until the 25th Congress, which was elected in 1836. The length of time it took for this label to solidify reflects the immaturity of the party system at the time.

It's useful to understand the evolution of the American party system in terms of *structuring*. The First Party System, which lasted roughly from 1792 to 1824, was not very well structured, because parties were not seen as an essential part of the system. Sartori explains how a structured party system differs from an unstructured one:

> So long as the voter votes for the local notable or for some kind of local chieftain (in the *personalismo* context spoken of in Latin America), parties remain labels of little, if any, consequence. Hence, as long as these conditions prevail, the party system is not structured. However, when allegiance is

---

[86] Hofstadter 1969, p. 251.

given to the party rather than to notables or chieftains, that is, when the voter relates to abstract party images, at this moment it is no longer the individual boss or leader that 'elects' the party, but the party that 'elects' the individual, i.e., that puts the individual into office. As the process develops, it is the party system that becomes perceived as a natural *channelling system* for the political society. And when the electorate takes a given set of electoral routes and alternatives for granted very much as drivers take a given system of highways for granted, then a party system has reached the stage of structural consolidation qua system.[87]

Although the original partisan division between Federalists and Democratic-Republicans was a sort of channeling system, with an ideological dimension of centralized vs. decentralized democracy, it was also somewhat defined by notables such as Hamilton and Jefferson. And it became more so after the waning of the Federalist party, when factions became organized around powerful men like John Quincy Adams, Henry Clay, John Calhoun, and of course Andrew Jackson. Also, suffrage was less extensive during this time. In 1824, 365,928 Americans voted in the presidential election — about 3.4 percent of the total population. In 1828, 1,149,216 voted — about 9.5 percent.[88] The Second Party System, beginning around 1828, marks the first establishment of mass structured parties as a subsystem of the overall representative system.

The structuring that Sartori writes about is helpful for understanding why certain multiparty systems fail to perform well. Brazil's system, for example, is still largely organized around political leaders rather than "abstract party images". This has led to a very fragmented party system, with 28 parties seated in the lower house of parliament in the 2014 elections. Such fragmentation indicates that the party system is failing to function as a channeling system — a pitfall to be avoided in our transition from two-party to multiparty.

---

[87] Sartori 1997, p. 37.
[88] Source: Leip.

One of the most striking things about figure 2.6 is the variety of parties that succeeded in winning congressional seats from the 1830s to about 1900. This shows that even though there have almost always been two dominant parties in government, the system was not always as duopolistic as it is now — there was real competition. In fact, some early political analysts viewed third parties as a key component of the system — even if they almost never replaced one of the two dominant parties, they gave voice to parts of the electorate that were not satisfied with their choices, and thus pressured the dominant parties into adapting to the needs of the time.[89] The one time in American history that a mass party, one of the dominant two, was replaced by another was in 1854, when the Whig Party collapsed in the face of the new Republican Party, marking the end of the Second Party System.

A 20th century turn

What happened around the turn of the 20th century to put an end to this "golden age" of minor parties? I'm not sure I know the full answer, but I think it has a lot to do with certain well-intentioned reforms of the Progressive Era. One of these was that electoral fusion was banned in most states (as discussed in chapter 1).

Another important milestone was the introduction of the direct primary to reduce the power of party bosses. This had the unintended effect of creating an avenue *within* the two major parties for dissenters to be heard and for them to have a chance to take over the party — and this dissent might otherwise have been channeled into developing a new party. The primary system absorbs the energy of political innovators (or "entrepreneurs"). The election of 2016 illustrates this dynamic with the prominent examples of Bernie Sanders and Donald Trump, both of whom were at odds with the mainstream of the party whose nomination they sought, and in another system would've been likely to run under different party banners.

According to political scientist Leon Epstein, the institutionalization of the direct primary

---

[89] Disch 2002.

discouraged [new] interests and groups from seeking power by establishing new parties or by persisting in efforts to build up existing minor parties. The latter course was also made more difficult by legal burdens that states imposed on new and minor parties as well as independents. For them to gain the ballot access automatically granted Republicans and Democrats on the basis of prior votes, they were required to submit petitions signed by large numbers of registered voters.[90]

So in the process of taking power from party bosses, it seems that Progressive-Era reforms erected barriers to outsiders — political entrepreneurs with the potential to shake up the party system — and encouraged the development of duopoly.

"Sore loser" laws, passed in many states in more recent decades, may compound the problem. These laws prohibit a candidate who loses in one party primary from running as an independent or under another party line in the general election. They force candidates to choose, sometimes many months ahead of the election, whether to run as a minor-party candidate or go for a major party's nomination through the primary process. Most choose the latter option.

I suspect that today it would be nearly impossible for one of the dominant two parties to be replaced, as happened in the 1850s. When one of them goes into a period of decline, it remakes itself along new political lines, without ever allowing space for a new party to blossom. The primary system facilitates this process. It also contributes greatly to the polarization of the two main parties, since primary voters tend to be fewer and more ideological than voters in general elections.

In a multiparty system, where voters had more meaningful choices in general elections, primaries would not be so important. There are benefits to letting party leaders have more say in choosing their candidates. It would help to keep candidates better aligned with party platforms, thus promoting ideological consistency. As E.E. Schattschneider[91] wrote, "Democracy is not to be found *in* the parties

---

[90] Epstein 1986, p. 173.
[91] Schattschneider 1942.

but *between* the parties." When party organizations are able to take more control of their destinies, they would provide a more stable environment for the cultivation of political leaders.

Figure 2.7 shows a timeline of the effective number of parties in the U.S. Congress (both houses combined), using the same sources as figure 2.6 (i.e. primarily Martis). Based on this chart, it's hard to see much difference between the late 19th century and the 20th century: With a few exceptions, ENP seems to stay roughly between 1.5 and 2.0. But this simple number masks the real variety in the allocation of congressional seats.

For example, in the 47th Congress, which was elected in 1880 and served from 1881 to 1883, the three measures of ENP range from 2.01 to 2.14. There were four parties represented in Congress: aside from Democrats and Republicans, 10 seats were held by the Greenback Party, and three were held by Readjusters or Readjuster Democrats. These numbers are a small fraction of the total number of seats, which was 369 at the time, so they don't affect ENP that much. But even a small amount of representation means a party can be heard and may change the terms of debate. How relevant the party is depends on the division of seats, and what kind of coalition potential it has. I'm not sure how relevant the Greenbacks and Readjusters were in the 47th Congress, but the point is it wasn't such a duopolistic system. Minor parties had a chance — if not to become a major party, at least to get their point across.

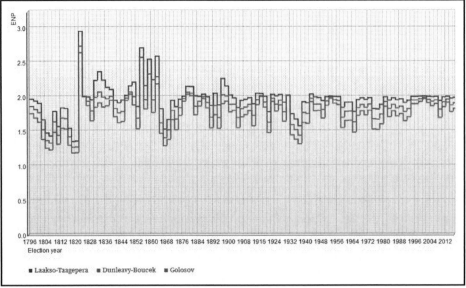

Figure 2.7. Effective number of parties in the U.S. Congress, 1796-2017 (simplified) (Full-color version: daneckam.com/book/btp/figures.)

Compare that to the 83rd Congress, which served from 1953 to 1955: The measures of ENP range from 1.97 to 2.0, but this time no minor parties were represented. Two seats (out of 531) were filled by independents. This is essentially a picture of duopoly, though ENP looks similar to what it was in the 47th Congress. With only minor exceptions for the Progressive Party and a few other parties (and, of course, a few independents), congressional seats have been exclusively filled by Democrats and Republicans since around 1900.

In an interview with Paul Jay of the Real News Network, historian and political analyst Thomas Frank makes some of the same points I've made about how the two-party system changed after the 19th century:

> **Thomas Frank:** If you go back and look at American political wars in the 19th century, whenever the two main parties would get too close to each other, you'd have a third-party challenge. On the issue of slavery, the Democrats and the Whigs at the time had basically agreed among themselves not to debate this issue openly, and what happens? You have the Republican

118

Party that rises up and says no, this is the main issue before us and we have to debate it. The Whigs in that case crumbled and fell apart, and were replaced by the Republicans. [...] In game theory, the two parties coming together and deciding to have a consensus, and not to debate certain things, this is going to happen. So you need this outside competition to keep things honest. This is an important element, is that you have to be able to form third parties and challenge these two guys when they do this. Because they're going to do it. And they're doing it right now, I mean, up until this year — like, say, the issue of trade and globalization — the two parties, everybody in charge in Washington, whether it's Bill Clinton or whether it's Barack Obama or whether it's George W. Bush or whether it's Ronald Reagan — they all think these trade deals are great. They all agree on this. [...] they keep this consensus by agreeing with each other within Washington, D.C. How do you smash that? Well, in the 19th century, you had third parties. Unfortunately, after Populism died down, almost every state in America passed laws forbidding the various electoral techniques that the Populists used, and that other third parties...

Paul Jay: For example?

Thomas Frank: It's called fusion. It was a technique they used to use at the state level in order to win elections. In the South, they would align with the Republican Party, [which] in the South in the 1890s was not very big. But there were still a lot of people that voted Republican in the South back then. And in the North, in a place like Kansas, they'd align with the Democratic Party, and they would cross-endorse each other's candidates, and they would win this way. That's illegal now [...] — as a result, it's extremely difficult to build a third party. You can run a candidate for President, like a Ross Perot or a Ralph Nader, or something like that, but to build a real third-party challenge in every state — you know, all over the country, building local power, electing members of Congress, governors, that kind of thing — that's pretty much impossible.[92]

We had the raw, messy beginnings of a competitive multiparty system in the 19th century. Then it was stamped out — duopoly took over. Now, we need to re-inject greater competition and representativeness into our party system, and with them greater accountability.

Conclusion

The phrase "two-party system" can be used to mean either a system that tends to be dominated at any given time by two parties, or one that systematically locks out minor parties, that disallows challenges by outsider parties, and thus is always dominated by the *same* two parties. It's the latter sense that this book is mainly about.

The American two-party system is more than just political reality; it's also an article of faith, a sort of "civic religion", for many people — a key element of so-called American exceptionalism. Lisa Jane Disch identifies this special status as the two-party *doctrine*, which has three tenets:

1. **Originality:** that the two-party system has been with us since the beginning of the Republic.
2. **Immutability:** that regardless of political winds of change, the system itself stands as a constant, both "a foundation of United States politics and a force that transcends it". Combined with the tenet of originality, it carries the notion "that the condition that prevails today — that third parties do not stand a chance in our winner-take-all system — has never been otherwise."
3. **Democratic progress:** that the two-party system aids popular sovereignty by narrowing the choices presented to voters to just two, which "fosters clarity and stability".[93]

None of these tenets stands on firm ground. The first two can be dismissed by examining history, and I hope that the facts I've

---

[92] Real News Network 2017, at 13:56 to 17:35.
[93] Disch 2002, pp. 4-7.

presented of American political history convince you that they do not withstand careful scrutiny. The third tenet is likewise very questionable, though as it's a bit more subjective than the others, it is somewhat harder to disprove. But as I've explained in this chapter, having just two choices is wholly inadequate to the expressive needs of voters. We need to reject the two-party doctrine if we are truly to have popular sovereignty.

The idea of representative democracy is that the people elect leaders who represent their preferences for public policy. A healthy party system provides a channeling system for the interests of the people, allowing them to express their views and for these views to be advocated in the halls of government. Ours is not a healthy party system. By locking out third parties, and thereby limiting competition, it limits the accountability of the government to the people.

We're the world's longest continuously running major democracy. Yet we have one of the most dysfunctional of all advanced democracies, and our politics seem only to be getting more dysfunctional. It seems odd that we don't give more consideration to the idea that our party system may be to blame. No other advanced democracy in the world has such a restrictive party system. If we took the time to compare the vibrancy of our system with that of other democracies, we might begin to realize just how deprived we are. The good news is that we have the power to change the system, to bring it more into line with the sort of accountability-promoting practices found in other democracies. And we don't even need to amend the Constitution to do it.

In chapter 1, I outlined some changes we could make to our electoral system, which would dramatically improve the chances for minor parties and lead to a political system in which voters would have more meaningful choices, and which included enough variety (in the cybernetic sense) to offer true representation. In this chapter, I've tried to show how healthy party systems function, and to dispel the myth that our system has always had its present duopolistic character. This is the starting point for developing the political will needed to make the change to a multiparty system. In the next chapter, I will continue this effort by explaining just how much the two-party system costs us, and how much better off we'd be with multiparty democracy.

3. Why Bother? The Benefits of a Multiparty System

"It is an essential part of democracy that minorities should be adequately represented. No real democracy, nothing but a false show of democracy, is possible without it." — John Stuart Mill

Isn't it ironic that of all the world's major democracies, it's only in America, the land of free enterprise, where the party system suppresses competition to such an extreme extent? Why do we tolerate such a paucity of choice in our politics, when we wouldn't stand for a similar restriction of consumer choice? Consumers don't have to pick between Coke and Pepsi — there are also Dr. Pepper, A&W, Orange Crush, 7-Up, Mountain Dew, Sprite, and on and on. Having the option to *defect* — to stop buying one thing and switch to something else — is crucial if we want consumer products to be responsive to our preferences. Say you like Coke and absolutely hate Pepsi, and one day, Coke changes its formula to something you don't like. Thanks to a competitive marketplace, you have a chance to find something else you like, without having to become a Pepsi drinker. You have *defection options*. And Coke knows this — so they know they need to work hard to keep you as a customer.

It's similar in politics, where voters are expected to choose from a set of alternatives, and thereby set the policy direction of the government. The alternatives compete against each other in a *marketplace of ideas*. The concept is that the best ideas will win, sooner or later, against less truthful, less compelling ideas. But when voters can only choose between two parties, the marketplace doesn't work so well. When there's a lack of defection options, accountability suffers.

As Sartori[94] writes, "If no party market, and thereby no party exit, is available, then 'voice' [of the citizens] is either powerless or can easily be silenced."

Schattschneider makes a very similar point: "The sovereignty of the voter consists in his freedom of choice just as the sovereignty of the consumer in the economic system consists in his freedom to trade in a competitive market."[95] For popular sovereignty to mean something more than a slogan, it's essential that voters have meaningful choices.

Market failure

A lot of voters in the U.S. are primarily concerned about one political issue. When they know where the parties stand on that issue, they don't need to know anything more. Abortion is probably the classic example because it inspires such passionate feelings on both sides. If a voter is strongly pro-life, they are likely to vote Republican, regardless of what they think of the party's other positions. And the reverse is true for strongly pro-choice voters. Neither type really has defection options: To switch to another party would mean to support a position that is anathema to their core beliefs. This means they don't have much reason to question the party's other positions, and no leverage to apply pressure if they would prefer changes. In fact, there's not even that much reason to learn what the party's other positions are.

But parties don't like to acknowledge that their supporters don't necessarily support their whole platform. When they win, they point to the number of people who voted for them and use it to claim a "mandate" for every part of their agenda. And this promotes misunderstanding and distrust between one side and the other. "How could so many people have voted for this?!", people often wonder. In many cases, the answer is that they didn't. It just looks like they did.

This is a "bundling" problem — among the many permutations of policy positions that exist, only two viable ones are on the ballot. The position that a voter prefers on one issue is combined, or bundled, with a lot of other issue-positions that they may or may not support.

---

[94] Sartori 1976, p. 58.
[95] Schattschneider 1942, p. 60.

Unfortunately, in our two-party system, there's no way to "unbundle" — no way to express support for part of the platform without also implying support for the rest of it.

A multiparty system would allow voters to be clearer about what they support. Imagine, for example, a pro-life party that was also pro-immigration, or a pro-choice party that wanted to limit immigration. What you think about abortion is (or at least, could be) independent of your views on immigration. More permutations would mean more choice, and more defection options, which would mean more chances to hold parties accountable.

Accountability also applies to intra-party affairs. For example, there's evidence that the Democratic National Committee showed favoritism to the Clinton campaign in 2016, which they aren't supposed to do.[96] Many Democrats were appalled by that — but what could they do about it? Defection, the ultimate expression of disapproval, is not an option for most, when the only viable alternative is the Republican Party.

The 2016 Republican National Convention was another scene of a party not playing by its own rules. The convention's presiding officer, Arkansas congressman Steve Womack, refused to allow a roll-call vote on a rules issue, ignoring objections from the floor and showing partiality in judging a voice vote in which both "ayes" and "nays" were loudly expressed.[97] Former Senator Gordon Humphrey (R-NH) didn't mince words when he expressed his frustration with the process:

> I sought to be recognized to raise a point of parliamentary inquiry and was immediately drowned out by people I would refer to as "brownshirts" in my surroundings. [...] You just saw the second most important item of business rushed through in a split second with no opportunity for debate, no opportunity for questions, no opportunity for points of order and no roll call vote although nine states under the rules requested a roll call vote, demanded a roll call vote, and should have been accorded that. So this was pretty shocking and shameful, I've

---

[96] H.A. Goodman 2016.
[97] McCormack and Warren 2016.

seen a lot of, but this is not a meeting of the Republican
National Committee. This is a meeting of brownshirts.[98]
Virginia Republican Ken Cuccinelli was similarly frustrated: "They
cheated. I mean, that's what you just saw. You saw them violate their
own rules. And, if the rules don't matter, I'm not quite sure why we
spend all this time writing them."[99]

The 2016 conventions weren't the only ones where such
controversies have erupted. Ron Paul supporters felt cheated in 2012
by an unfriendly (and, many would argue, unfair) interpretation of
the rules.[100] Were they right? I can't say for sure (the byzantine
convention rules make it difficult to judge conclusively), but clearly,
there was significant dissatisfaction with how the process played out,
and without meaningful defection options, those who were
dissatisfied were left with no recourse.

Job security for the elected

One way to measure the lack of competition in our system is to look
at the rate incumbents are reelected. After the November 2014
elections, PolitiFact reported that Congress's incumbent reelection
rate was about 95 percent, while its approval rate was roughly 14
percent.[101] A difference that big tells us that something is amiss. (I'd
expect there to be some gap even in a well-functioning system,
because people don't always get what they want, and they like to
complain — but more than 80 points?)

In figure 3.1 below, I chart the incumbent reelection rate (defined as
the percentage who won of those incumbents running for reelection)
over our history. It doesn't surprise me to see that this rate was lower
from the 1830s through the 1890s — the only period in American
history when it tended to be below 80 percent. Compare this finding
to the variety of congressional parties during the same period, in
figure 2.6. Is it merely coincidence that when there was a more

---

[98] Matthews 2016.
[99] Hanchett 2016.
[100] LoGiurato and Wyler 2012.
[101] Jacobson 2014.

vibrant, robust competition between parties, the rate of incumbent reelection was lower?

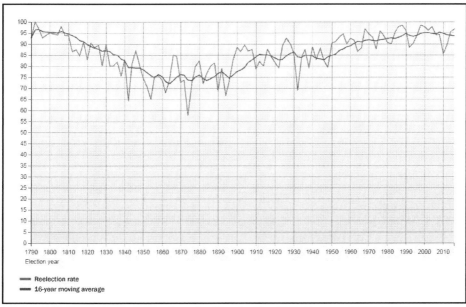

Figure 3.1. Incumbent rate of reelection in the U.S. House, 1790-2016

Sources: Huckabee 1995, *Vital Statistics on Congress* 2017 (table 2-7), Kondik and Skelley 2016.

Is 75 percent a healthy rate? I don't know; maybe it should be even lower. It shouldn't be *too* low, because the system needs stability. Too much turnover could be a problem. But it shouldn't be too high, either. On the one hand, a better electoral system would be more competitive, depriving representatives of their ability to dodge accountability. On the other hand, it would do a better job promoting effective representatives, who, as incumbents, will have proved their mettle, and thus would be expected to have an advantage over challengers, on average.

Many people advocate term limits for elected representatives, and I understand where they're coming from: They want more accountability. But I would suggest that a more competitive multiparty system would be a better solution, one that deals with the problem at its roots rather than attacking symptoms. It would give voters more options, including the option to keep a representative in office for another term if they're doing a good job. Term limits can be a bit like tying one arm behind your back.

Responsiveness
One of the main points of democratic government is to be *responsive* to the demands of the people — that is, to give them what they ask for. Responsive parties make promises to the electorate and, if given the power, work to deliver on them.

In our two-party system, both parties do their best to be "big tent" parties — to include enough different groups to win a majority of seats. Evangelical Christians and Wall Street financiers unite under the Republican banner. Environmentalists and labor unionists share space under the Democratic tent. But these diverse elements of the coalition have different interests. So, to keep them together, a big-tent party needs to hedge — it needs to maintain a delicate balance of interests so it doesn't lose any part of the coalition. Sometimes this is an impossible challenge — but when hedging fails, people have no option but to feel frustrated and complain, because they have no meaningful defection options.

Some groups suffer more than others from this lack of options. For example, since the 1960s blacks have voted overwhelmingly for the Democratic party. Their support for it is so strong that their interests may well be taken for granted when Democratic leaders develop and advocate policy positions.[102] After all, what would the Democratic Party gain by being more responsive to the interests of black people, if it already has their votes? As in presidential races, where most of the candidates' attention is focused on swing states, some segments are taken for granted because there's not much strategic advantage to courting their votes. (Sure, turnout matters, but at least Democrats can be fairly confident that the votes won't go to Republicans.)

It may seem controversial to say that certain groups are taken for granted by the parties — and I suppose it would be a hard thing to

---

[102] Chideya 2016.

prove. But even if you don't buy the claim, the main point is that the system has a structural tendency to promote this taking-for-granted. Imagine a left-to-right axis divided into two halves: Those on the extremes, far from the boundary, are unlikely to defect, because of their distance from any other viable option. That lowers their strategic value for the party on their side.

"Big-tentism" implies a certain degree of slipperiness when it's time for candidates to take issue positions. It's considered *de rigueur* in American politics for candidates to pander to their base during primary season, then tack to the center for the general election. The fact that they so easily get away with this is a testament to systemic slipperiness. For example, the Republican Party is generally associated with a stand against government subsidies; they claim to believe in a small-government philosophy. Yet when they go to Iowa during presidential primary season, they advocate for ethanol subsidies (a major issue in a state that grows so much corn). In the 2016 Iowa Republican caucus campaign, Ted Cruz was the only candidate who opposed ethanol subsidies — the rest of the field all pandered to the audience, as is typical.[103] So, what does the label "Republican" tell us about government policy on subsidies? This built-in slipperiness is not, to quote from a great song by the Smiths, "natural, normal or kind".[104] It's not what representative democracy is supposed to look like. If we're to take seriously the idea of the people as sovereign, voters need to know what they're voting for. A multiparty system would allow enough variety for party labels to be more significant.

Ted Cruz actually won the Iowa caucus in 2016, which would seem to undermine the example. But the point is that most of the candidates felt so free to shift in their positions and to obfuscate their connection with what is supposed to be a simple, clear doctrine of the very party they aspire to lead. Or, put another way, the party may advertise the simple clarity of its positions in one arena (say an audience of small-government libertarians), but in reality it generally

---

[103] Worland 2016.
[104] "Meat Is Murder", from the 1985 album of the same name.

insists on a remarkably large amount of "wiggle-room" when it comes to campaigning — not to mention governing.

Also, such issues change over time. Maybe ethanol subsidies will no longer be such a "third-rail" issue in the future as they were in the past. But there are bound to be other issues where campaign considerations are allowed to trump party principles — because of the nature of the system. And it's not just the Republicans, of course. Democratic candidates often pander to organized labor (or just take them for granted), but in government often fail to hold their interests close to heart. NAFTA is a good example of that — whether you think it was good or bad, it wasn't what organized labor wanted, and they got it anyway, from their own side. That's what I'd call "slippery".

That the parties don't firmly stand for a coherent set of principles is one kind of unresponsiveness. Another is simply not delivering what voters want. Gun control is a great example. In the wake of the mass shooting at Sandy Hook Elementary, an overwhelming proportion of American voters supported universal background checks — 91 percent, including 88 percent of those in households with guns.[105] Yet the government still did not pass them. That's a serious lack of responsiveness.

Law professor and activist Lawrence Lessig points to

> the endless list of troubles that sit on our collective plate but that never get resolved: bloated and inefficient bureaucracies; an invisible climate policy; a tax code that would embarrass Dickens; health care policies that have little to do with health; regulations designed to protect inefficiency; environmental policies that exempt the producers of the greatest environmental harms; food that is too expensive (since protected); food that is unsafe (since unregulated); a financial system that has already caused great harm, has been left unreformed, and is primed and certain to cause great harm again."[106]

---

[105] Quinnipiac 2013.
[106] Lessig 2011, pp. 1-2.

In other words, in many ways, our government fails to respond to the needs of the people. We look to government for solutions. When it doesn't provide them, some of us decide it isn't capable of solving anything — and so cynicism grows.

Sometimes unresponsiveness comes in the form of a missed opportunity. For example, I think most Americans would prefer that we tried to reduce the number of nuclear weapons in the world. In fact, the nuclear Non-Proliferation Treaty (NPT), which went into effect in 1970, requires the signatory nations to work towards nuclear disarmament. Now, I know it should ideally be a multilateral disarmament, and that's not always easy to negotiate, but it doesn't seem to me that we've even been trying. It's as if we like having thousands of nuclear weapons just because it enhances our stature. Someday one or more of these weapons may be used in an unexpected way, and we'll wish we had worked harder on disarmament. You don't hear a lot of demand for this from voters, but I think that's largely because neither party is willing to put it on their agenda. They'd be worried it would make them look weak. In a multiparty system, on the other hand, this public interest could be served by a smaller, more "entrepreneurial" party, which might then find that taking a stand for disarmament gets a lot of traction in the electorate, and doesn't necessarily make the party look weak, but rather makes it look responsive and responsible.

Unresponsiveness can come from pandering to a strategic minority while neglecting the majority. For example, consider the embargo against Cuba. Most of the Cuban exile community favors it, and they happen to be concentrated in Florida, a very important swing state. Though a few are opposed to it, most care a lot about and strongly support it. But these people are less than one percent of the U.S. population. Most Americans don't think much about the embargo, but if they were to learn a bit more, and you pressed them on it, I suspect they would mostly be against it.

It seems to me that if we can trade openly with a communist country like China, then why can't we do the same with Cuba? Having the export market would be good for American business. And has the embargo really accomplished anything worthwhile? Many would argue that it has actually been counterproductive, that it has helped to entrench the authoritarian regime. So I think that if the issue were fully debated and explored in a national dialogue, most people would decide that they'd rather end the embargo.

But in our two-party system, both parties pander to Cuban-Americans for strategic reasons, due to their importance in a swing state. The flip side is that the majority of Americans have no channel to express their opposition. The system is unresponsive to their interests. To be sure, President Obama began the process of opening relations with Cuba in 2014 — but why did it take so long? And why are we now heading back in the other direction? I think it has a lot to do with the two-party system. It's worth noting that Obama only undertook this change in his second term, when he had no possibility of reelection.

It's not that the government is *totally* unresponsive to the citizens. Representatives do have beliefs of their own, and are subject to incentives to act in certain ways and not in others. Whose interests do they respond to the most? The answer will come as no surprise to anyone who's been paying attention: the *affluent*. Political scientist Martin Gilens systematically studied the relationship between citizens' policy preferences and subsequent policy outcomes, based on survey data collected between 1964 and 2006. He found that "American citizens are vastly unequal in their influence over policymaking, and that inequality is growing. In most circumstances, affluent Americans exert substantial influence over the policies adopted by the federal government, and less well off Americans exert virtually none. Even when Democrats control Congress and the White House, the less well off are no more influential."[107]

However, Gilens also found that "political competition increases the responsiveness of policymakers to the views of the public and generates policies that more equally reflect the preferences of all Americans" — which is exactly what I'm saying, although he doesn't go beyond the confines of two-party competition.

---

[107] Gilens 2012.

Is there such a thing as too much responsiveness? Yes: sometimes the public's demands are short-sighted. We would not want our representatives passing laws that infringed on certain people's rights, for example. Needless to say, we wouldn't want them to be responsive to bribes or other forms of corruption. How about a "tax holiday" for a whole year? That is, nobody pays any taxes! That might sound good in the short term, but would be very harmful in the long term — in short, it would be *irresponsible*.

Responsibility

Responsibility, as many democratic theorists recognize, is another important feature of good governance. The word has multiple meanings. In one sense, to act responsibly is to be prudent, applying careful judgment, considering long-term consequences as well as short-term benefits. When brewers exhort their customers to "drink responsibly", they mean it in this sense. It's the opposite of impulsive.

In another sense, to be responsible means to be *answerable* or *accountable*. To take *responsibility for* something means to be willing to accept blame or credit for it. When politicians play the "blame game", when they would rather "pass the buck" than accept their part in something, we say they are dodging responsibility. When Harry S. Truman famously said, "The buck stops here", he was asserting responsibility in this sense.

Perhaps these meanings can be unified by saying that responsibility means a commitment to take seriously the duties that one has been given. This would entail prudence and giving due consideration to consequences, as well as being answerable and accountable for one's conduct. In terms of democratic governance, it's clear why responsibility is crucial. Unfortunately, the two-party system does a poor job of delivering it. Let's consider a few examples from recent history.

In September 2016, Congress passed the Justice Against Sponsors of Terrorism Act, or JASTA, a law intended to allow 9/11 families to file lawsuits against Saudi Arabia, although it doesn't mention that country by name. Politically, that's a clear winner — no politician wants to be seen as opposing the interests of the victims of 9/11. But it's shortsighted because it compromises the principle of sovereign immunity, the legal doctrine which says that a country's actions don't fall under the jurisdiction of foreign courts — and this sets a precedent which could later harm U.S. diplomats. As then CIA chief John O. Brennan wrote in a statement upon passage of the bill:

> I believe that the "Justice Against Sponsors of Terrorism Act" (JASTA) will have grave implications for the national security of the United States. The most damaging consequence would be for those US Government officials who dutifully work overseas on behalf of our country. The principle of sovereign immunity protects US officials every day, and is rooted in reciprocity. If we fail to uphold this standard for other countries, we place our own nation's officials in danger. No country has more to lose from undermining that principle than the United States—and few institutions would be at greater risk than CIA.[108]

President Obama took much the same view, and vetoed the bill. But his veto was overridden by Congress — the only time in his presidency that this occurred — by votes of 97-1 in the Senate (with Senator Harry Reid casting the lone dissent) and 348-77 in the House. The clincher is that many of those voting for the bill knew that it was problematic, having received letters from the President, defense secretary Ash Carter, and chairman of the Joint Chiefs of Staff Gen. Joseph Dunford. They voted for it anyway. "I don't think the Senate nor House has functioned in an appropriate manner as it relates to a very important piece of legislation," said Sen. Bob Corker (R-TN), chairman of the Senate Foreign Relations Committee. "I have tremendous concerns about the sovereign immunity procedures that would be set in place by the countries as a result of this vote."[109] Yet rather than take the time to get the bill right, Congress rushed headlong into passing it, for political reasons, without regard for long-term consequences. That's reckless and irresponsible behavior.

---

[108] Brennan 2016.
[109] Steinhauer et al 2016.

The JASTA story also illustrates another form of irresponsibility, the tendency of some elected leaders to point the finger at others instead of accepting their part in the process. In spite of the administration's warnings, some members of Congress appeared to try to blame President Obama for their own failure to take appropriate care in crafting the bill. For example, CNN reported the following comments by Senate Majority Leader Mitch McConnell (R-KY):

> "That was a good example of the failure to communicate early about a piece of legislation that was obviously very popular," McConnell said.
>
> McConnell explained that lawmakers were very focused on the needs of the 9/11 families and didn't take the time to think through the consequences.
>
> "Because everyone was aware who the potential beneficiaries were, but nobody focused on the potential downside in terms of our international relationships. And I just think it was a ball dropped," McConnell said. "I wish the President — and I hate to blame everything on him and I don't — but it would have been helpful had... we had a discussion about this much earlier than the last week."[110]

With the aid of groupthink, legislators found it easy to dodge responsibility. With more parties at the table, maybe the "bandwagon effect" would not have been as strong, because the problem could have been identified from more perspectives.

Another stark example of irresponsibility can be seen in Senator McConnell's long-running campaign to say "no" to everything put forward by President Obama. "The single most important thing we want to achieve," McConnell said before the 2010 midterm elections, "is for President Obama to be a one-term president." Now, checks and balances are one thing, but blind, reflexive opposition is not how American democracy is supposed to work. The typical expectation is that he'd have some policy ideas he prioritized, and that he'd want to leave the door open to working together with Democrats on them, even given slim chances of succeeding. Would that not be the

---

[110] Barrett and Walsh 2016.

responsible stance — because taking seriously the duties of office means engaging in the governing process? But McConnell made a strategic decision to block the Democrats at every turn, with the goal of returning Republicans to control of Congress:

> Many times in the past, when the country has gotten into real trouble, the parties have come together to do what is necessary to set things right again. A good recent illustration is the Troubled Asset Relief Program (aka "the bailout"), which kept the economy from collapse, was supported by both party leaderships and was signed into law by President Bush in October 2008. McConnell called TARP's passage "one of the finest moments in the history of the Senate." Obama took over expecting this spirit to endure. But from the outset, McConnell blocked or frustrated just about everything the administration tried to do, including the government's distribution of TARP funds, in January 2009, just three months after McConnell voted to authorize them.[111]

This is "seesaw" politics — foiling the opposition simply because you can, for reasons of teamsmanship. Choosing a zero-sum approach because it works for you in the short term.

As it happened, even winning control of both chambers of Congress, as the Republicans did in the 2014 midterm elections, was not enough to convince some of them that they should govern in good faith — because they still did not control the White House. "If Republicans proclaim that they have to govern now that they run Congress," reasoned the editors of *National Review*, "they maximize the incentive for the Democrats to filibuster everything they can — and for President Obama to veto the remainder. Then the Democrats will explain that the Republicans are too extreme to get anything done." Here the editors seem to presume a cynical gamesmanship, where the point is not the pursuit of policy goals but a kind of posturing, in which not being portrayed negatively by one's opponents is paramount.

---

[111] Green 2011.

They also point out that trying to govern would be divisive for the party, "on the same tea-party-vs.-establishment lines that Republicans have just succeeded in overcoming" in the 2014 elections. And, that even if the Republicans succeed in governing, it wouldn't do them any good. It might just convince voters to continue with a Democratic president and Republican Congress when it came time to choose in 2016. The thing to do, they say, is to build "the case for Republican governance after 2016. That means being a responsible party, to be sure, just as the conventional wisdom has it. But part of that responsibility involves explaining what Republicans stand for — what, that is, they would do if they had the White House."[112]

This kind of thing is so stunningly contrary to the usual expectations of governing in good faith that it's hard to know what to say in response. Stephen Colbert did a good job lampooning it in his *Colbert Report* segment "The Word", on November 10, 2014: "Yes! It's time to show the American people that Republicans are capable of bold, decisive action — sometime later."[113] But in the seesaw American political system, many people on the Republican side don't see the essential irresponsibility and cynicism at work here, both because their media sources and friends and family aren't likely to bring it up and because their partisan loyalties encourage them to approve.

Ironically, the editors of *National Review* got their wish for a Republican president — but not of the sort they imagined.[114] It appears that the party is much more comfortable being in opposition than being in charge — a thought captured five months before the election in a *Texas Monthly* piece entitled "The Conservative Case for Hillary Clinton":

> If Clinton becomes president, Republicans will be members of the opposition, meaning they can oppose her agenda openly and even, despite this Trump disaster, with occasional credibility. If Trump becomes president, they'll be the loyal members of a party led by a dangerously impulsive president.

---

[112] "The Governing Trap" 2014.

[113] "The Word — It's a Trap!" 2014.

[114] For an example of their disapproval of Trump, see "The Republican Crisis", published Oct. 10, 2016.

They'll be chronically torn over whether they should summon the temerity to express their discomfort with whatever Trump decides to do in response to something mean he saw someone say about him on the internet, or to accept the reality that he is their leader, and they are tools he feels free to use to serve his ego. I know which lifestyle I'd prefer.[115]

Essentially, a party has gained the power it has been seeking, in the name of certain policy goals, then, rather than pursue those goals in good faith, clung to its posture of opposition and obstruction for cynical short-term benefits. This is irresponsibility, enabled by seesaw politics.

Abdicating responsibility

Have you ever wondered why the president and his administration propose the budget that Congress debates, revises and passes? The federal budget is the most important recurring piece of legislation passed by Congress. So you might expect that the process would begin in the legislative branch, not the executive. That's what the Founding Fathers thought. And that's how it was until 1921.

The Budget and Accounting Act of that year, which established the modern, so-called "executive" budget, was the fruition of the work of the Commission on Economy and Efficiency, which had been set up by President Taft in 1910 and had delivered its report, *The Need for a National Budget*, to Congress in 1912. At that time, there was no centralized budgeting process; rather, individual federal agencies each sent budget requests to the appropriate committees in Congress, who then voted on appropriations. With the responsibilities of the federal government growing in the late nineteenth and early twentieth centuries, this process had become increasingly unwieldy. One of the members of the Commission wrote about this old system in 1927:

No attempt was made to consider the whole problem of financing the government at one time. Expenditures were not considered in connection with revenues. Even the idea of balancing the budget did not exist. ... Though the law required

---

[115] Grieder 2016.

all the estimates to be submitted by the Secretary of the Treasury, that officer acted as a mere compiling authority; he had no power to modify proposals transmitted to him by the heads of the administrative departments. The estimates thus represented little more than the individual desires of the department heads. ... Their financial needs being met from a common fund, each inevitably sought to secure as large a share as possible.[116]

The 1921 act created the Bureau of the Budget in the Treasury Department, physically, but "under the direct control of the President and not of the Secretary of the Treasury".[117] It was moved in 1939 to the Executive Office of the President, and in 1970 was renamed the Office of Management and Budget (OMB).

Clearly, the old system called out for consolidation, centralization, rationalization. But why centralized in the *executive* branch instead of the *legislative*? One of the problems of our democracy is what's sometimes called the "imperial presidency" — the fact that the executive branch has too much power, relative to Congress. It's debatable when this phenomenon came fully into effect — perhaps with World War II and the ensuing Cold War. Or maybe it was earlier, with FDR and the New Deal, as political theorist James Burnham claims:

> We do not need an exact gauge [of power] to inform us that— relative to the executive, the bureaucracy and for that matter the judiciary—the legislature's share has during the past generation not merely somewhat declined but dropped to an altogether different level. [...] Throughout most of our history there has been congressional predominance within the central government. Since 1933, Congress has not been even the peer of the executive, but a mere junior partner.[118]

The executive budget is one of the anchors, or prerequisites, of the imperial presidency. Locating the responsibility of writing the federal budget in the executive branch has arguably abetted the establishment

---

[116] Dews 2016.
[117] Congressional Digest 1940, p. 38.
[118] Burnham 1959, p. 128.

there of the so-called "deep state" — the hidden, largely classified world of the intelligence community, national security establishment and connected contractors[119] — or, more broadly, any secretive part of the bureaucracy that could conceivably be in a position to subvert the will of the elected officials above it.

Insulating certain parts of the bureaucracy from changes of elected officials seems like a good idea, and secrecy is needed for some government functions, such as intelligence and national security. Continuity is important. But so is accountability. Both the executive and legislative branches have bureaucratic institutions that don't change with every election. An example on the legislative side is the Congressional Budget Office, a nonpartisan agency created in 1974. Perhaps if more of the bureaucratic state were located in the legislative branch, it would be more accountable. One piece of this would be for Congress to take more responsibility for the budget, as the Founders would have expected.

I am not saying the president should never have the chance to make proposals at the beginning of a budgetary review process. Nor am I advocating a return to how budgeting happened before 1921. But I am saying that in allowing the executive branch to take over major parts of the budgeting process, the legislative branch has, at the institutional level, abdicated some of the responsibility given to it by the Constitution.

The balance of power between executive and legislative branches has shifted in favor of the executive. Many experts feel this threatens our system of checks and balances. For example, in launching the "Article I Project" with other political leaders in 2016, Senator Mike Lee (R-UT) wrote:

> The authors of the Constitution intended Congress to be first among the federal government's three co-equal branches. Endowed with the power to legislate, tax, spend, and oversee the weaker Executive and Judicial branches [...] Congress was meant to be the driving force in federal policymaking.

---

[119] That is, the "military-industrial complex" — the thing that Dana Priest & William Arkin detailed in their report "Top Secret America" (2010).

In recent decades, however, Congress has surrendered too much of that role to the Executive Branch, and relegated itself to the backseat of American politics. This upending of our constitutional order has led not only to bad policy, but inexorably to greater public distrust for our governing institutions.[120]

Our founders wanted a balance of power, with a strong legislative branch, able to stand up to the executive when necessary. They didn't want us to elect kings (or queens) — but we've been getting dangerously close to that in recent decades.

Deficit spending

Budget deficits are a key test of responsibility. Figure 3.2 shows the deficit as a percentage of GDP, from 1792 to 2020 (projected, in later years). We can see that up until the 1930s, the budget was often in surplus, and when it did go into deficit to a large degree, it was usually because of war — the Civil War in the 1860s, World War I in the late nineteen-teens, and World War II in the 1940s.

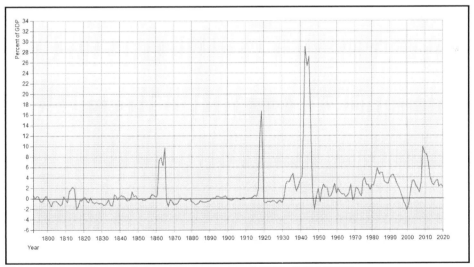

Figure 3.2. Budget deficit as percentage of GDP, 1792-2020
Source: USGovernmentSpending.com (Chantrill).

---

[120] M. Lee 2016.

Since the 1930s, though, the budget has rarely been in surplus. Deficits have become typical. While there may be good arguments for them in the short term, such as when the economy is in recession, or in certain "emergency" situations, in the long term running continually in the red causes problems. It can crowd out private investment, for one thing.[121] It can erode the government's credit rating, which has already been downgraded by several agencies to below AAA, beginning in 2011.[122] And taking a long-term view, deficits represent a shift of burden from current to future generations — a refusal to take responsibility.

One of our two main parties made a lot of noise about taking the deficit seriously and reducing the national debt, to the point that it was widely believed to be the party of fiscal responsibility. Then, when it finally found itself in control of both houses of Congress and the White House in 2017, it went on a spending spree, adding about $1.2 trillion in deficits just for fiscal year 2019, and $7.2 trillion over the next decade.[123]

The state of affairs is dire: "Saying that Congress has abrogated its power-of-the-purse duties gives it way too much credit. In reality, the House and Senate have been running away almost at full speed from their legally required budget responsibilities ... with impunity," said budget expert Stan Collender to a House budget committee hearing in May 2016.[124] So our current system doesn't function very responsibly on the issue of deficits.

Would a multiparty system function better? It's reasonable to worry that party fragmentation could lead to irresponsible behavior, since parties may have an incentive to propose higher spending, with little matching incentive for fiscal discipline. I will address the issue of fragmentation generally in chapter 5. For now, though, I would say that with more competition, voters will have better chances to provide a disincentive for irresponsibility — by voting representatives out of

---

[121] Kurtzleben 2013.
[122] Berlau et al 2011.
[123] Taylor 2018.
[124] Arkin 2017.

office for it. Obviously, this depends on voters *valuing* responsibility — a basic problem for democracy. One way to view this problem is through a lens of representation: The interests of future generations may not be adequately represented. When we spend too freely today, we incur debts due tomorrow. So, would a multiparty system give better representation to the interests of future generations? I think it would, because from more variety of perspectives would come more opportunities for such interests to be voiced.

Also, perhaps under a multiparty system, the presidential veto would work more effectively, and more in line with how the Founders envisioned, as a check on the legislature. As Hamilton wrote in 1788:

> [The veto power] not only serves as a shield to the executive, but it furnishes an additional security against the enaction of improper laws. It establishes a salutary check upon the legislative body calculated to guard the community against the effects of faction, precipitancy, or of any impulse unfriendly to the public good, which may happen to influence a majority of that body.[125]

The presidential veto is designed, he says, "to [i]ncrease the chances in favor of the community, against the passing of bad laws, through haste, inadvertence, or design." In other words, it's meant to promote responsibility.

The theory of responsible party government

One of the most frequently cited articles in 20th century American political science was published in 1950 by the Committee on Political Parties of the American Political Science Association (APSA), with the title "Toward a More Responsible Two-Party System". The authors, led by committee chairman E.E. Schattschneider, argue that parties in America were too weak, as organizations, to perform the functions required of them in a healthy, modern democracy. As they write in the foreword of the report:

> Historical and other factors have caused the American two-party system to operate as two loose associations of state and

---

[125] *Federalist* no. 73.

local organizations, with very little national machinery and very little national cohesion. As a result, either major party, when in power, is ill-equipped to organize its members in the legislative and the executive branches into a government held together and guided by the party program. Party responsibility at the polls thus tends to vanish. This is a very serious matter, for it affects the very heartbeat of American democracy. It also poses grave problems of domestic and foreign policy in an era when it is no longer safe for the nation to deal piecemeal with issues that can be disposed of only on the basis of coherent programs.[126]

The Committee makes many recommendations for improving the parties, including many measures designed to improve *intraparty* democracy — that is, democratic decision-making within the parties. Some of these were taken to heart by the parties, while others weren't. As critics of the report[127] pointed out, it fails to spell out exactly who should qualify as a member of a party, or how its leaders could effectively act responsibly with respect to the membership while at the same time developing coherent programs of public policy and enforcing party discipline.

For the purposes of this book, though, the key point is the Committee's view that a system of two — and *only* two — parties is best for producing responsible party government. The idea is that one party should be given a chance to implement its program so that the voters can see how it works and decide whether to support or oppose it. And voters should be given a simple choice, an either-or, yes-or-no sort of choice. Ronald Reagan, in his 1980 campaign, boiled down the question for voters into just this sort of choice, asking, "Are you better off now than you were four years ago?" Voters who answered "yes" would presumably approve of the incumbent president, Jimmy Carter; those who answered "no" should vote for Reagan — and of course, Reagan thought (correctly, it seems) that more voters would answer "no".

---

[126] Committee on Political Parties 1950, p. v.
[127] E.g. Ranney 1951.

As the argument goes, if no party could win a majority of seats and thus control the levers of power, the voters would be unable to tell who to hold responsible for governmental decision-making. Those in power but not fully in command would tend to "pass the buck", to blame others for their inability to carry out the policies they favor. As Alexander Hamilton wrote in *Federalist* no. 70, "one of the weightiest objections to a plurality in the Executive [...] is, that it tends to conceal faults and destroy responsibility."

The Committee frames its ideas in terms of the party in power and the party in opposition. To make the parties accountable to the public requires "a two-party system in which the opposition party acts as the critic of the party in power, developing, defining and presenting the policy alternatives which are necessary for a true choice in reaching public decisions". They're skeptical of having more than one "opposition party":

> When there are two parties identifiable by the kinds of action they propose, the voters have an actual choice. On the other hand, the sort of opposition presented by a coalition that cuts across party lines, as a regular thing, tends to deprive the public of a meaningful alternative.[128]

But they don't seem to have considered the possibility that parties should *share* power — that is, that the very idea of a single "party in power" (as applied to a legislative assembly) deserves to be questioned.

There's no doubt that it's part of human nature to try to dodge responsibility when things don't go well (and try to claim credit when they do). Hamilton was right, I think, to want executive authority to be centralized in one official. But the legislative branch is different. There, the name of the game is to craft laws that the executive will carry out. The crafting of laws should be a matter of deliberation between officials who *represent* the nation. Representation is paramount — so John Adams's words seem more pertinent than Hamilton's:

---

[128] Committee on Political Parties 1950, pp. 18-19.

> [T]o do strict justice at all times, it [a representative assembly] should be an equal representation, or in other words equal interest among the people should have equal interest in it.[129]

In a just crafting of the law, the people must be accurately represented (in their diversity of political viewpoints, not necessarily in their background or superficial features). Legislative assemblies that are unrepresentative are more likely to produce law that is unjust. This is a fundamental principle of representative democracy, but it seems to me that it doesn't get enough attention, since our own representative assemblies are actually not so representative.

Adams wasn't the only thinker of the revolutionary era who understood the idea of representation in this way. The anti-Federalist known pseudonymously as the "Federal Farmer" wrote, in October 1787:

> The essential parts of a free and good government are a full and equal representation of the people in the legislature, and the jury trial of the vicinage in the administration of justice—a full and equal representation, is that which possesses the same interests, feelings, opinions, and views the people themselves would were they all assembled—a fair representation, therefore, should be so regulated, that every order of men in the community, according to the common course of elections, can have a share in it.[130]

Of course, it's notable that women, and (I presume) men without property, were left out of this reckoning. But the basic principle, it seems to me, holds: A representative assembly, being meant to act in the name of the people, should reflect the interests and public-policy demands of the people. Another anti-Federalist, "Brutus", wrote this in November 1787:

> [A] representation of the people of America, if it be a true one, must be like the people. It ought to be so constituted, that a person, who is a stranger to the country, might be able to form a just idea of their character, by knowing that of their

---

[129] Adams 1776.
[130] Kammen 1986, p. 270.

representatives. They are the sign—the people are the thing signified.[131]

James Madison saw the danger of one party (or faction) being able to exert full control over the government. "When a majority is included in a faction," he wrote in *Federalist* no. 10, "the form of popular government [...] enables it to sacrifice to its ruling passion or interest both the public good and the rights of other citizens." And so the government was designed with checks and balances in mind — the executive separated from the legislative power, the legislative branch split into two chambers, a separate judicial branch, and local government separated from national.

It was designed, in other words, to protect us from the danger of a faction that includes a majority. But Madison and the other Founders failed to foresee the two-party system, which gives too much power to a broad-based (but not so broadly controlled) faction.

It's a different story in countries with parliamentary systems of government, especially when dominated by two main parties, as in the U.K. In such systems, it's the norm for one party to have a majority of seats. There is no separately elected executive branch; rather, the majority party "forms a government", empowering its leader to be prime minister and other members of parliament to take on other specific roles, in what is known as *cabinet government*. So, as long as one party has a majority of seats in the House of Commons, government cannot be divided, as it often is in the U.S. The responsible-party model is a better fit for parliamentary systems, and especially those dominated by two parties, such as Britain's.

Woodrow Wilson, who was a political scientist before he became a politician, greatly admired the British style of cabinet government — and hoped it could serve as a model for the U.S. While he was a senior in college, Wilson wrote an essay titled "Cabinet Government in the United States", and managed to get it published in *International Review*, a magazine edited by Henry Cabot Lodge, in August 1879.[132] In the essay, Wilson advocates selecting members of the president's

---

[131] Kammen 1986, p. 322.
[132] Cooper 2009, pp. 30-31.

cabinet from members of Congress, and giving them at least some of the powers of committee chairmen to initiate legislation. Adopting such a system would, in his view, lead to more responsible government, because cabinet members would feel pressured to take responsibility for their actions, and to resign when they were unsuccessful in achieving their legislative agenda. They would also bring more open, honest debate to the floors of Congress than happens under the committee system.[133]

Wilson's ideas on cabinet government weren't deemed very practical, in the end. But the example shows that the idea of responsible party government long predated the work of the mid-twentieth-century Committee on Political Parties. Wilson was not the only early political scientist who wrote on the subject. A. Lawrence Lowell (1856-1943), Henry Jones Ford (1851-1925), and Frank J. Goodnow (1859-1939), prominent American political scientists of the late 19th and early 20th centuries, all in various ways sang the praises of responsible party government.[134] So this is a significant part of the history of how Americans think about our party system. It's a doctrine we need to reckon with.

Does the doctrine match the terrain?
We all want our political leaders to act with prudence, and not impulsively. But do we need to give the reins of power to one (and only one) party, so that the voters may know who to assign credit or blame for how we're governed? Wilson thought so — in 1885, he wrote:

> If there be one principle clearer than another, it is this: that in any business, whether of government or of mere merchandising, *somebody must be trusted*, in order that when things go wrong it may be quite plain who should be punished.... *Power and strict accountability for its use* are the essential constituents of good government.[135]

---

[133] Wilson 1879.
[134] Ranney 1962.
[135] Wilson 1885, pp. 283-284; quoted in Ranney 1962, p. 29.

It's interesting that he puts this in terms of "when things go wrong". Is it so inevitable? What if we would rather things *not* go wrong?

Letting one party have full control does not necessarily promote responsibility in the sense of prudence and careful consideration. How many times have we Americans discovered that our elected leaders are voting on legislation that they haven't even read? For example, in December 2017, when one party controlled both houses of Congress as well as the White House, Sen. Bob Corker (a member of that party) had this to say about part of a tax bill that was rushed through the legislative process:

> I don't really know what the provision does to be honest. I would need an accountant to explain it. I had no knowledge of this and would have no knowledge of it except for you guys are calling me about it. I have no idea whatsoever whether it impacts me or doesn't impact me.[136]

That's not very responsible, if you ask me. Yet it seems that a lot of people believe in the idea that our system should allow a single party to take full control.

As an example of this belief, I'll quote David Frum, a leading conservative writer, from a conversation with Sam Harris and Andrew Sullivan recorded in January 2018. Harris proposes that convergence of views, among people who disagree, is possible given enough time for conversation. Frum explains how he sees it differently:

> **Frum:** I don't think the goal in politics is to converge. If you were told that Comcast and Time Warner had decided to lay aside their differences and work together to create the best possible cable system for all Americans, [audience laughter] you would understand that's probably not going to go well for you.
>
> **Harris:** But they could agree on a framework in which they can compete fairly.
>
> **Frum:** Exactly. It is not to banish differences. It's to create frameworks by which differences get arbitrated by democratic vote. And that the parties are given incentives to present the

---

[136] Ecarma 2017.

best versions of themselves. Cause at some level, you know, "more government services at higher cost", [vs.] "less government services at lower cost" — that's a choice; and we don't want to blur it, you want to sharpen it. But you want it to be done in a way that's ethical, that's honest, without foreign intervention, subject to constitutional rules, and where the owners of the country — the voters — get ultimately to make the decision, to be given meaningful choice. But meaningful choice not on policies, because that's unworkable, but between which set of political actors will get to implement their program.[137]

Up until the very end of this passage, Frum seems to be singing the same tune I am. The second sentence captures the undesirability of monopolies (and by extension duopolies) and draws an analogy between the economic marketplace and the "marketplace of ideas" in politics — which is exactly how I began this chapter. To sharpen choices for voters is what I was talking about in terms of "unbundling" — more parties with more coherent ideologies mean the voters (the "owners of the country") have more control over the direction of the country. Ethical, rule-based decision-making is connected to responsibility (in the sense of being prudent, deliberate, and conscientious). And in saying that it's "unworkable" for voters to choose policies directly, I think he simply means that we need representative, not direct, democracy — something I fully agree with.

But in the second half of the final sentence, he seems to reveal his allegiance to the doctrine of responsible party government when he implies that one "set of political actors" (which I read as "party") should be able to "implement their program". This is a common understanding of how democracy should work — and a flawed one, that entails great risks. It's time to examine those risks in greater detail.

---

[137] Harris 2018, at 2:03:58.

Hijacking and hostage-taking

When one party has majority control of Congress, it has the opportunity to abuse its power in service of its partisan goals. I think it makes sense to describe this as "hijacking". Congress is supposed to act in the public interest. When a party steers it away from this purpose to the service of partisan goals, it is subverting its proper function.

Hostage-taking is a type of hijacking, in which one faction takes as a "hostage" some aspect of government function and refuses to relent until it gets its way. The classic example of this is shutting down the government. Let's briefly review some of the major shutdowns that have occurred in the United States.

In 1990, the government was forced to shut down for a weekend in October when Rep. Newt Gingrich (then House Minority Whip) led a revolt against a budget deal struck between President George H.W. Bush and Congress which included a tax increase (in spite of the president's earlier promise that there would be none). In 1995, Gingrich, now Speaker of the House, tried to force President Bill Clinton to accept his efforts to reduce the budget deficit; when this failed, the government shut down for five days in November, reopening after a temporary measure was passed. When a more lasting agreement could not be struck, the government shut down a second time, this time lasting 21 days. The Republicans came out of the confrontation bruised in the court of public opinion.[138]

The next federal government shutdown happened in 2013 and lasted for 16 days. In this case, House Republicans tried to insist on defunding the Affordable Care Act, even though they knew that President Obama would veto any such defunding. When the House and Senate failed to agree on a budget (or actually, a continuing resolution), the government was forced to shut down.

In January 2018, the federal government shut down again, this time over a Democratic demand to include, in a continuing resolution required to keep the government open, a provision to "protect young people who came to the country illegally as children", which President

---

[138] Kessler 2011.

Trump had earlier seemed to support.[139] Senate Republicans were unable to overcome a Democratic filibuster to pass a bill lacking the provision. To end the impasse, Senate Majority Leader Mitch McConnell agreed to allow debate on the DREAM Act.

Besides these major shutdowns, and a few smaller ones in the 1970s and '80s, the *threat* of shutting down the government — or of failing to raise the debt ceiling, thus leading to a shutdown — has been used many times. For example, in 2006, Senator Barack Obama voted with other Democrats against raising the debt ceiling.[140] (He later called this a "political vote" that he could not support as president.) In 2015, Senator Ted Cruz led a sizable group of Senators, along with dozens of House Republicans, in using the threat of a government shutdown to try to defund Planned Parenthood.[141]

This system incentivizes bad behavior not only to extort concessions from the other side, but also as a way of signaling virtue to a party's base. But it can also backfire. Commenting on what seemed like a threat by Senator Marco Rubio to shut down the government over immigration policy in 2014,[142] political analyst Ryan Grim noted,

> We're in a strange place where, politically at least, nobody would benefit more from a government shutdown than Democrats. And if that's the political incentive, then they actually have, you know, every incentive to go forward and kind of tweak the Republicans — so the President is actually incentivized to come with the strongest immigration proposal that he can come up with, because it will gin up the Republicans, who then gin up the Democratic base.[143]

This is not the way grown-ups are supposed to conduct the process of legislating. This is gamesmanship — seesaw politics: Don't bother with trying to govern responsibly, just do whatever you can to make the other side look bad.

---

[139] Elliott and Jenkins 2018.
[140] Mikkelson 2015.
[141] Everett 2015.
[142] York 2014.
[143] Sharpton 2014.

The debt ceiling, like the government shutdown, is clearly seen by both parties as a potential weapon. Could that be the main reason we keep it around? Other democratic countries don't have a debt ceiling. Why do we? Political scientist Alan I. Abramowitz, among many others, suggests that we abolish it:

> The debt ceiling serves no useful purpose because the money owed by the federal government has already been committed by Congress, but it has regularly been used by both parties to engage in political gamesmanship. In today's polarized political environment, however, these political games have become much more dangerous.[144]

But he also writes that this reform will not be easy to implement. He doesn't explain precisely why, but I suppose it's because of the benefits the two major parties derive from having this device available as a political weapon — or a "high-stakes bargaining chip".[145]

My point is that however hard or easy it is to abolish the debt ceiling, it will be easier in a multiparty system, because there will be a greater incentive to do so. Imagine Congressional seats split, say, five ways: You're a member of the leading party, but you only have 39 percent of the seats. Now you decide to use the debt ceiling as a political weapon to gain advantage for your party. But there's a problem: You're going to have to frame it as serving some higher purpose, because you're going to need help from the other parties to get it done. How to do that, when what you want is the irresponsible move of shutting the government down? Any party that tried it on its own would be risking the scorn not just of "the other side", but of *all* the other parties.

Given the diminished utility of the debt ceiling as a political weapon, I think the chances would improve for it to be recognized as useless, and abolished. The same goes for government shutdowns.

---

[144] Abramowitz 2015, p. 205.
[145] Shabad 2017.

Majority of the majority: the Hastert rule and the speakership
Since the 1990s, we've been living through increasingly polarized times in America. One of the symptoms (as well, no doubt, as a cause) of this polarization is the so-called Hastert rule, named for Dennis Hastert, Speaker of the House from 1999 to 2007. It is not an official rule of the House of Representatives; rather, it's a guideline used by some Speakers, which says that a bill should only be brought up for a vote if it has majority support within the majority party.

Imagine a bill with a lot of cross-partisan support, favored by moderates of both parties, that could pass if the whole House had the chance to vote on it, but which only 45 percent of the Speaker's party — the majority party — supports. If the Speaker follows the Hastert rule, the bill won't be brought up for a vote — essentially, it will be blocked. That's one way hijacking and hostage-taking are enabled, by allowing a majority faction to block what would otherwise be the sort of deliberation and decision-making that the idea of representative democracy is based on. And it's not because the majority faction is united ideologically, it's just that they play for the same team — a team which has arrogated unto itself the exclusive power of deciding which bills get a vote and which don't.

In a multiparty system, with no single party likely to control a majority of seats, there'd be more incentive for all the parties to choose a fair-minded, moderate Speaker, who wouldn't follow the Hastert rule. If he were a consensus-minded candidate, he might do his best to rise above politics, at least part of the time, which Speakers of recent history very rarely do. Even if, on occasion, one party did have a majority of seats, and could thus choose a Speaker on its own, soon a norm would develop of picking fair-minded, consensus-oriented ones, and the party would only override such a norm at its peril.

To help ensure a consensus pick for Speaker, the House could decide to use a voting method such as Condorcet IRV, which I described in chapter 1. Or they could use the exhaustive ballot, which would allow time for negotiations between rounds. It would be up to them — and the more parties with seats, the more the choice of voting method would tend towards something fair.

In the 34th Congress (1855-1857), there was no majority party. (It was a transitional period between the collapse of the Whig Party and the solidification of the new Republican Party.) The contest for Speaker was one of the longest ever, lasting from December 1855 to early February 1856. After 129 ballots, no candidate had a majority, and the House felt forced to settle the election by plurality instead of the usual requirement of a majority. On the 133rd ballot, they finally elected Nathaniel P. Banks of Massachusetts, who had come up in the Democratic party but had switched to the American Party (the so-called Know Nothings) after adopting an anti-slavery stance.

Banks was apparently a very capable Speaker:

> Supporters and opponents alike gave him high praise. Stephens of Georgia, who had seen Banks's victory as evidence of sectional enmity, thought him "one of the ablest if not the ablest Speakers I ever saw in the chair." Another southerner and former Speaker, Howell Cobb, said that "Banks was in all respects the best presiding officer he had ever seen." Although a few said the Speaker was too kind to slaveholders, and although some antislavery representatives felt that he neglected them in the distribution of committee posts, all seemed to agree that Banks was "a just and honest presiding officer."[146]

If he had been elected with a majority instead of merely a plurality, Banks would've had even more legitimacy and authority as Speaker. His example bolsters my argument that our system for selecting a Speaker of the House tends to work better when it doesn't follow the Hastert rule, that is, when the decision isn't hijacked by a single party for itself but rather is made by the whole chamber — as the Founders expected it would be.

Spiking the punch

Another example of hijacking the institutions of government can be seen in the actions of the North Carolina legislature between the defeat of Governor Pat McCrory in 2016 and the beginning of newly

---

[146] Hollandsworth 1998, chapter 2.

elected Governor Roy Cooper's term on January 1, 2017. McCrory's party had majority control of both houses of the state's General Assembly, and would continue to control a majority of seats under Cooper. In what the *New York Times* called a "brazen power grab", the legislature passed several measures to limit the new governor's powers. For one thing, the governor's cabinet appointments would henceforth have to be confirmed by the Senate. Many temporary positions in the executive branch, serving at the pleasure of the governor, were converted into permanent civil-service jobs, which the new governor could not fire without cause. The legislature had allowed Gov. McCrory to designate up to 1,500 positions as "political appointees" that could be hired and fired at will. Once Cooper was elected, they lowered this maximum to 425. The majority party also changed the composition of the state election boards to give themselves an advantage, among several other changes that seemed designed to deprive the new governor of some of the power he would normally assume upon taking office.[147]

Much of this power grab was blocked in court a few months later.[148] But it's the attempt itself that supports my point that majority factions can be hazardous to the responsible practice of democracy. Hijacking and power-grab mean essentially the same thing. The two-party system makes it much more likely to happen, because (a) taking power from "the other guys" is easier when there is only one group of them, and (b) more importantly, the system not only allows but *normalizes* the ability of a single party to legislate on its own.

The same sort of thing happened after the November 2018 elections: an effort by one party to reduce the powers of an incoming governor of the opposite party.[149] Not much was said (as far as I could tell) about how such happenings are related to the structure of our party system. But I think they clearly are.

---

[147] Stern 2016, Campbell 2017.
[148] Stern 2017.
[149] Michaels 2018.

Blocking a Supreme Court nomination

Merrick Garland was nominated for the Supreme Court on March 16, 2016, following the unexpected death of Antonin Scalia a month earlier. According to the Constitution, it was then up to the Senate to give "advice and consent" on the nomination. But the Senate was controlled by the Republican Party, and they didn't wish to cooperate on this issue during an election year. On the very day that Scalia's death became known — more than a month before President Obama announced his nomination — Senate Majority Leader Mitch McConnell said, "This vacancy should not be filled until we have a new president."[150]

This did not mean considering Judge Garland and then voting his nomination down. (He was considered moderate by most pundits.) Rather, Republican senators blocked hearings for the nominee, and refused to allow a vote to confirm or reject him. The Supreme Court vacancy continued until April 2017, when Neil Gorsuch was confirmed. The nomination was before the Senate for a total of 293 days — blowing away the previous record of 125 days for Louis Brandeis in 1916.[151]

This partisan blockade was a major departure from institutional norms. The Senate had never before refused to consider a president's Supreme Court nomination, with just six exceptions during the 19th century. In all of those cases, either (a) the nomination was made *after* the election of a new president (i.e. during a president's lame-duck last months in office), or (b) the nomination was made by a president who came to office via succession rather than election — such as Andrew Johnson, whose 1866 nominee was not considered by the Senate (partly because they were busy reducing the number of seats on the court). In those times, "there was still some ambiguity over whether a Vice President literally became the President or merely acted as President".[152]

Some Republican senators seemed prepared to go even further. John McCain of Arizona, Ted Cruz of Texas, and Richard Burr of

---

[150] Everett 2016.
[151] Ware 2017.
[152] Kar & Mazzone 2016.

North Carolina expressed support for leaving the Supreme Court seat vacant throughout the term of Hillary Clinton, should she be elected.[153] This would have effectively reduced the number of Supreme Court seats to below nine for the first time since 1869.[154]

Here we see again how our system makes hijacking and hostage-taking rewarding for political parties. In a multiparty system, it would require more than one party to team up for this kind of obstruction, and since the rewards wouldn't necessarily flow to any of them it would be less likely to happen.

Incidentally, some[155] have said that when the Senate declined to exercise its power of advice and consent, it forfeited its prerogative, and so the seat could have been filled without Senate confirmation. This makes sense from a systems perspective — because it prevents the system from "locking up". (Whether it makes as much legal sense, I'm not sure.[156])

Asymmetric polarization

Perhaps it's time we talked about the "elephant" in the room. Although I criticize both parties in this book, you may have noticed that more of my examples (at least in this chapter) involve the Republican Party than the Democratic one. That's not because I'm being partisan, it's because the Republican Party has become more extreme in recent decades, as several authoritative sources have concluded.[157] In the process, it has become much more likely to put issues of teamsmanship above acting responsibly.

The party used to be more moderate, even progressive, at times. Republican President Dwight D. Eisenhower, in office from 1953 to 1961, presided over years of massive infrastructure investment, with marginal tax rates as high as 91 percent. Richard Nixon created the Environmental Protection Agency in a 1970 executive order. Even Ronald Reagan, who greatly increased defense spending and the

---

[153] Siddiqui 2016.
[154] Levitsky & Ziblatt 2018, p. 166.
[155] E.g. Diskant 2016.
[156] See Adler 2016.
[157] See Mann & Ornstein 2012, Hacker & Pierson 2015, Levitsky & Ziblatt 2018.

national debt, made some attempt at fiscal responsibility, raising government revenue by closing tax loopholes and increasing Social Security taxes. He also maintained a cordial relationship with the Democratic Speaker of the House, Tip O'Neill, though they strongly disagreed on many issues. As Mann & Ornstein write, "Reagan was a serial violator of what we could call 'Axiom One' for today's GOP, the no-tax-increase pledge: he followed his tax cuts of 1981 with tax increases in nearly every subsequent year of his presidency."[158]

In opposition, the modern GOP has placed more emphasis on obstruction than on governing. Even before Obama took office in January 2009, Republicans charted a course of unrelenting obstruction against the new president. "If he was for it, we had to be against it," said former Senator George Voinovich.[159] A few days into the new administration, House Republicans voted unanimously against the president's economic stimulus plan,[160] in a time of extraordinary national crisis — the depths of the Great Recession, with two major wars still dragging on overseas. (During the last four months of 2008 and the first four months of 2009, over 5.4 million jobs were lost — an average of almost 700,000 per month.)

Republicans may also benefit from voter disgust with Washington politics, because of the anti-government stance they've increasingly adopted since the Reagan years. "Unless dysfunction is clearly attributable to a particular set of politicians affiliated with the GOP, it generally hurts the party associated with an active use for government (that is, Democrats)."[161] That's seesaw politics: Just make the other side look bad, and you automatically gain, because there are no other viable options.

So, convenient though it might be to blame both sides equally for the polarization of present-day politics — because it would allow writers like me to more easily portray ourselves as neutral and unbiased — it would also be misleading. It would be to fall into the trap of false equivalence. The fact is that we're afflicted by *asymmetric*

---

[158] Mann & Ornstein 2012, p. 53.

[159] Grunwald 2012.

[160] Capehart 2012.

[161] Hacker & Pierson 2015, p. 63.

polarization: The Republican Party has moved further to the right than the Democrats have moved to the left.

But I hope it's clear that I'm calling attention to systemic problems in structural terms. The identities of the parties are not the point. It happens to be the Republican Party that became more extreme in our recent history, but in another time and place it could be another party. The structure of a party system creates incentives and disincentives. In our case, there are too many incentives for hijacking and hostage-taking, and the result is seesaw politics — parties striving to give their team an edge regardless of the demands of responsibility.

To those Republican readers who still feel offended by what I've said, you can take some solace from the fact that I'll be offending Democrats as well. Keep reading.

Strategic non-cooperation
The series of charts below (figure 3.3) show how cooperation between the two main parties has declined since the mid-20th century. For each Congress, starting with the 81st which convened in 1949, each member of the House of Representatives is shown as a circular node, red for a Republican and blue for a Democrat. Lines (or *edges*, in graph lingo) are drawn between every pair of nodes to represent cooperation between those two legislators on roll-call votes — the more votes the two agree on, the thicker the line. (If the two never vote the same way, there is no line between them.) This is a *force-directed graph*, in which nodes are positioned according to an algorithm, which uses the metaphor of a repulsive force between nodes, and a balancing attractive force proportional to the strength of the connections between nodes, i.e. the lines. The algorithm tries to keep lines as short as possible through positioning the nodes.

As you can see, in some Congresses, such as the one beginning in 1969, you can hardly even say there are separate red and blue clusters — the red and blue nodes are all mixed up. But from the 1980s to the present, the clusters have become increasingly isolated from each other as cross-party cooperation declined. The main exceptions in recent years have been conservative Democrats. For example, in the 2011 graph, shown at the lower right, the blue node near the top center, but hovering closer to the Republican cluster than to the Democratic one, is Rep. Collin Peterson (D-MN), a member of the conservative Blue Dog Coalition of Democratic legislators. (You can see legislators' names in the large versions of the charts.)

You might be saying, "That doesn't look so asymmetric to me. With just a few exceptions, both the red and the blue clusters look about equally clustery — or clumpy, or coherent." But the graphs depict cooperation, not polarization — they are agnostic about the content of the roll-call votes they are based on. And because they are only based on votes, they leave out various kinds of obstruction that are designed to avoid votes. What this series of graphs really depicts is the decline of cross-party cooperation and the rise of partisanship, or teamsmanship, among House legislators. It takes two to tango, as they say, and these charts don't answer the question of who does most of the refusing.

The relative moderation of the parties at the time of the Committee on Political Parties' report, in 1950, may hint at why they were so convinced of the value of the responsible party government model, with two and only two parties. Perhaps they took for granted that in a two-party system, both parties would gravitate towards the center. They didn't foresee that teamsmanship would come to predominate over the need for governing in good faith. Circumstances such as the Cold War may have helped maintain the ability of both parties to work together, and to compromise when necessary for the greater good. But things have changed since then.

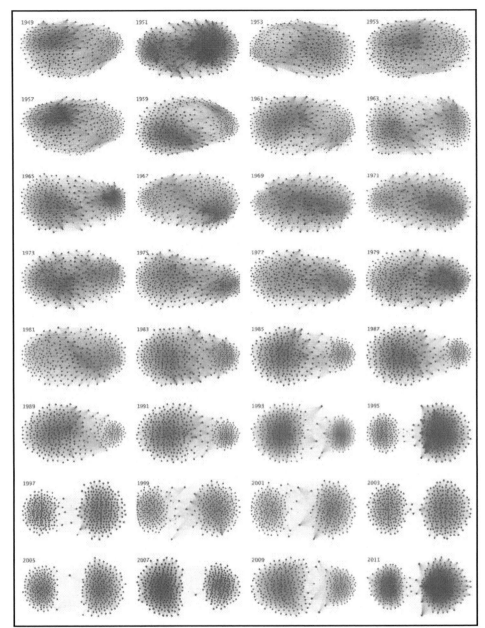

Figure 3.3. Division of Democratic and Republican Party members, 1949-2011
(Full-color version: daneckam.com/book/btp/figures.)
Source: Andris et al. 2015.

The above series of charts shows us something else that's very important, concerning the ideal of individual responsibility versus the ideal of party government. Many Americans don't trust political parties; they believe in voting for the person, not the party. In other words, they don't accept the doctrine of party government when it comes to electing representatives. This ideal of individual, not party, responsibility is understandable, of course, especially given our slippery (ideologically vague), big-tent major parties. But if we're going to move to a multiparty system, we're going to have to move past this idea; we're going to need to put more trust in parties as reliable vehicles for voter expression. And the good news is that when we have more coherent, more disciplined parties under the framework of a multiparty system, they will be more reliable, because they will be more accountable to the demands of voters.

That's not to say that individual responsibility will have no place whatsoever in the new system: it will. But it will partly fall to the parties themselves to groom high-quality candidates, and get rid of those who falter. Voters shouldn't have to research every single candidate for every single race to know how to vote. They don't do it well, either — if you need proof, read *Democracy for Realists* (2016) by Christopher H. Achen and Larry M. Bartels. There's a lot of depressing news in there. The average voter knows very little. So the ideal of individual responsibility doesn't really work.

And as the charts show, government is run by parties. It wasn't so much that way in the mid-20th century. Back then, elected officials worked together as individuals. But today, the parties cohere, as teams, to a far greater extent than before. They behave like "parliamentary" parties (in the sense of party discipline). Voters should recognize this as a fundamental reality of modern democracy. If the "cogs" of the wheels of government are political parties, then voters should be choosing from a selection of cogs.

Filibustering: obstructionism par excellence
One of the best-known, most classic types of congressional obstruction is the filibuster. In its canonical form, it features a lone senator monopolizing the chamber's time by standing for hours on

end, speaking about the need to block some vote that they find deeply troubling (or about pretty much anything, to fill time). For example, in the 1939 film *Mr. Smith Goes to Washington*, the eponymous character, played by Jimmy Stewart, speaks from the floor of the Senate for 24 hours before collapsing from exhaustion. In the end, the senator is vindicated against his corrupt enemies.

In the real world, a notorious example is Senator Strom Thurmond's filibuster to block passage of the Civil Rights Act of 1957, which lasted for 24 hours and 18 minutes. This was the longest spoken filibuster in American history, although Thurmond allowed some interruptions for Senate business after being assured he would be allowed to resume. He didn't change any senator's vote, and the bill passed 72-18.[162]

On February 7, 2018, Rep. Nancy Pelosi stood in the House of Representatives and spoke for more than eight hours, fitting the "colloquial" definition of a filibuster, if perhaps not the technical one: Filibusters have not been allowed under House rules since the 1890s. Pelosi used the privilege of her "leadership minute" to speak as long as she wanted, though the Republicans could have cut her off had they chosen to.[163]

In recent times, use of the filibuster as a tactic of obstruction has increased dramatically. I wish I could simply show you a chart of the number of filibusters in each Congress, but it's not that simple, because the definition of filibuster is a matter of debate. Senate expert Sarah Binder[164] says that when counting filibusters, we should include "extended debate on the floor, objections to requests for consent to move measures and nominations to a floor vote, and threats to filibuster or to object (sometimes in public, sometimes not)". This gets complicated.

One proxy for the number of filibusters in a legislative session is the number of cloture motions filed. Cloture is the ending of debate on a matter, so as to bring it to a vote. By Senate rules, it takes 60 votes to invoke cloture — that is, 60 votes to end a filibuster, to overcome

---

[162] Hickey 2013.
[163] Huder 2018.
[164] Binder 2014.

obstruction of the majority by a minority. The figure below shows the number of attempts to invoke cloture, and the number of those that were successful, from 1919 through 2016.

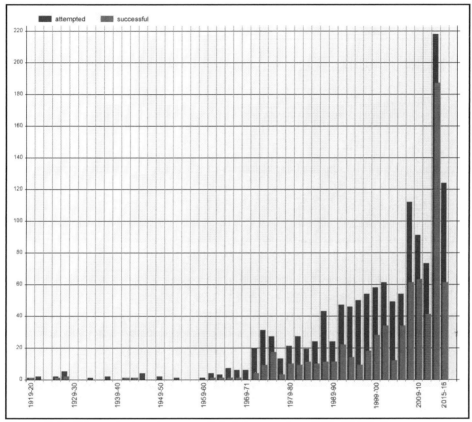

Figure 3.4. Attempted and successful cloture votes, 66th-114th Congress, 1919-2016

Source: *Vital Statistics on Congress* 2017 (Table 6-7).

We've reached the point where 60 votes are needed in the Senate to get most things done. The main exceptions are presidential nominees for the executive and judicial branches, which only require a majority since Senate Democrats invoked the so-called "nuclear option" in 2013 and Senate Republicans extended it to Supreme Court nominees in 2017. The other exception is the complex reconciliation process, originally meant to allow adjustments to the budget but which has increasingly been used for more significant pieces of legislation.

> The filibuster, once a rarity, has become omnipresent. The reasons for this are many, but political scientists mostly blame the rising polarization of the two parties, and particularly the tactical obstructionism pioneered by Republicans. The bottom line, though, is that basically nothing passes the Senate now without 60 votes, and the bipartisanship necessary to find those 60 votes is in sparser supply than ever before.[165]

This 60-vote rule is not built into either the Constitution or the institutional design of the Senate. The filibuster, says Binder, "was created by mistake." Originally, in 1789, both chambers of Congress had the same rules. They both had a rule concerning what's known as the "previous question" motion. Later, this became the chief way in the House to cut off debate and call for a vote on the issue at hand: A member would *move the previous question*. But in these early days it was not fully appreciated as a way of ending obstruction, and when Aaron Burr suggested eliminating the rule from the Senate, they complied without question, and dropped it in 1806.

This created the possibility of filibustering in the Senate, but it wasn't until 1837 that the first real filibuster occurred, and they remained rare up until the Civil War. Later in the 19th century, they became more common and more controversial, until finally, in 1917, the Senate adopted a new cloture rule requiring a two-thirds vote. (This was changed in 1975 to three-fifths.) As Binder explains, they chose a supermajority rule "not because senators were uniformly committed to the filibuster," but "because a minority blocked more radical reform." In other words, it was a matter of politics more than principle.[166]

Every new Congress has the opportunity to pass new rules. The filibuster can be eliminated anytime there are enough votes for reform. To claim that the current rule matches the Founders' vision of how the Senate should operate is to misread history. The Senate

---

[165] Klein 2017.
[166] Binder 2010, Binder and Smith 1997.

can function perfectly well with majority rule rather than supermajority. And it should, as I'll argue below.

Most filibusters are not about high principle. Look at an example from 1995. As head of the Senate Foreign Relations Committee, Sen. Jesse Helms (R-NC) blocked 18 ambassadorial nominations that year by the Clinton administration, to countries including China, Pakistan, South Africa and Lebanon. His aim was to consolidate and shrink the U.S. foreign policy establishment, by abolishing three foreign policy agencies and merging them with the State Department. He also blocked a vote on the START II arms-control treaty, which had been signed in January 1993 by President George H.W. Bush and Russian President Boris Yeltsin, and the international Chemical Weapons Convention, also signed by Bush in January 1993. In early December, Sen. Jeff Bingaman (D-NM) got fed up with Helms's obstruction, and filibustered an unrelated issue, an amendment to the Constitution to prohibit desecration of the national flag. After two hours of filibustering, Bingaman accepted assurances from Senate Majority Leader Bob Dole (R-KS) that there would be votes on the nominations and START II treaty by the end of the year. From the Congressional Record:

> **Mr. BINGAMAN.** Madam President, I wish to state a couple of questions and ask for the majority leader's response, if I could, at this time. Madam President, I know that there has been an agreement worked out with regard to the voting on the nominations and on the START II Treaty. I know that yesterday we had another discussion on the Senate floor, and the majority leader referred to his intention to, also in addition to the nominations for ambassadors, clear the rest of the items on the Executive Calendar before we left. I just wanted to once again ask for his assurance that that is his desire and his intention before we adjourn this fall.
>
> **Mr. DOLE.** Madam President, if the Senator will yield, I will just say, as I did yesterday, that it is certainly my hope that we can clear everything on the Executive Calendar before we leave this year. I cannot give a 100 percent guarantee. Somebody might have a hard hold on something. They may

not be able to get it up, and we might not be able to get cloture. But my view is we ought to accommodate where we can the executive branch, and I have always tried to do that.

Senator Bingaman relented, and the ambassadorial nominations and treaty votes went forward. The flag amendment also got a vote — it was defeated, with 63 Senators voting in favor and 36 against (it needed 66 votes to pass).[167]

It's interesting that an obstructionist tactic, the filibuster, was used to counter another obstructionist tactic, Senator Helms's use of his power as committee chairman to control the calendar. Hostage-taking to counter hostage-taking. It's almost like two wrongs making a right — but not really. There's nothing about the deliberative processes of a legislative assembly that should require such convoluted maneuvering.

This story is just one (or do we count it as three — or twenty?) of countless examples of obstructionism in the Senate. And we haven't even talked about less conspicuous parts of the problem, like *holds* (which were mentioned by Senator Dole in the quotation above). A hold letter is a request from a senator to the majority leader to delay a vote on a particular motion or bill. The original idea was apparently to extend a courtesy to senators who would be out of town and didn't want to miss a vote, or who needed more time to study a bill, or to negotiate a provision with its authors. But it can also be used to signal the intent to filibuster, and if the majority leader (who is in charge of scheduling votes) honors it, often it is tantamount to a filibuster, without the need to actually hold the floor and speak. Holds may be secret, meaning the senator who requested the hold may be anonymous — which is very useful for avoiding the political costs that more visible obstruction may incur.[168]

And how did this system of holds arise? "It is unclear when the hold system began," writes Gregory Koger, author of an authoritative book on the history of the filibuster and related forms of obstruction in the House and Senate. But he identifies the earliest known reference to a

---

[167] Dewar 1995a.
[168] Koger 2010, pp. 173-176.

hold as being in 1958, when Senate Majority Leader Lyndon B. Johnson (D-TX) mentions a hold letter received from Sen. Dennis Chávez (D-NM) regarding a bill on construction-contract policy.[169]

To fully understand the history and variety of congressional obstruction, you'd need a whole book (such as Koger's). But why should it be so complicated? Why should it take months or years for senators to master the rules of their chamber? Why should we be the only country to tolerate a legislative process so extensively burdened by the ability of a minority to obstruct?

In the British House of Commons, the practice effectively ended in the early 1880s, after a series of clashes between Irish nationalist Home Rulers and the British government.[170] Common sense would seem to support the view of the Speaker of the House of Commons in 1877, Henry Brand:

> [T]he House is perfectly well aware that any Member wilfully and persistently obstructing Public Business, without just and reasonable cause, is guilty of a contempt of this House; and is liable to punishment, whether by censure, by suspension from the service of this House, or by commitment, according to the judgment of the House.[171]

By contrast, in America some proclaim the filibuster as a sacred tradition, a hallowed senatorial "right" to unlimited debate. In reality, it is no such thing. It's an illegitimate power of a minority to obstruct public business. As James Madison recognized in *Federalist* no. 10, the "republican principle" — i.e. the rule of majority decision — should suffice to overcome a minority faction. Surely this applies as well to obstruction as to other actions in Congress.

I'd say it's a sign of our decrepitude as a democracy that it's so difficult to tell what the rules are and how they are manipulated. (Senator John Kennedy of Louisiana: "I've read a lot about the rules but I will tell you most of them seem to have been written right about the time of Moses and nobody completely understands them."[172]) It's a

---

[169] Koger 2010, p. 174.
[170] Chafetz 2011, pp. 1018-1023.
[171] Chafetz 2011, p. 1019.
[172] Williams 2018.

sad reflection of governmental obscurantism that a so-called "minute" can last for over eight hours, or that even political scientists sometimes have trouble following what goes on in Congress. We can do a lot better.

Hardball vs. restraint

Hijackings, hostage-takings, and obstructionism are all kinds of what Steven Levitsky and Daniel Ziblatt call "constitutional hardball" — "playing by the rules but pushing against their bounds and 'playing for keeps' ... a form of institutional combat aimed at permanently defeating one's partisan rivals—and not caring whether the democratic game continues."[173]

One example they cite is the disenfranchisement of African-Americans after Reconstruction: "after the Fourteenth and Fifteenth Amendments formally established universal male suffrage, Democratic-controlled legislatures in the South came up with new means of denying African Americans the right to vote. Most of the new poll taxes and literacy tests were deemed to pass constitutional muster, but they were clearly designed to counter its spirit".[174] Finding it difficult to win by fair rules, the governing party found ways to make the playing field unlevel.

Such hardball tactics go against long-held, unwritten democratic norms of institutional *forbearance*, which they define as "the idea that politicians should exercise restraint in deploying their institutional prerogatives".[175] When norms such as this, or the acceptance of electoral competitors as legitimate rivals, are neglected or subverted, democracy is weakened.

Constitutional hardball is not so easily played in a multiparty system, where no single party can govern on its own. When there are more parties, the rules, and the need for the rules to be fair, become more important. There's less scope for shenanigans, because there are more parties to cry "foul" when one of them gets out of line.

---

[173] Levitsky & Ziblatt 2018, p. 109; Tushnet 2004.
[174] Levitsky & Ziblatt 2018, p. 111.
[175] Levitsky & Ziblatt 2018, pp. 8-9.

We want our political parties to compete vigorously with each other, and to pursue their policy goals vigorously — that is, to use what power they have to strive earnestly for the policies they espouse. But such exercise of power goes too far when it undermines the democratic game itself. And this is more likely to happen in a seesaw two-party system than in a multiparty one.

Structural benefits of pluralism

I've been arguing that a multiparty system would work against some of the dysfunctions promoted by a bipolar system, including in the areas of responsiveness and responsibility. I've claimed that the debt ceiling would be more likely to be abolished under a multiparty system, and that hijackings and hostage-takings in general would be less likely and/or less well-rewarded. But maybe some readers haven't found these claims to be fully convincing. It's time to establish a firmer underpinning for them.

To do so, I'm going to rely on two brilliant papers. The first is from 1983: "Pluralism and Social Choice", by Nicholas R. Miller, published in *The American Political Science Review*. The second is from 2002 and draws heavily on Miller's paper: It's titled "The Tyranny of the Super-Majority: How Majority Rule Protects Minorities", by Anthony J. McGann, published by the Center for the Study of Democracy at the University of California, Irvine. Both papers are available online and are readable for non-experts in social choice theory.

Miller argues that social choice theory values too highly what is known as "collective rationality", meaning transitivity of social choice, which in many elections does not hold (see chapter 1 on the Condorcet paradox). Collective irrationality, he says, does not imply political instability. Rather, it leads to unstable social choice, but this instability itself "fosters the stability of pluralist political systems".[176]

A large society, with a wide diversity of interests and preferences, will tend to have many cross-cutting cleavages: Two random people will likely "have conflicting preferences with respect to one or more

---

[176] Miller 1983, p. 744.

issues but almost certainly agree on many issues as well".[177] So, although on any given two-sided issue there will be a majority and a minority, on different issues the majority will consist of different people. In a pluralistic society, there will not be one monolithic majority group who always wins — think of it as "the Majority", with a capital 'M'.[178] There will instead be *shifting* majorities — different groups of winners on different issues. One may lose today but win tomorrow on another issue, as part of a different coalition. But if there were not cross-cutting cleavages, but instead a permanent Majority, then the losing side would have little prospect of ever getting its way; it could easily become disillusioned and turn against the system. And this would be a problematic kind of instability — of the system itself, not just of political outcomes. In a pluralistic society, Miller says, "political outcomes are brought about by shifting coalitions of smaller [preference] clusters. Political outcomes probably please and displease nobody all the time; rather they please almost everybody some of the time. Political satisfaction, although probably nowhere total, is widespread."[179]

In a 1920 book, sociologist Edward A. Ross compares sets of cleavages to the interaction of waves, interfering or reinforcing each other depending on their alignment. "Every species of conflict interferes with every other," he writes, except when lines of cleavage coincide, when rifts in society are reinforced, "crest meet[ing] crest while trough meets trough". Therefore:

> A society [...] riven by a dozen oppositions along lines running in every direction, may actually be in less danger of being torn with violence or falling to pieces than one split just along one line. For each new cleavage contributes to narrow the cross clefts, so that one might say that society *is sewn together* by its inner conflicts.[180] [emphasis in original]

---

[177] Miller 1983, p. 735.
[178] Guinier 1994, p. 4.
[179] Miller 1983, p. 737.
[180] Ross 1920, p. 164-5.

Miller writes that arguments supporting this point of view are "standard in academic political science literature"[181] and provides many references. He quotes social anthropologist F.G. Bailey on how pluralism promotes moderate behavior:

> [T]hose who are enemies in one situation are sometimes required to act as allies in another situation. With an eye on future cooperation, they restrain their behavior in present competition.[182]

So pluralistic preference patterns, arising from cross-cutting cleavages, lead to moderation because no single preference cluster is numerous enough to take control of policymaking on every issue. Instead, different groups must work together, forming shifting majority coalitions on each issue — so they have an incentive to maintain good relations with people outside their preference cluster. The workings of this system, the way it is "sewn together by its inner conflicts", provide a source of restraint.

Hijacking and hostage-taking are what we too frequently get when we allow one faction to wield power on its own. James Madison would have recognized these problems as symptoms of majority faction. Consider these words from *Federalist* no. 10:

> The smaller the society, the fewer probably will be the distinct parties and interests composing it; the fewer the distinct parties and interests, the more frequently will a majority be found of the same party; and the smaller the number of individuals composing a majority, and the smaller the compass within which they are placed, the more easily will they concert and execute their plans of oppression. Extend the sphere, and you take in a greater variety of parties and interests; you make it less probable that a majority of the whole will have a common motive to invade the rights of other citizens; or if such a common motive exists, it will be more difficult for all who feel it to discover their own strength, and to act in unison with each other. Besides other impediments, it may be remarked that,

---

[181] Miller 1983, p. 736.
[182] Bailey 1970, p. 129; quoted in Miller 1983, p. 736.

where there is a consciousness of unjust or dishonorable
purposes, communication is always checked by distrust in
proportion to the number whose concurrence is necessary.

Of course, in his day travel and communication were much slower;
regions had more distinctive and divided interests than today.
Madison naturally thought of regional differences as a primary source
of factious disputes. But not the only one; he also recognized policy-
based differences:

> A religious sect may degenerate into a political faction in a part
> of the Confederacy; but the variety of sects dispersed over the
> entire face of it, must secure the National Councils against any
> danger from that source; A rage for paper money, for an
> abolition of debts, for an equal division of property, or for any
> other improper or wicked project, will be less apt to pervade
> the whole body of the Union, than a particular member of it;
> in the same proportion as such a malady is more likely to taint
> a particular county or district, than an entire State.[183]

It's the differences of viewpoint (arising, sometimes, from regional
differences) that matter. Variety of interests continues, as Madison
recognized it, to be a key to preventing tyranny.

Madison wanted shifting majorities, not a permanent, and
potentially tyrannical, Majority. But a Majority is what we have —
more precisely, a party system that promotes the idea of Majority by
its very structure (while at the same time celebrating "minority rights"
via Senate rules, which actually amount to obstructionism). And in
fact, the Majority that plagues our system, consisting of the more
numerous party in Congress, doesn't truly reflect majority opinion in
the populace, because the parties hedge and claim mandates that
don't actually exist. It's a synthesized Majority that is largely an
outcome of structuring things in a duopolistic way.

In a multiparty system, parties would more accurately represent
what their supporters actually want, because of the finer granularity of
representation. We'd expect our pluralistic preference patterns to be

---

[183] *Federalist* no. 10.

reflected in our parties, so that none of them would have the power of majority. They would have to share legislative power.

Stability is an important feature of any good political system. It's sometimes argued that a multiparty system would be less stable than a two-party one, and that one of the features of the two-party system is its stability. But in some important ways, this is not so. For one thing, to apply the market analogy again, competitive markets tend to be self-stabilizing: If producers fail to respond to consumers' demands, entrepreneurs may come along to disrupt things and restore the market's natural responsiveness. A market with excessively high barriers to entry locks out potential disruptors and suppresses innovation. And our duopolistic party system certainly locks out third parties. In a superficial sense, the system is "stabilized" — arrangements become frozen, change becomes more difficult — but in a deeper sense, the system becomes less stable as its responsiveness declines. It calcifies and grows brittle.

Miller writes that "*the* question of political stability" is "how to induce losers to continue to play the political game, to continue to work within the system rather than to try to overthrow it".[184] A pluralist political system, operating as shifting majorities under the majority rule, has better stability as a system than a dualist one. To see why, consider the following diagram:

---

[184] Miller 1983, p. 742.

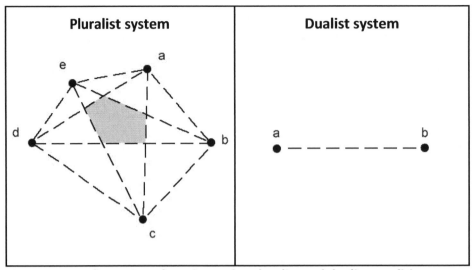

Figure 3.5. Configuration of parties under pluralist and dualist conditions

These two diagrams depict an abstract, two-dimensional ideological/policy space, in which each labeled point represents the ideal position for a certain legislator (or, by extension, a group of them). We assume that each legislator follows a simple utility function for determining how much they like a given position, which can represent either the status quo or some proposed new policy. The utility function says that the closer a point is to their ideal position, the more they prefer it.

On the left we see a simplified, abstract version of a multiparty system. The shaded area in the middle represents what political scientists (and game theorists) call the "core": the set of policy positions that cannot be defeated — in this case, assuming majority rule. For example, suppose each of the five parties has equal strength — or that there are five legislators, each representing a different party. Consider two points, one representing the status quo, which is inside the shaded area, the other representing a proposed new policy, which is outside it. The proposal will not be able to win a majority (three out of five in this example), because it cannot be closer to the ideal for more than two legislators. Try it — choose any point outside the core, and ask yourself how many legislators would consider it an improvement over a point inside the core. You'll see that it can never be more than two — and that's less than a majority. So the core represents the range of stable policy outcomes for a given legislative body.

On the right, we see a simplified version of a dualist party system. It actually gives more credit than is due to our two-party system because it presumes that each party has coherent ideological preferences, which they really don't, as I've previously explained. But this is an illustration of its structural tendencies, so it will help explain the point about system stability.

Where is the core, in the right diagram? Assuming there are only two legislators, with ideal points a and b, the core would be any point on the line connecting them. But let's add a bit of realism and suppose that there are more than two legislators, and a majority of them have point a as their ideal. Then the core would simply be at point a. No other point could defeat it under majority rule. And if a majority preferred point b, then the core would simply be at point b. The core becomes just a point, not a region. That doesn't leave much room for negotiation. The game becomes a winner-take-all struggle to command a majority. Under one party, policy will tend to move to one point, and then later under the other party, it will move to the other point. If you add the passage of time, and picture the diagram in animated form, it starts to resemble a seesaw.

In a pluralist system, policy also shifts over time. Pluralist politics, Miller writes, does not "authoritatively allocate values in a stable fashion". Rather, it permits volatile outcomes, ones which are reversible under shifting coalitions, but which tend to be within the bounds of the core, i.e. can be considered reasonable in light of the competing parties' preferences. But this "generic instability", Miller writes, "may contribute to the stability of pluralist political systems" — by ensuring that there are no permanent losers. Instability of political outcomes, when they are all reasonable, is not as bad as instability of the system itself. And in fact, this volatility may be less in practice than in theory, perhaps because the parties recognize the potential and try to avoid it. As McGann points out, some of the most majoritarian of western democracies, such as the Netherlands, Austria, and Sweden, do not appear to be especially unstable.[185]

In the last sentence of the passage quoted above, Madison points out something else I've hinted at — that the more parties need to be involved in some corrupt or misguided initiative, the more difficult it will be to pull off. Distrust, he writes, will rise "in proportion to the number whose concurrence is necessary". Collusion is harder the more people are required for it. (The "people" here would most likely be party leaders, representing their parties.)

Along the same lines, having multiple groups involved in considering a question makes it more likely that lies and mistakes will be revealed and more widely understood. In engineering terms, it improves the function of "sanity checking" — i.e. making sure that we haven't made an obvious or dumb mistake. When there are only two parties, they may take opposite positions on an issue without really illuminating their reasons — and voters then aren't very clear who's right and who's wrong.

For instance, some leaders say that we need to reform our entitlement programs — mainly Social Security, Medicare and Medicaid — if we are to preserve any semblance of fiscal health in the future. Others say we don't. An uninformed voter doesn't know who to believe. If one party says one thing, and the other party says the other, the voter will probably just stick with their side, and not think very hard about it. But if there are more parties, and a lone party says one thing while all the rest say the other, then voters who identify with the minority-opinion party may decide to examine the position a little more closely to make sure they're not wrong. That's not to say that the majority is always right, just that it helps to have more perspectives.

Another way of expressing the idea of sanity checking is "bullshit detection". Have you noticed that a surprising amount of bullshit seems to go undetected? Might this not be connected to the exclusion of alternative voices in our bipolar system?

---

[185] Note: by "majoritarian" he means following majority rule, not "winner-take-all", which is what some political scientists mean (unfortunately) by that word.

Table 3.1 summarizes these differences between a dualist and a pluralist system:

System feature	Dualist system	Pluralist system
1. Power sharing	Not encouraged	Encouraged
2. Political satisfaction	Winner-take-all contests; semi-permanent losers	Today's loser may be tomorrow's winner
3. Political system stability	Less responsive government eventually threatens system stability	Potential for instability of outcomes, but enhanced system stability
4. Political socialization	"Us" versus "them"; demonization of enemies	Promotes moderation, understanding other views
5. Resistance to bad moves	Low	Higher

Table 3.1. Social choice in dualist and pluralist political systems

Now you might be saying that yes, we have a two-party system, which sounds dualist, but in fact it's fairly pluralist, because the parties are so loose in their ideological coherence. If you're saying that, please look again at figure 3.3, which shows the increase in teamsmanship in our two parties. Even if they're not ideologically coherent, on a team-playing level they've become quite coherent. Of course, the institutional structure partly dictates how the game of politics is played — and our party leaders have been more and more willing to exploit the game.

Majority rule and tyranny

Do we have something to fear from majority rule? What is the concern of those who talk about the "tyranny of the majority"? What do they mean by that phrase? To begin to deal with these questions, it will help to notice that "rule" can be understood in two different ways:

1. rulership — authority over others. To *rule* is to wield power.
2. a principle for decision-making — the *rules* of the game.

As discussed in the previous section, when power is controlled by a Majority, that is, one faction that persists over time and across many issues, the system lacks much resistance to hijacking and abuse of power. The fact that this Majority may alternate between parties every two years, or every four years, helps keep it somewhat in check, but in its basic structure such a system neither reflects nor promotes the interests of pluralism in our society. This is the main legitimate concern embodied in the phrase "tyranny of the majority" — a majority faction. And the answer to this is a pluralist system in which shifting majorities — not a unified Majority — shape government policy. Civil rights theorist Lani Guinier calls them "Madisonian Majorities"[186] — what Madison envisioned as the happy outcome of an extended republic, or, as we might interpret it, of a diverse society.

What about majority rule as the rule of voting — of deciding? We can also call this the majority *criterion*, because it means that the criterion for deciding when something is passed is that a majority votes for it.

Does the majority criterion promote a tyranny of the majority? In his paper, McGann shows that it doesn't. The majority criterion, he writes, "is the decision rule that provides most protection for the worst-off minority".[187] Why? Because:

> it makes it easiest for a minority to form a coalition that can overturn an unacceptable outcome. Super-majority rules can certainly protect (or rather privilege) some minorities, but only at the expense of others. It is not logically possible for every minority to be privileged over every other minority. Super-majority rules make the status quo hard to overturn and thus privilege minorities who favor the status quo over those who favor changing it.[188]

---

[186] Guinier 1994, pp. 3-6.
[187] McGann 2002.
[188] McGann 2002, p. 15.

Super-majority rules are one kind of "checks and balances", designed to impede unwise government action — "hasty and partial measures", as James Madison termed it in *Federalist* no. 58. But Madison also wrote that "these considerations are outweighed by the inconveniences in the opposite scale. In all cases where justice or the general good might require new laws to be passed, or active measures to be pursued, the fundamental principle of free government would be reversed. It would be no longer the majority that would rule: the power would be transferred to the minority." As McGann says, not using the majority rule unfairly privileges a status-quo-favoring minority.

Defenders of the Senate filibuster often emphasize the fact that it protects the status quo against rash and unwise action — in other words, it performs a *restraint* function. Here, for example, is Senate Majority Leader Mitch McConnell, writing in the *New York Times*:

> Yes, the Senate's design makes it difficult for one party to enact sweeping legislation on its own. Yes, the filibuster makes policy less likely to **seesaw wildly** with every election. These are features, not bugs. Our country doesn't need a second House of Representatives with fewer members and longer terms.
>
> America needs the Senate to be the Senate.[189] [emphasis added]

I would suggest that there's a better way to keep policy from seesawing wildly, a more natural way, baked-in at a structural level: a multiparty system, which would provide the desired restraint without the expense of using a decision rule less fair than the majority criterion.

This is not to say that there's no place for checks and balances, and other forms of restraint, in our system. There are many such inhibitory mechanisms — including bicameralism, the presidential veto power, the power of judicial review, and the power of Congress to impeach. Federalism, too, provides a check on federal-government overreach: States have the standing to sue when necessary. Our system has many protections for minority rights. We don't need supermajoritarian rules for decision-making. In fact, it could be that

---

[189] McConnell 2019.

congressional inaction creates more scope for pseudo-legislating by the executive branch (in the form of executive orders) and the judicial branch (in the form of judicial activism, also known as "legislating from the bench").

If we've established that the majority criterion is the fairest rule to use for democratic legislating, is there any room left for potential "tyranny"? We come here to another crucial matter of definition. What does the word "tyranny" actually refer to?

The best way to understand this word is as a violation of *rights* — human and civil rights, the right to due process under law, but also the political right of opposition. Sartori writes that tyranny of the majority is "first and foremost, a constitutional problem", concerned with safeguarding minority rights against the power of a majority: "If the opposition is hampered, harassed, or stamped on, we may thus speak of 'tyranny of the majority' in the constitutional meaning of the expression."[190]

Related to, but distinct from, this is another constitutional problem, which Madison and Jefferson called "elective despotism":

> What they feared was the despotism of an assembly government unrestricted by division of power: an elective body (a parliament, but specifically its lower house) that would concentrate in its hands an unlimited and, by this token, a tyrannical power. That their fear was well justified was shown soon after by the French revolutionary *gouvernement conventionnel*, indeed a perfect incarnation of elective despotism. However, the elective despotism envisaged by Madison and Jefferson does not really bear on the majority-minority relationship but on the principle that undivided power is always an excessive and dangerous power.[191]

In principle, the Constitution protects our rights. The powers of Congress, the president, and the judicial branch are limited in scope; if they infringe on rights recognized by the Constitution, they should be (and generally are) overruled. And we have separation of powers —

---

[190] Sartori 1987.
[191] Sartori 1987.

three equal branches of government, each with checks on the others. This is an effective barrier to the sort of despotism seen during France's Reign of Terror in the 1790s. So, in the constitutional context, we seem to have most, at least, of what we need to avoid tyranny.

In the "electoral-voting" context, Sartori writes that the concern about tyranny does not really apply, for the reasons I have outlined above. The majority principle does not imply the exclusive rulership of a concrete majority. It is simply a decision rule, and in any decision (except those taken unanimously), some will be on the winning side while others will be on the losing side. "[I]n voting," Sartori writes, "the *minority has no rights*: It consists of those whose vote was lost — period. The implication is that in electoral-voting contexts the expression 'majority tyranny' is inapplicable and meaningless." And this is especially true when issues are decided by shifting majorities rather than a more lasting faction — a Majority — of the sort whose formation the two-party system promotes.

There is also a social context for the phrase "tyranny of the majority" — a tyranny of conformity to dominant social values. This was a prime concern for Alexis de Tocqueville and John Stuart Mill. The latter wanted protection "against the tyranny of prevailing opinion and feeling, against the tendency of society to impose... its own ideas and practices as rules of conduct on those who dissent from them... and to compel all characters to fashion themselves upon the model of its own."[192] This is indeed a problem, but it doesn't have much to do with democracy — it has been a problem since before democracy was invented. But we should be vigilant against letting majoritarian decision-making give "an element of legitimacy, a *right*, to what is otherwise a sheer *fact*, namely, that social tyranny exists and entails costs and excesses".[193]

In the most relevant sense, then, tyranny refers to the oppressive violation of rights. As such, we are already protected from it, to a large degree, by our constitution and the checks and balances built into our system (although, for reasons explored in this book, they are not

---

[192] Mill 1859.
[193] Sartori 1987.

always exercised effectively). We don't need to worry about the majority principle being a source of tyranny. And to the extent that a majority *faction* (that is, a Majority) does have the potential for tyranny, a multiparty system will protect better against it than a two-party system.

Yet some people seem to think that somehow, the two-party system helps protect us against a tyranny of the majority. How is it that they believe such a thing?

Calhoun vs. Madison: the concurrent majority

The issue of tariffs seems to come up frequently in discussions of the tyranny of the majority. Perhaps by taking a closer look at the history of the tariff issue, we can learn something about how people view majorities.

Beginning in the 1820s, the United States faced a major crisis when southerners, especially South Carolinians, objected to a series of tariffs passed by Congress, including one passed in 1828 that was known to its detractors as the "Tariff of Abominations". The idea was to promote domestic manufacturing, which was concentrated in the northern states. Unfortunately for the South, these tariffs hurt their regional economy, which was based on cotton and other crops (and on slave labor). By the early 1830s, South Carolina would become split between unionists, who wanted to go along with the federal government, and nullifiers, who believed in the right of their state (and all states) to *nullify*, i.e. invalidate, any federal law that infringed on the state's sovereign powers.

In the middle of this controversy was a brilliant politician from South Carolina, John C. Calhoun. Having been elected to the House of Representatives in 1810 at the age of 28, he originally viewed the idea of tariffs favorably, as part of what became known as the "American System" — a set of ideas building on those of Alexander Hamilton for strengthening the new nation, which included a national bank and funding for internal improvements such as canals and roads. But Calhoun's position shifted in the 1820s, after economic difficulties hit his home state hard, and he developed a theory of nullification based on a concept he called the "concurrent majority".

A concurrent majority, Calhoun said, stands in contrast to the *numerical* majority of the whole, of the people of one unified nation. He thought of the people less in terms of their national identity than of their state. In his view, the states retained a high level of sovereignty, such that if one state found a law to be unconstitutional, it could unilaterally nullify it, i.e. render it null and void within its borders, subject only to the limitation that three-fourths of all the states could override such a "state veto".[194] Unlike Madison, who believed in a sovereignty divided between the national and the federal (see *Federalist* no. 39), Calhoun located the sovereignty of the people in the "distinct political communities" of the several states.

> Unless the people of the states retained their original sovereignty that conferred on them the authority to decide which powers to delegate to the federal government and which to retain for themselves, Calhoun maintained, the federal government would gain by default the fundamentally unrepublican power to determine the extent of its own authority. Neither the Supreme Court through judicial review nor the president through his veto could be trusted to determine the extent of federal power since they were themselves branches of the federal government. The final authority of constitutional review lay not with any part of the government but with the governed in their original sovereignty.[195]

A concurrent majority is a unanimous concurrence of interest groups all of which favor, by majority decision, a certain policy. In the case of nullification, the interest groups were the states, but the idea of concurrent majorities can be applied more broadly to include almost any kind of interest group. This essentially means that every recognized interest group has a veto on government policy. Here are Calhoun's own words, from *A Disquisition on Government*, published in 1851, the year after he died:

---

[194] Ford 1994, p. 48.
[195] Ford 1994, p. 49.

[T]he government of the concurrent majority, where the organism is perfect, excludes the possibility of oppression, by giving to each interest, or portion, or order — where there are established classes — the means of protecting itself, by its negative [i.e. veto], against all measures calculated to advance the peculiar interests of others at its expense. Its effect, then, is, to cause the different interests, portions, or orders — as the case may be — to desist from attempting to adopt any measure calculated to promote the prosperity of one, or more, by sacrificing that of others; and thus to force them to unite in such measures only as would promote the prosperity of all, as the only means to prevent the suspension of the action of the government — and, thereby, to avoid anarchy, the greatest of all evils. It is by means of such authorized and effectual resistance, that oppression is prevented, and the necessity of resorting to force superseded, in governments of the concurrent majority — and, hence, compromise, instead of force, becomes their conservative principle.[196]

It sounds good, in theory — we all want to prevent oppression. Wouldn't it be nice if we had a way to exclude the possibility of it? Calhoun was pretty sure he'd found one — and he thought that James Madison, the last of the leading Founders, who lived until 1836, would concur with his view. He was wrong about that. In 1830, responding to a letter from an ally of Calhoun's, Madison denied that he contemplated nullification as part of the Constitutional framework devised in 1787. "What the fate of the Constitution of the U. S. would be," he wrote, "if a few States could expunge parts of it most valued by the great majority, and without which the great majority would never have agreed to it, can have but one answer." And that answer would be the sort of dysfunction that had plagued the Confederation which preceded the Constitution of 1787:

A political System that does not provide for a peaceable & authoritative termination of occurring controversies, can be but the name & shadow of a Govt: the very object & and end of

---

[196] Calhoun 1851.

a real Govt. being the substitution of law & order for uncertainty confusion & violence.

That a final decision of such controversies, if left to each of [the states], would make the Constitution & laws of the U. S. different in different States, was obvious; and equally obvious that this diversity of independent decisions must disorganize the Government of the Union, and even decompose the Union itself.[197]

Madison thought that questions of constitutionality should be decided by federal courts, and that if states objected to any part of the Constitution, they had the right to push for amendments to it. But they did not have the right to simply ignore or invalidate laws they didn't like. Courts have agreed; they have repeatedly refused to recognize the validity of nullification.

By the spring of 1833, the Nullification Crisis was over. Along the way, it had spawned a new party to advance the cause — the Nullifier Party, founded by Calhoun in 1828, which elected a few members of Congress in the 1830s, and whose presidential candidate won South Carolina in 1832. (That's a nice illustration of the power of a party system to give expression to a newly formed interest group — dimly though we may view the interest.) And nullification continued to figure in the thought of some political leaders, especially in the South. But as a legal doctrine of constitutional interpretation, it was thoroughly rejected.

Nevertheless, the idea of the concurrent majority has lived on. In fact, I get the feeling that behind much of the worry over majoritarian tyranny are ideas based on, or inspired by, the idea of a concurrent majority. For example, the tariff issue is construed as tyranny, even though the Constitution gives the power of tariffs to the federal government and it was decided by a duly elected representative assembly (and even though the whole objection is premised on an explicitly white-supremacist justification of slavery). That's why it's important to explain what's wrong with this concept. I hope that this chapter has done that, by explaining the anti-democratic nature of

---

[197] Madison 1830.

supermajoritarian rules. To allow any single actor, whether a Senator, a state, or another interest group, a veto on policymaking is to unfairly privilege the status quo and turn the principle of democratic decision-making on its head — a point also made by Madison in his letter:

> That the 7 [states, of 24 then in the Union] might in particular cases be right and the 17 wrong, is quite possible. But to establish a positive & permanent rule giving such a power to such a minority, over such a majority, would overturn the first principle of a free Government, and in practice could not fail to overturn the Govt. itself.[198]

Calhoun held deeply illiberal views (in the Enlightenment sense). He saw the "peculiar institution", slavery, as a "foundation for the construction and maintenance of a thoroughly republican social order that was crudely egalitarian for white males" — a guarantor of equality among white men.[199] The historian Richard Hofstadter summed up Calhoun's concerns as follows:

> Not in the slightest was he concerned with minority rights as they are chiefly of interest to the modern liberal mind—the rights of dissenters to express unorthodox opinions, of the individual conscience against the State, least of all of ethnic minorities. At bottom he was not interested in any minority that was not a propertied minority. The concurrent majority itself was a device without relevance to the protection of dissent, but designed specifically to protect a vested interest of considerable power. Even within the South Calhoun had not the slightest desire to protect intellectual minorities, critics, and dissenters... it was minority privileges rather than rights that he really proposed to protect. He wanted to give to the minority not merely a proportionate but an *equal* voice with the majority in determining public policy.[200]

It's true that minority rights should be protected. Minorities deserve representation (and they would have it in a multiparty system). But

---

[198] Madison 1830.
[199] Ford 1994, p. 41.
[200] Hofstadter 1948, pp. 116-117.

that doesn't justify not making decisions according to the numerical majority. We have a Constitution that protects our rights, and an independent judicial branch of government to secure them. And the more our systems of representation accurately represent the interests of the people (which has much to do with the variety in our party system), the more we can rely on our legislative branch not to be under the control of a static Majority, which does tend to ignore minority interests. The more our legislative assemblies reflect the diverse interests of the people, the more they function based on shifting majorities that vary in composition from one issue to another, and thus tend to recognize the concerns of all (or at least all who have coalition potential — that is, who are considered reasonable — on some major issue).

Conclusion

The main point of this chapter is that we have a serious problem with representation in America — a structural problem at the root of much system dysfunction. When we consider John Adams's recommendation that our representative assemblies should be "portraits" of the people, and compare it with the system we have, it seems clear that we're falling short. Our assemblies aren't worthy of the label "representative". And a major part of the reason for this is our party system. In cybernetic terms, it simply lacks the *variety* needed to adequately perform its essential functions — that is, channeling the will of the people, providing a vehicle for the expression of voters' desires. It's a "steering" problem: In a democracy, the government is supposed to follow the will of the people. Elections are the primary mechanism for that will to be expressed, channeled, and translated into action. But when voters have only two viable choices, as they do in most elections, it's not enough to make clear the diversity of opinion. Public opinion is "over-channeled" into just two giant camps, ones so big that for at least some issues it's impossible to know what people are saying with their vote.

   This chapter has also explained why majoritarian decision-making is the fairest system, and why supermajoritarian rules tend to be unjust in denying the policy preferences of the majority. It's true that minority rights are important, and that's why they are protected by constitutional rights as well as by checks and balances. But the 60-vote Senate was never part of the Founders' plan, and devices such as Calhoun's concurrent majority are no substitute for what Madison recognized (in *Federalist* no. 58, among other places) as democracy's "fundamental principle" — that a numerical majority should have more power than a minority.

Congress is the most dysfunctional of the three branches of our federal government, and one of the most important reasons is that it's so bogged down by obstruction. Another important reason is a duopolistic party system that creates structural disincentives for consensus-seeking, and promotes hijacking and hostage-taking, which are all too common in the U.S. Opening up the party system would tend to reduce such abuses, and also lead to less obstructionism. If there is no Majority faction to rule on its own, it's more likely that the Speaker and other agenda-setters in Congress will be consensus-builders, skilled at assembling shifting majorities issue by issue, instead of hostage-takers who abuse the leverage given them by their Majority position — a position not reliably reflective of majority opinion in the electorate.

But Congress also has functions beyond legislating. It's also meant to act as a check on the other branches of government — the executive and judicial. In this capacity, too, it has failed — and the failure is closely connected to the nature of our party system. In the next chapter, we'll explore this idea in greater depth.

4. Teamsmanship Versus Principle

"We've been spinning our wheels on too many important issues because we keep trying to find a way to win without help from across the aisle. That's an approach that's been employed by both sides, mandating legislation from the top down, without any support from the other side, with all the parliamentary maneuvers that requires. We are getting nothing done, my friends, we're getting nothing done." — John McCain[201]

Although our parties don't represent very much in coherent ideological terms, they cohere all too well as teams. The two-party system, as entrenched in congressional and electoral rules, practices, and customs, imposes a structure that creates certain incentives, disincentives, and opportunities to reap gains from team-oriented play. The two major parties have increasingly been exploiting these potentials, leading to irresponsible government. In this chapter, we'll explore how this happens and how it would be different in a multiparty system.

An important part of the checks and balances designed by the Founders is the power of impeachment given to Congress — over the president, the vice president, members of the cabinet, and federal judges. This is a very important function because the power to remove someone from office helps ensure accountability.

The Founders knew that the president and Congress would need to work together. But they didn't foresee that they would be bound together by common interests of party. What they *really* didn't foresee was that we'd have a two-party system in which the president would be co-partisan with around half of Congress — sometimes more,

---

[201] Farrington 2017.

sometimes less, but usually more than enough so that strong partisan interests would be able to block impeachment and removal from office, thus thwarting accountability.

If you're a member of Congress and the president is the leader of your party, it means you're going to be very reluctant to support impeachment hearings even if they are warranted. This is a major flaw in our system that greatly diminishes accountability. A great example, in my opinion, is the failure to impeach George W. Bush and Dick Cheney over their use of misleading information to get approval for the Iraq War.

A foreign policy debacle

To briefly review what happened, on September 11, 2001, the U.S. was attacked by al-Qaeda, which was then based in Afghanistan. The U.S. responded by invading Afghanistan, with congressional approval. Eighteen years later, that war is still going on. But already by August of 2002, the Bush administration was pushing for war in Iraq, based mainly on charges that Saddam possessed weapons of mass destruction (WMDs). Vice President Dick Cheney claimed there was "no doubt" that Saddam had WMDs and that he was preparing to use them, and National Security Adviser Condoleezza Rice raised the specter of nuclear weapons, saying "we don't want the smoking gun [of evidence of WMDs] to be a mushroom cloud".

A key part of the claimed evidence for Saddam's nuclear weapons program was that he had tried to acquire aluminum tubes used for enriching uranium. Secretary of State Colin Powell testified, at the U.N., to the reliability of this evidence, and therefore of the need to act. But in reality, the evidence that the tubes could only be used for uranium-enriching centrifuges was very thin, and chosen selectively. Many experts did not believe they were well-suited to uranium enrichment and were probably designed for use with rockets. The Department of Energy, which has responsibility for our nuclear weapons and thus knows a few things about centrifuges, found it highly unlikely that the tubes Saddam had acquired were used for enrichment. Experts in the state and defense departments concurred;

some of them urged Powell not to include dubious claims in his U.N. presentation, but the Secretary ignored them.[202]

Similar distortions of the truth were used to explain how Saddam was acquiring uranium. According to documents given to the CIA by Italian military intelligence, he had tried to buy a large quantity of yellowcake uranium from Niger. These were widely recognized as forgeries, and this finding was confirmed by Joseph C. Wilson, a former ambassador to Gabon who was well-acquainted with the region. When the CIA sent him to Niger to investigate the claims in February 2002, Wilson found there was no "there" there. The CIA knew that the connection between Saddam and Niger was highly dubious.

But, under pressure from the White House and Vice President Cheney's office, the agency approved the president's 2003 State of the Union speech, which included these notorious words: "The British government has learned that Saddam Hussein recently sought significant quantities of uranium from Africa." This was technically true — the British government had published an unclassified report to that effect — but it was a cop-out because our own intelligence experts viewed that report as unreliable. As Senator Carl Levin said, "The only purpose [...] of telling the American people that the British have learned that Saddam was seeking uranium in Africa was to create the impression that we believed it. But we didn't believe it. The intelligence community did not believe it." CIA director George Tenet admitted, almost six months after the speech, that the words should not have been approved.[203]

Such failings seem to have been purposeful, the result of persistent pressure from high levels of the administration. In the words of Powell's former chief of staff, Colonel Lawrence Wilkerson, "What I saw was a cabal between the vice-president of the United States, Richard Cheney, and the secretary of defense, Donald Rumsfeld, on critical issues that made decisions that the bureaucracy did not know were being made."[204]

---

[202] Conyers 2006, pp. 63-72.
[203] Tenet 2003.
[204] Alden 2005.

Saddam's possible nuclear capability was not the only concern; some also expressed fear that he had a biological weapons program. An Iraqi defector codenamed "Curveball" had applied to Germany for asylum in 1999, selling a fabricated story that he'd worked at mobile bioweapons labs in Iraq. German intelligence passed the information on to counterparts in the United States, where it was used by both President Bush in his State of the Union speech and Secretary of State Colin Powell in his presentation at the U.N. But U.S. intelligence knew that Curveball was not reliable; in fact, as early as September 2001, Britain's MI6 had warned the CIA that his behavior seemed typical of a fabricator. A fabricator warning was posted in U.S. intelligence databases in May 2002. When the CIA's European operations chief asked the Germans to let him question Curveball, he was warned that they thought he was "probably a fabricator".[205]

What all this, and much more, points to is that the case for war was exaggerated, that the administration led us into it without good reason. As the Downing Street memo, based on a July 23, 2002 meeting of high-level British officials, noted, "Military action was now seen as inevitable. Bush wanted to remove Saddam, through military action, justified by the conjunction of terrorism and WMD. But the intelligence and facts were being fixed around the policy."

On top of all this, the Iraq War was a *preemptive* war, based on a dubious principle allowing one nation to attack another based only on the belief of an imminent threat. This is a dangerous precedent for a world that respects the idea of national sovereignty, and aspires to some basic rule of international law — so it should at least imply that a higher standard of evidence is required. If there was any standard in effect here, it went ignored (a failure of both the executive and legislative branches). The Iraq War is undoubtedly one of the biggest misadventures in American history. And if we were deliberately misled into it, that's an extremely grave "high crime" and exactly the kind of abuse of power our Founders wanted to avoid, by giving Congress the ultimate check on the executive branch: the power of impeachment.

---

[205] Stein and Dickinson 2006.

Even the Republican Party seemed to finally acknowledge the mistake of going into Iraq, after years of denial — and they did it in an oddly unexpected way. In 2015, Jeb Bush, as a candidate for president, said that even with the benefit of hindsight, he would have supported the invasion. Soon after, he had to backtrack, and eventually admitted that he would not have invaded.[206] That he would fumble so badly what should've been a predictable question is remarkable. So too is the almost incidental way the party seemed to shift, as David Brooks noted on the PBS NewsHour:

> The final, most surprising thing to me is that the rest of the party seems to have switched to the idea the Iraq War was a mistake. I was really struck by all — a lot of the other candidates came out and said obviously it was a mistake, given what we know now about the weapons of mass destruction. And that is how parties shift sort of accidentally. Suddenly, they have decided the war was a mistake, after not admitting that for a long period of time. And so I'm mostly struck by how the whole party seems to have pinioned on this issue in about three days.[207]

This is not how most of the democratic world's political parties shift their positions. This is not healthy party operation. Responsible and responsive parties would be working to figure this out, probably with a certain degree of transparency. Their active members, at least, would understand that change was coming, instead of being blindsided unpredictably by shifts based on cynicism and ideological vagueness.

There were probably other impeachable offenses too, such as torturing enemy combatants through the use of waterboarding, or wiretapping American citizens without a warrant. But I focus on the misleading case for war because it so clearly matches the deep fear our Founders had that the president would be like a king in all but name. And also because it had such massive and dire consequences — hundreds of thousands of Iraqis killed, thousands of American

---

[206] Jacobs 2015.
[207] PBS NewsHour 2015.

casualties, and a cost running into trillions of dollars. As a nation, we cannot afford to repeat such a mistake. So in my opinion, we should have held the Bush-Cheney administration to account, by impeaching them. By not doing so, we gave a signal to future administrations that they may be able to get away with similar crimes.

The thing is, the two-party system had a lot to do with this failure of accountability. Republicans did not want to consider the possibility that the leader of their party could have misled the nation into war. So they blocked impeachment hearings. To a certain extent, that's predictable: We would expect members of a certain team to be the last to recognize a mistake made (or crime committed) by their team leader(s). But it's a problem for representative democracy because we depend on our elected leaders to speak out against irresponsibility when they see it. We need them to judge issues on their merits, and according to principled values, not on partisan interests — gaining short-term political advantage for their team. When teamsmanship is elevated over principle, irresponsibility often goes unchecked. This is a major defect in how the system functions.

But it gets worse. Not only did the president's party defend him from impeachment hearings, so did the Democratic Party. Although Rep. John Conyers, Democrat of Michigan, held hearings about the Downing Street memo in the basement of the House, and a few other representatives, such as Dennis Kucinich (D-OH), advocated impeachment hearings, on the whole the party preferred to avoid the subject of impeachment. Famously, about six months before the 2006 elections, House Minority Leader Nancy Pelosi (D-CA) declared that impeachment was "off the table" — meaning that if Democrats won a majority of seats, they would not be pursuing it.[208] Conyers went along with the plan. Pelosi thought that if the Democrats pushed for impeachment, it would hurt their chances of winning a majority in the 2006 midterms.

And here's the *really* weird thing: She may have been right. In 2006, not that many Americans believed that the president and/or vice president deserved impeachment. So if the Democrats had made a big

---

[208] Babington 2006.

deal of it — as big a deal as they knew, or should have known, it actually was — it was a genuine risk that the electorate would judge that unfavorably. Maybe they would've viewed it as merely partisan vindictiveness, or seen it as too negative to be running a campaign on. Such concerns could have made the difference between Democrats winning a majority and not doing so.

But notice that the concern here depends on the two-party structure of our government — that one party or the other will be in the majority, and thus able to govern more or less on its own — as a Majority, as I described it in chapter 3, a faction that claims nearly all the levers of power for itself. In the context of the two-party system, Pelosi's decision had a convincing logic to it — and it's a logic that doesn't apply in a multiparty system. Under multiparty conditions, no party would expect to have a majority of seats on its own. The lack of such an expectation would free the party from certain electoral pressures, such as taking a big chance on pushing for impeachment. With more parties in competition, it's likely that at least one would see an opportunity for electoral success in the idea of impeachment. It could present itself as a defender of the Constitution, of the system of checks and balances which is a foundational value of American democracy.

Accountability failure

Even if it were true that most Americans did not want impeachment during election season in 2006, that's not reason enough not to follow where the truth leads. When serious, important questions are raised, they should be investigated — meaning that hearings should be held. And as hearings are held, they reveal more and more information, and if there are impeachable offenses, it would become more and more undeniable. This would change the political calculus. Impeachment would go from being a dangerous "third rail" of divisive partisan politics to being seen as necessary, perhaps to the point that parties obstructing impeachment without good reason would be seen as irresponsible. In this way, the issue could be initially pushed by a fringe party, then, if deemed worthy, be taken up by other parties, resulting in a proper investigation of the truth and an increase of accountability.

The gap between the level of accountability we should have, as a healthy democracy, and the level we actually have under the two-party system is one of the strongest indicators, to my mind, of the need for reform. The fact that Pelosi's decision to take impeachment off the table was strategically defensible illustrates precisely why the two-party system is fundamentally incompatible with an effective system of checks and balances. If we want to make sure that future presidents do not feel that they can get away with misleading the country into war, the two-party system won't cut it. It doesn't give us the protections we need.

In 2018, with midterm elections approaching, Nancy Pelosi again felt compelled to announce that impeachment was "off the table". The strategic thinking seems to have been the same as in 2006: She didn't want to let Republicans use the threat of impeachment to "gin up" their base. And once again, given the seesaw structure of our system, the strategy makes sense. But we need a system that doesn't punish parties for taking the more responsible stance, that presidents should be impeached when they need to be impeached — so party leaders should keep an open mind.

In April 2019, *The Economist* recognized the problem, in writing about the just-released Mueller report. On the one hand, they said, not sanctioning the president would signal to future presidents that "the lying, the footsie with Russia and attempts at obstruction are just fine". On the other hand, the risk of President Trump being acquitted in the Senate could boost his chances of re-election. The Founders "did not foresee the rise of a rigid two-party system that mirrors the rural-urban divide" which makes it very hard to remove a rogue president.

> The result is that one man is, in effect, above the law for all but the most serious and readily understandable crimes, such as murder, which would surely be too much even for the committed partisans of either side.[209]

---

[209] "After Mueller, what next?", 2019.

As I finish writing this book in the fall of 2019, the House has launched an impeachment inquiry, and it looks probable that President Trump will be impeached. Assuming that he is, the outcome will go one of two ways: he'll be removed from office, or he won't. I don't know what will happen, but I don't think it will have any effect on the argument of this book. If the president is not removed, it will be more evidence that teamsmanship is systematically elevated above accountability in our two-party system. If he is removed, it will have to be because the case against him is so strong that even Republicans have ditched him. Thus it won't be a very useful test case.

Trigger happiness
Let's consider an "opposite problem" — how do we ensure that Congress doesn't try to impeach presidents too often? Again it appears that a multiparty system would help, at least in some ways. Consider the impeachment of Bill Clinton — which most Americans don't think was well-justified. Yes, he committed perjury, and that's a serious offense; but his crime had nothing to do with the national interest. There's no comparison between lying about an extramarital affair and misleading a country into war. But with a Congress dominated by the Republicans, who had taken an extremely negative stance towards the Democratic president, there was nothing structural standing in the way of impeachment.

Contrast that dynamic with what would be likely in a multiparty system, that no party would be in control of Congress on its own. Under such conditions, impeachment wouldn't get far unless it was supported by two or more parties. That would make it much less likely unless the crime was serious — that is, unless it was truly a case of "high crimes and misdemeanors". Political gains for removing a president from office would not be so clear. In a two-party system, discrediting one party automatically benefits the other. But when there are more than two, if one is discredited it's not clear which of the others benefits.

Would that be enough to make sure that impeachment isn't always "on the table" for one party or another? And wouldn't that be extremely divisive, even traumatic, for political society? At first, under multiparty politics, some parties might perceive short-term benefits to pursuing impeachment, even knowing that it would not end with the president's removal from office. But over time, "playing the impeachment card" without solid justification, as a cynical political strategy, would be seen for what it is.

It's also worth mentioning that the power of impeachment can function as a strong *deterrent* against presidential misconduct. Its value as such has waned under two-party politics. But if restored, under multiparty politics, to the prominence it was intended by the Founders to have, it would naturally help presidents to see that they'd be better off not antagonizing Congress. The divisive, traumatic potential of impeachment can help all sides better understand how to avoid it.

Moving beyond the seesaw will shift the decision-making process towards judging situations on their merits. Cybernetically speaking, we can say that the system lacks the variety it needs to judge questions of impeachment fairly and effectively. Thus, adding party variety would help.

The politics of hate
Politics today is practiced too much as a zero-sum game: My gain is your loss, and your gain my loss. Teamsmanship has been on the rise in recent decades. As we've seen in figure 3.3, showing the decline of cross-partisan cooperation, for most of the post-war 20th century, the parties exhibited a kind of centrism. Perhaps the Cold War, by providing an impetus for party unity in foreign policy, had something to do with it. But starting, I think, somewhere between the beginning of the Clinton administration and the Republican victory in the 1994 elections, a new style of teamsmanship has seemed to emerge in our politics. In the lingo of political science, centrifugal forces (that is, pushing away from the center) have become more significant relative to centripetal (that is, center-seeking) ones.

Frances E. Lee writes in depth about this phenomenon, in a book titled *Beyond Ideology: Politics, Principles, and Partisanship in the U. S. Senate* (2009). She documents the fact that "parties-in-government have become stronger as institutions over the past 25 years",[210] and finds compelling evidence that the increase of party conflict in Congress can be attributed to more effective teamsmanship:

> [P]arty conflict *regularly* occurs on issues that do not involve conventional ideological distinctions in American politics. Other issues account for a very substantial amount of partisan conflict in Congress [...] 45 percent of roll-call votes on issues not involving typical left-right cleavages divided the Senate along party lines. Republicans and Democrats disagree about a lot more than liberals and conservatives do.[211]

In other words, for today's elected officials, more than at many times in the past, teamsmanship plays a role as big, or perhaps even bigger, than ideology in shaping their legislative behavior. "Rather than seeking to bridge their differences, the vast majority of legislators in each party now reflexively vote against any initiative that originates with the other."[212] Even when our representatives might be able to agree, based on their ideological principles, they would rather disagree, to support their team's political game plan.

Lee doesn't explore the connection between this behavior and the structure of our two-party duopoly. But I think there's a strong one. Modern American politics are played too much as if the parties are on opposite sides of a seesaw. What harms the fortunes of one side helps those of the other. This has a lot to do with the norm, and structural tendency, for one party to control most of the levers of power — to act as a Majority. The parties are locked in a struggle for domination, which is always, potentially, around the corner, after the next election. In the view of democratic theorists Gary W. Cox and Mathew D. McCubbins, our legislative parties, "especially the majority party" (notice the premise) behave as "legislative cartels" which "usurp the power, theoretically resident in the House, to make rules governing the structure and process of legislation."[213] As I've tried to make clear, this "usurpation" (or "hijacking") would have seemed very troubling to

---

[210] Lee 2009, p. 164.

[211] Lee 2009, p. 185.

[212] Brownstein 2007, pp. 14-15.

[213] Cox and McCubbins 1993, p. 2.

our Founders. Why not try structuring our legislature more closely to how they would have envisioned — without giving the power of majority to any one faction?

The structure of our party system encourages us to ask, "Who do I hate?" — not "Who do I love?", or "What am I for?" Given only two viable party choices, to figure out which party you hate is to pick the other side. As Senator Lindsey Graham (R-SC) said, "You are one team versus the other and never the twain shall meet. If it's a Democratic idea, I have to be against it because it came from a Democrat. And vice versa."[214]

Senator Ben Sasse (R-NE) made the same point in a public radio interview:

> We're not thinking about where we are in economic history — the transformation to the digital, mobile, post-industrial economy where the average duration in a job is going to get shorter and shorter. That has huge policy implications. We're not talking about any of that stuff, because it's usually a shirts-and-skins exercise of the weirdos in Washington who are kind of the one percent that are so politically addicted that they want to take from the 99 percent the ability to have a longer-term conversation. [...] D.C. isn't focused on serious, future things, it's sort of Republican-versus-Democrat hackery most of the time, without even having clarity about what particular policy fight we're arguing about.[215]

It's easy to be against something. Opposing shouldn't be the end of the story of choosing which side to support. Representative democracy depends on the people being able to communicate what they want to their representatives. The fallacy of our system is that negative feelings towards one side mean support for the other side — a short-circuiting of the tough questions we voters need to be considering if we're to have a well-functioning democracy.

---

[214] Brownstein 2007, p. 12.
[215] Sasse 2017, at approx. 10:40 to 11:30.

A judicial appointment example

As a way to illustrate how the seesaw quality of our party system affects government, let's consider three scenarios concerning the Senate's duty to confirm the president's appointments to the judiciary. I'll outline two scenarios that can occur under a two-party system, then one under a multiparty system.

In the first scenario, suppose there are only two parties in government, and that the Senate is controlled by the one opposite to the president's party. Given bitter partisan polarization, what can happen (and did, in the case of Merrick Garland) is that the Senate simply refuses to consider the president's appointment, obstructing the seat from being filled at all. This is clearly not how the system was intended to work.

In a second scenario with only two parties, suppose that the Senate is controlled by the president's party. Then the president can appoint someone with a partisan orientation and count on the Senate to confirm. Short shrift may be given to the other side of the aisle, to the need for moderation and restraint. But members of the judiciary are meant to be impartial — above politics — not partisans. So this, too, is far from ideal. The only thing that keeps it sort of balanced, in theory at least, is the alternation in power of the two parties. But this works very imperfectly. Seesaws don't gravitate towards balance.

Now let's consider a third scenario, this time under a multiparty system. Given proportional voting, as I'm recommending in this book, and enough time for the party system to adjust to it, it will less often happen that one party controls a majority of seats on its own. So the president will need to appeal to more than just the narrow partisan interests of his own party, by nominating someone well-qualified, impartial, and moderate. And if he does, most parties will accept that, knowing that they're unlikely to achieve a better result by obstructing the appointment.

(There's a valid objection here: The Senate cannot be elected by proportional representation because Senate races are single-seat elections. We could change the staggered six-year terms so that both senators from a state are elected at the same time. But short of that, the Senate will probably have a more two-party complexion than the

House. I will address this objection in three ways: One, the culture will have changed, and although two parties may dominate, they won't exist in the same sort of duopolistic system we now have. They will be subject to more pressures of accountability. Norms of party behavior will change in a multiparty system. Second, different states may have different dominant parties — so single-seat elections won't necessarily mean just two parties to represent the whole nation. Let's remember that Duverger's law works primarily within a district, not across districts. Finally, if we use the Condorcet IRV method for single-seat elections, as recommended in chapter 1, responsible, moderate and consensus-seeking candidates will be favored, reducing polarization.)

One more difference between the second and third scenarios: the process. In our current system, the president's nomination is first taken up by the 21-member Judiciary Committee, which holds hearings to vet the nominee. Under the partisan management of the committee chair, the candidate is eventually given a committee vote. If she wins a majority, the matter is referred to the Senate floor. Then, a cloture vote is usually held to limit debate on the issue. If that succeeds, then after a 30-hour waiting period the whole Senate finally gets to vote on the nominee. This is a convoluted and not very transparent process. Many citizens will be confused: They will hear of a vote on the nominee and think it's a final vote, when in fact it's a procedural one, for a procedure they don't understand. This lack of understanding is a problem for democracy, whose workings depend on the polity being able to judge how their government is performing.

In a multiparty system, vetting would still be needed; it could be done by either a standing or an ad-hoc committee, or perhaps another way. There wouldn't necessarily be a requirement for the committee to vote to refer the issue to the whole Senate, so there wouldn't have to be a "choke point" where the nomination could be derailed. Once enough vetting was done, every Senator would have a chance to vote on the nomination. The rules would be up to the Senate, and there are many possibilities. But they would probably be fairer, less convoluted, and more transparent, because they would have to be to win approval from more than one party. (See the section "More parties, more fairness" in chapter 5.)

Analyzing the system failure

In my high-level system overview of our democracy (figure 2.1), I depicted the main structures involved in constituting our federal government, and how that government is structured. Let's zoom in on the governmental part of this diagram, and review the problems we've been considering in terms of it.

Figure 4.1 shows three important arcs in red — the ones most heavily impacted by the duopoly in our party system. Arc H represents the cooperation or conflict between the legislative and executive branches. When Congress is dominated by the president's party, there is far too much potential for collusion — cooperation gone too far. When it's dominated by the other party, there is potential for knee-jerk, ill-considered opposition and obstructionism of the president's agenda. In either case, it's not how our Founders intended for this relationship to work.

Arc J represents the checks of the legislative branch on the executive. As we have seen in the case of the Iraq War and the failure of the Democrats to hold impeachment hearings, this restraint on presidential action is not functioning as intended. And arc K, representing the checks of the legislative branch on the judicial branch, is colored red because Congress is too polarized to ensure that judges are impartial and non-partisan.

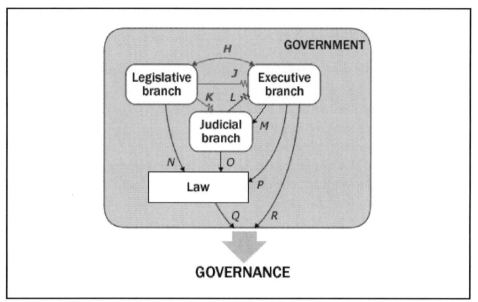

Figure 4.1. System malfunction between branches of government (Full-color version: daneckam.com/book/btp/figures.)

These are serious defects in the system, and of course they have effects on other parts of the diagram too. Arc *M*, for example, could have been shown in red, because when arcs *J* and *K* aren't working as designed, presidents are free to appoint partisan judges. Arcs *N*, *O*, and *P* also work less well than intended, as an indirect result of how Congress is constituted and its interactions with the other branches.

Teamsmanship in the electorate

So far, we've been talking about parties in government. The other main aspect of parties is how they function in the electorate. Here, a certain amount of teamsmanship is expected, since the game is all about competing to win seats.

In this domain, we need to promote healthy competition between political parties by allowing them to develop their own "sales pitches" for the electorate. That implies a certain amount of independence — parties should be free to define themselves. And this means that the idea of open primaries doesn't make much sense. In a state with open primaries, voters who don't consider themselves members of a party are able to participate in the process of choosing its nominees for a general election.

Most democracies don't have anything like this. Usually they have a far more precise idea of party membership, including the payment of dues. Only fully paid, card-carrying members of the party are allowed to participate in the nomination process. Most voters are not dues-paying members of any party. The U.K.'s Labour Party, for example, has slightly more than half a million members, in a country of over 65 million. It's the largest party in the country.

If this seems undemocratic to you, it's probably because of what you're used to. Remember Schattschneider's dictum that democracy is "between the parties", not within them. Our notions of intraparty democracy have been conditioned on the two-party system as context. Given our duopolistic system, widespread participation in primaries has been an adaptation designed to increase representation. But as an adaptation, it's shortsighted. Far better would be the sort of multiparty system I'm describing, in which it's not preordained who the major party contenders will be, therefore elections are decided on bases more responsive to voter interests.

To see how zany our primary system is, imagine a 100-meter race in the Olympics, in which instead of each country competing against all the others, there were just two competitors — one labeled "West", the other "East", let's say — and there was a preliminary race to determine which two runners would compete. In such a situation, many people would not be interested in the final race because their country would already have been eliminated. And if the runner for "West" was from the northern hemisphere while "East" was a southerner, that might be the most relevant geopolitical confrontation yet the labeling would fail to capture it. But this is a silly way to run a 100-meter race. There's no good reason to do it this way. And given that we have voting methods that escape from the spoiler effect, the same is true of elections.

Another analogy might be to the steering mechanism of a car. The idea of representative democracy is for the people to steer, by their choice of representatives, the policies of their government. So the people are the driver, and government policy is the direction the wheels are pointed in. What if, instead of being connected to the tie rods and other usual pieces of a steering system, the steering wheel was connected to two smaller steering wheels, which were connected to the tie rods, etc.? It's really not a well-designed system: It's not how any competent engineer would propose to solve the problem of steering. But it is a bit like how our party system works.

We should be less concerned with primaries and more concerned with how to hold a general election in which multiple parties can compete fairly. Let parties decide for themselves how they choose their nominee. If they value democratic decision-making they will want to consult their own members on the question. Maybe they'll even invite non-members to participate — I doubt they'd want to, but it should be up to them. If they want the decision to be made only by party leaders, that should be okay too, as long as there are ways for new parties to come along and compete on a level playing field. If party members are unhappy with intraparty processes of decision-making, they would be free to join another party, or start a new one.

The need for party self-control is one reason why "top-two" primaries, such as the one used in California, are not such a great idea: Since all voters vote in the same contest, the concept of party membership vanishes in significance. This way of structuring elections is bad for minor parties, as well, who rarely make it to the second round, between just two candidates. There's no good reason for reducing the number so drastically, when we have better voting methods. Sometimes, the top two candidates come from the same party, depriving voters of party choice in the second round.[216]

Freedom of association, infiltration, and absorbency
Giving parties this freedom, as private associations of people, to choose who will represent their views will help prevent embarrassing situations such as in 2018 state and federal legislative elections, when five candidates running under the Republican banner were white supremacists or Holocaust deniers — or both.[217] The Republican Party

---

[216] See Winger 2018.
[217] Coaston 2018.

doesn't really want to be associated with such ideologies, as its leaders well know. Let fringe elements have their own party, if they can organize it. If the "fringe" is sizable enough, it may get some representation, and the fringe ideology can be criticized openly using more meaningful terms of debate. If it's not big enough it will fail to meet the threshold to gain seats.

Kesha Rogers is an example on the Democratic side. Based in Houston, she is a follower of Lyndon LaRouche, whose movement during the Obama years liked to display a picture of the president with a Hitler-style mustache at public events. Running for the House in 2010 and 2012, she won the Democratic nomination for the Texas's 22nd congressional district both times before being defeated by the Republican. She called President Obama's healthcare reforms "fascist" and called for his impeachment. In 2014, she came second (out of five candidates) in the Democratic primary race for senator.[218]

A party that cannot kick someone out when they need to is not fully in control of its own positioning in the marketplace of ideas. This seems loosely analogous to a company that cannot easily fire an employee. In some countries there are labor laws that make it very difficult — and these countries usually have weak economies. Although it may seem counter-intuitive, when restrictions on firing are loosened, companies feel freer to *hire* — and they become nimbler as a result, more responsive to the demands of the marketplace, more competitive. It also helps workers because more companies decide to hire. By analogy, if we had parties able to dissociate themselves from views they dislike, it would make their associations more meaningful — help them refine their ideological appeal and thus compete more effectively against other parties.

One of the problems with the system is that the two dominant parties tend to soak up energy that would otherwise be directed to creating and developing new parties. We can think of this tendency as "absorbency". Suppose you're a potential candidate who doesn't fit in too well with the "establishment" wing of one of the major parties, but who does appeal to a sizable "activist" wing. Since you know that third

---

[218] Mock 2010.

parties almost never win elections, you decide to try for the major party's nomination instead of joining with or founding a minor party. This is the most rational way for political outsiders to pursue their ambitions. And so new and small parties are starved of the best political talent.

I think, by the way, that a certain amount of this absorbency, on the part of big parties, can be a good thing. To keep in touch with changing times, parties naturally have an interest in updating their ideas. If that means picking up, or co-opting, a good idea put forward by a small outside group, so be it — that's one of the ways innovation happens. But when a party is so absorbent that it really can't be identified with any lasting ideological commitments, maybe that's when it goes too far.

To many people, "establishment" is a dirty word, an insult thrown by party activists against party bigwigs. But an establishment should be a good thing — it means a solid foundation or mooring. We should want our parties to have strong establishments, as long as it's clear what ideological principles they represent, and as long as those principles still appeal to party members. The problem with major-party establishments today is that they tend to be ideologically incoherent — more concerned with holding power than with being true to their beliefs. A well-founded, coherent party establishment would have a certain amount of power to resist outsiders who are out of alignment with its ideological orientation. And a healthy multiparty system would give them this power.

Bernie Sanders, who came close to winning the Democratic Party's nomination in 2016, is a classic example of an outsider able to infiltrate one of the major parties due to their weakness as organizations (and their ideological vagueness, or slipperiness).

> Sanders has defined himself as a socialist throughout his political career and always run as an independent, and even as he sought the Democratic Party's presidential nomination he refused to clearly label himself as a member of the party. That he could nevertheless run so strongly, in spite of nearly united support of the Democratic leadership, says a great deal about the party's vulnerability. One might see Democrats' ability to

fend off and then ultimately coopt Sanders as a sign of good organizational health, but doing so was extraordinarily costly in terms of ongoing partisan cohesion.[219]

Another great example is Donald Trump, who won the Republican Party nomination as an outsider. He became a vehicle for many voters disenchanted with both major parties, and as a result the country went through a gigantic political "earthquake" which turned a lot of things on their head. From the point of view of party establishmentarians, such tumult must be very unsettling. How much better would it be if disenchantment in the electorate were channelled naturally into ideologically coherent parties, where they could be openly seen and understood, and where they would rise or fall on their own distinct merits?

In other established democracies, parties do a more effective job getting rid of members who don't represent their values. For example, in October 2018 in Australia, it emerged that neo-fascists had tried to infiltrate the Young Nationals, the youth branch of the country's National Party. The party didn't have much trouble expelling the infiltrators.[220] It could be the same here in the U.S. if we respected the autonomy of parties as private political associations.

Gerrymandering

One area in which teamsmanship clearly goes too far is the way electoral districts are drawn. As I mentioned in chapter 1, we took a wrong turn in the 1960s when we collectively decided to require single-member districts for all congressional elections. It may have been well-intentioned — historically, multi-member districts had been used (without proportionality) to dilute minority voices. But the best answer would have been (and still is) to use *proportionally* elected MMDs, instead of winner-take-all, single-member districts. This wrong turn has profound consequences for the quality of representation. It opens the door to gerrymandering, and given the extreme teamsmanship of the two-party system, results in our

---

[219] Wallach 2017.
[220] Haydar and Sas 2018.

politicians being able to choose their voters, rather than the other way around. Not quite literally, but clearly too much inclined in that direction.

Our courts have taken an active role in trying to make sure that ethnic minorities get a fair shake within the framework of single-member districts — promoting, for example, the creation of majority-minority districts through packing (sometimes called "gerrymandering for good"). These districts are designed to ensure seats for politically cohesive minorities, such as African-Americans. But when you pack members of a certain group into one district, you also take away their strength in neighboring districts. It's far from clear that this really helps those minorities overall — in fact, some studies show the opposite.[221] And this sort of "good" gerrymandering is more feasible for minorities that are geographically concentrated. When a group is geographically dispersed, it is much more difficult, if not impossible, to draw a district for them. So, could the structure of single-member districts be acting as an impediment to racial integration? It seems very possible to me. The basic idea of integration seems to demand geographic dispersal, but if dispersal means a loss of voting power, as it does in a framework of single-member districts, then we have set two goods against each other.[222] Ditching winner-take-all and electing officials proportionally would sidestep this quandary.

Also, while the Supreme Court has shown a willingness to override racial gerrymanders, it has been very reluctant to impose a remedy for *partisan* gerrymanders — ones designed to favor one party or the other, based not on race but on partisan voting patterns. In its 2019 decision in *Rucho v. Common Cause*, the Court seemed finally to close the door on hopes that it would rule them unconstitutional — it declared the issue "non-justiciable", meaning a political question beyond the purview of federal courts to adjudicate. "Federal judges," in the words of Chief Justice John Roberts, "have no license to reallocate political power between the two major political parties, with

---

[221] Matthews 2013.
[222] See Amy 2002, pp. 140-141.

no plausible grant of authority in the Constitution, and no legal standards to limit and direct their decisions." So it's up to the states, and/or Congress, to deal with the problem.

Reformers are looking to independent redistricting commissions, composed of citizens of both parties, along with independents, to take over the process of districting. But while these help to prevent legislatures from being too lopsided in one direction or the other, they don't necessarily deal with another problem with gerrymandering — its potential to protect *incumbents*, of both parties, by creating "safe" districts for them.[223] Imagine, for example, a citizen redistricting commission composed of five Democrats, five Republicans, and five independents. If this group were to consider a proposed set of districts that helped keep seats safe for incumbents of both parties, they might very well approve it, because it insulates their co-partisans from competition. So the problems with gerrymandering go beyond just producing disproportionate results; They also include a general diminishment of competition, and thus of accountability.

Proportionally elected MMDs avoid all these problems, and do it by virtue of their basic structure. When an electoral system allows for both majorities and minorities to be represented within each district, the stakes of the districting game are radically lowered. It's no longer a matter, for a given party, of all or nothing — i.e. zero or one of their reps being seated. Instead, it becomes a matter of the difference between one and two seats, or between two and three, or three and four. There is less reward for manipulating district boundaries.

To see why, consider figure 4.2, below.[224] Here we suppose an electorate of 60 voters, each belonging either to the Red or the Blue party. There are 24 Red voters (40 percent) and 36 Blue (60 percent). There are six seats to fill. On the left side, we assume six single-member districts, while on the right we assume just two districts, each using a proportional method to elect three seats. We see two alternative sets of district lines in each scenario, which serve the interests of Red and Blue in different ways.

---

[223] See Amy 2002, p. 60.
[224] Adapted from Eckam 2019.

In map *A*, we've drawn what is perhaps the geographically simplest set of lines, creating single-member districts which each contain ten voters, six Blue and four Red. Note that the result is extremely unfair to Red, because Blue will be able to elect their choice in all six of the districts. Blue would get 100 percent of the seats based on 60 percent of the voters.

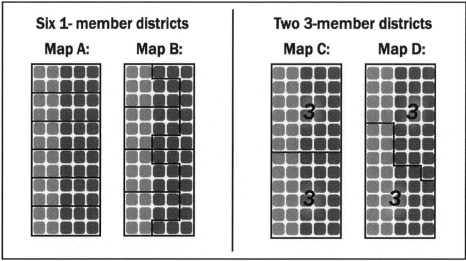

Figure 4.2. Drawing district lines under single-member and multi-member districting (Full-color version: daneckam.com/book/btp/figures.)

In map *B*, still assuming single-member districts, it looks like Red has managed to influence the line-drawing tremendously. By "cracking" and "packing" the Blue voters, they've created four districts where they are in the majority, versus only two for Blue. So Red would get 67 percent of the seats based on only 40 percent of the voters.

But if we divide the electorate into two districts of 30 voters each (as shown on the right), with each district electing three representatives, the "fidelity" of converting votes into seats increases dramatically. In map *C*, the simplest division, each district would elect one Red and two Blue representatives, thus Blue would get 67 percent of the seats — reasonably close to its 60 percent share of votes.[225]

---

[225] I'm assuming the D'Hondt method here — see chapter 1.

Map *D* represents an attempt by Red, presumably, to maximize its share of seats. By creating one district in which it has a slight majority, Red is able to win two of the seats in that district without losing its only seat in the other. The result is an even split of three seats for each party. Again that's not too far from the 60-40 split among voters.

If Red tried for more, by moving even more of its voters into its majority district, it wouldn't help because Blue would gain in the other district whatever it could gain in its own. And Blue can't do better than the 67 percent of seats it's getting in map *C*, which is already more than its share of voters. So with these multi-member districts, there is much less scope for manipulation.

In fact, it's partly because we're supposing such a small number (three) of representatives per district that there is still this much opportunity for gerrymandering. As the district magnitude rises, the fidelity of representation increases, meaning that the potential for manipulating seat share, relative to vote share, decreases to the point of insignificance: "When there are about five or more members in a district, PR can be regarded as completely immune from gerrymandering."[226]

By adopting proportionally elected MMDs, we would eliminate gerrymandering in a structural way, a way that would be more durable for the long term because it wouldn't depend on the intentions of either elected officials or citizen commissioners. And we'd do it in a way that inherently supports the representation of minority interests — not just ethnic minorities (divisions which, though politically salient now, are not guaranteed to be so in the future), but minorities of all types.

New formations

What parties would be likely to exist when we switch to a multiparty system? It's hard to say precisely, but there do seem to be, among humans, a few consistent worldviews, or styles of approaching politics, or, perhaps, "sensemaking frameworks". They change over time, as some "ism"s fade away while others become more popular.

---

[226] Lijphart and Grofman 1984, p. 7.

So, naturally, it would depend on the important ideas and cleavages of the time.

Imagine a spatial model of politics with several dimensions instead of just one (as with the left-right spectrum) or two (as with the Nolan chart created by libertarian activist David Nolan). Let's say there are three dimensions, for the sake of visualization, and that one axis is for social issues, one for economic issues, and one for foreign policy. Now we have defined a three-dimensional space in which every voter could, in principle, be positioned with (x, y, z) coordinates. What sort of distribution should we expect in this space?

It would surely be "lumpy", not uniform — that is, you'd find that if you mapped the whole population in the ideological space, there would be clusters, areas where a large group of people appeared. That's partly because of people's worldviews, partly because of personality types (perhaps) and social influences, and partly because some areas of the space are self-contradictory. The biggest (i.e. most populous) clusters could be considered the most obvious bases of potential political parties.

In 2016, *The Economist* came up with an imaginary party landscape for the U.S. if it had a parliamentary system. Based on polling data about presidential candidate preferences (from April 2016), they came up with these likely parties:

- Social Democratic Party (left) — led by Bernie Sanders — 26% of the vote: "protectionist, big government, socially liberal".
- Liberal Party (center-left) — led by Hillary Clinton — 28%: "pro-trade, pro-immigration, socially liberal".
- Conservative Party (center-right) — led by John Kasich — 9%: "pro-trade, socially conservative".
- Christian Coalition (right) — led by Ted Cruz — 11%: "pro-trade, socially conservative, religious".
- People's Party (populist) — led by Donald Trump — 26%: "nativist, protectionist, socially liberal".[227]

---

[227] "The world v the Donald" (sidebar) 2016.

I think this set of parties does a reasonably good job of depicting the strong, coherent clusters of political ideology in America (in 2016). It is certainly a far more accurate "portrait of the people" than our current party system allows at the party level.

Many people would fit much more comfortably into one of these alternatives than the big tents our two major parties represent, where they are supposed to make common cause with people they profoundly disagree with. Many conservatives, for example, have no sympathy for Trump-style populism. In some ways the Republicans are going through an identity crisis, one that probably wouldn't have happened under multiparty conditions. As former Speaker of the House John Boehner said:

> There is no Republican Party. There's a Trump party. The Republican Party is kind of taking a nap somewhere.[228]

On the other side, many centrist Democrats, who are essentially liberals, are concerned to see their party being led towards socialism by some of the more "progressive" members of their party. Conversely, many left-wing Democrats are weary of disagreeing with more centrist co-partisans. In a new configuration there would be less need for such accommodations.

The sociology of the seesaw: negative campaigning and wedge issues
American elections are plagued by mudslinging, and many of us feel that's just the way the game of politics is played. But it isn't necessarily so — and if we compared our system to other countries', we'd find that in some, negative campaigning is less prevalent than it is here. Could this have something to do with party systems? Political scientists Travis N. Ridout and Annemarie S. Walter decided to investigate the effect of a country's party system on negative campaigning by looking at the case of New Zealand. Recall from chapter 2 that New Zealand reformed its electoral system in the mid-1990s, causing a change from a classic two-party system to a multiparty one. Ridout and Walter compiled measurements of negativity in political campaigns both before and after this change,

---

[228] Icsman 2018.

and found evidence supporting their hypothesis that "[i]n a multiparty system the level of negative campaigning will be lower than in a two-party system."

In a multiparty system: "If Party A attacks Party B, support for Party B may decline, but instead of those voters turning to Party A, they may decide to support Party C or Party D."[229] By contrast, in a two-party system, if Party A attacks Party B, and Party B's support declines, Party A benefits because there are no other alternatives. So our two-party system incentivizes negative campaigning.

This structural incentive may also help explain why some issues are repeatedly exploited by the two major parties and why we can't seem to move on from past cleavages. "Since the 1960s, the key to winning elections has been to reopen the same divisive issues over and over again.... old resentments and angers are stirred up in an effort to get voters to cast yet one more ballot of angry protest."[230] The continuing centrality of *Roe v. Wade*, a 1973 court decision, may be a prime example. In Britain, according to *The Economist*, "controversy about abortion is now largely over. Rather than reflecting public opinion, though, America's lawmakers have for decades found it more useful to inflame it."[231]

This problem does not just affect how partisan leaders act in the electorate or in government. It also affects how the media frame political issues, and how voters think about the world — which seems increasingly to be in a very "tribal" way, prioritizing team play over a principled evaluation of issues. We can see an example in how Democrats and Republicans view the issue of climate change. Elected leaders of the Republican party and right-leaning media often push skepticism about climate change — either that it's really happening, or that humans are the main cause of it. It would be one thing if this reflected the true ideological interests of Republican voters. But according to research done by social psychologists Leaf Van Boven and David Sherman, "the problem is not so much that Republicans are skeptical about climate change, but that Republicans are skeptical

---

[229] Ridout and Walter 2015.
[230] Dionne 1991, p. 16.
[231] "A majority of Americans..." 2019.

of Democrats — and that Democrats are skeptical of Republicans. This tribalism leads to political fights over differences between the parties that either do not exist or are vastly exaggerated." As a former Republican congressman said of climate change policy, "All I knew was that Al Gore was for it, and therefore I was against it."[232]

We really need to get over such tribalism and start debating important issues based on the best knowledge available. A multi-party system would mean more opportunities for truthful, honest information to be understood, and more ways to question bad information. It might even reduce the frequency of perplexing statements like this tweet from Sen. John Thune (R-SD) on June 8, 2015:

> Six million people risk losing their health care subsidies, yet @POTUS continues to deny that Obamacare is bad for the American people.

At first glance it sounds like a typical Republican attack on Obamacare, except that the reason six million people faced the possibility of losing their healthcare subsidies was *because of Republican attacks on Obamacare*. The context was the Supreme Court case of *King v. Burwell*, an effort led by Thune's own party to render the Affordable Care Act unworkable. As Francis Wilkinson stated in *Bloomberg View*, "Thune's tweet is devoid of logic: His argument is that Obama denies that Obamacare is bad even though terrible consequences will ensue for millions of beneficiaries if Republicans destroy Obamacare."[233] Most of the coverage of this tweet was on the left side of the spectrum — meaning it went largely unremarked on the other side.

Dysfunction itself can be used to discredit the other party — something that Jacob S. Hacker and Paul Pierson[234] call "Newt Gingrich's fundamental contribution to American politics." They write:

> [T]he GOP may benefit if intensifying gridlock contributes to voter alienation and negative views of Washington. Unless dysfunction is clearly attributable to a particular set of

---

[232] Van Boven and Sherman 2018.
[233] Wilkinson 2015; see also Millhiser 2015, Dreyfuss 2015, Sargent 2015.
[234] In Persily 2015.

politicians affiliated with the GOP, it generally hurts the party associated with an active use for government (that is, Democrats).[235]

Seesaw politics help explain the rise of Donald Trump to the presidency and his continuing support among some segments of the population. Even when they don't agree with him, they support him as a giant "middle finger" to a culture of political correctness perceived, by many, as elitist. As Yascha Mounk commented in conversation with Sam Harris:

> It's sometimes puzzling, I think, to understand why things that he says that most Americans really do dislike [...] when he calls Mexicans rapists and so on, so forth, that is not something that the majority of Americans want to have any kind of truck with. But what happens is that all of the people who the majority of Americans hate [i.e. elitists] condemn Trump — and they have good reason to condemn Trump, when he says those things. But they look at that and they say, "Do I like what Trump said? No. But if all of *those guys* hate him, there must be something right with him." It's a very weird dynamic. I don't actually know how to get out of it.[236]

It's that old fallacy, that "the enemy of my enemy is my friend" — hatred and resentment outweigh questions of approval and agreement. I have a suggestion for how to get out of it: Get over the seesaw — move beyond the two-party system. That way, people would have more options to vote *for*, rather than simply voting *against* what they dislike.

Separate knowledges: the example of the wage gap
The need to maintain (and perhaps deepen) partisan cleavages also helps to explain the information "bubbles" that many voters live in — self-contained systems of knowledge resistant to information that doesn't align with the defined narrative. The issue of the wage gap between men and women gives us an example of how this works.

---

[235] Hacker & Pierson 2015, p. 63.
[236] Harris 2019 at 34:49.

In the 2012 campaign, President Obama and other Democrats made much of the fact that women earning full-time wages made 77 percent of what full-time wage-earning men made. According to a 30-second campaign ad, "President Obama knows that women being paid 77 cents on the dollar for doing the same work as men isn't just unfair, it hurts families." PolitiFact rated this claim "mostly false". Why? The problem is with saying it's "for doing the same work".[237] The statistics come from government agencies such as the Census Bureau and the Bureau of Labor Statistics, and they compare women in all types of jobs against men in all types of jobs. They make no attempt to define or determine what qualifies as "the same work".

The difference between men's and women's pay is portrayed as a direct result of discrimination — and no doubt sexism and discrimination are part of the story. But it's a lot more complicated than that. Men and women choose different careers. Men are disproportionately represented in software engineering, for example, while the field of nursing tends to be dominated by women. More men become lawyers than women. Doctors are more commonly male than female, while receptionists are the opposite. The reasons for these differences are complex and varied. They are influenced by cultural and socioeconomic biases, but individual preferences also have a lot to do with it.[238]

There are other differences. There seems to be some evidence that women, on average, are less assertive in negotiating for pay increases. Men work longer hours, on average, than women. (Note that "full-time" describes a range of hours per week.) And, of course, there's maternity, and the fact that women don't have a legal right to maternity leave in the U.S., as they do in some countries. In my view, this is a problem that should be corrected; it's another area in which we lag behind in securing the well-being of our citizens. But given that we currently don't have this guaranteed public good, my point is simply that it helps us to understand why the wage gap is so big. Having a gap in one's career can make a difference in compensation.

---

[237] Jacobson 2012.
[238] See Jussim 2017, Hakim 2011, Farrell & Glynn 2013.

Studies have found that when these and other relevant variations are accounted for, the *unexplained* wage gap falls to around five to seven percent.[239]

Now, *should* these differences matter as much as they do? Maybe our economic system shouldn't incentivize being so hard-nosed in pay negotiations, for example. On the other hand, maybe we shouldn't put too many constraints on the ability of employers and employees to reach a mutually beneficial arrangement. That's another worthy debate to have — something to be decided through the democratic (electoral and legislative) process. We could also ask whether software engineering should be so much more lucrative than nursing or teaching. That's a pretty big question, tied up deeply with the issue of capitalism itself — but we could have the debate.

The problem does not seem to be a lack of government action. The Equal Pay Act made gender-based pay discrimination illegal in 1963 — to be strengthened later, in 2009, by the Lilly Ledbetter Fair Pay Act. That seems like fairly strong regulatory action. And who, exactly, is arguing that a woman *should* be paid less for doing the same work as a man? I'm not aware of anyone reasonable who takes that position. *Of course* same work should be same-paid. Rather, the disagreement is about how to interpret the data, and what they imply about social structures extending beyond the labor market. (Should household work be financially compensated, for example?)

The point is, to pretend the issue is as simple as saying that women get paid 23 percent less than men *for the same work* is a major distortion. The issue isn't presented with the nuance it deserves — clearly our current system doesn't reward such illumination. A more consensus- and fact-based media culture, influenced by the structure of a more varied party system, could help to make it clearer to the public.

The reason has a lot to do with the seesaw structure of our party system. For many voters, especially progressives, the Republican party has low credibility on women's issues. That gives Democrats a strategic opening to reinforce their narrative that Republicans don't

---

[239] Hoff Sommers 2012; see also Bolotnikova 2016, "Are women paid less..." 2017.

care about such issues — driving and exploiting a wedge between women (and their allies) and Republicans. If a Republican questions the Democratic picture of unequal pay for equal work, the Democrats can question his credibility. Voters simply see two sides disagreeing on fundamental questions of fact and how they should be interpreted, and aren't encouraged to delve into the nuances. In a black-and-white world, shades of gray are misrepresented. As a system, the seesaw doesn't promote truth-seeking.

If there were other credible voices — a third major party, say — they could help explain what's really going on. They could make it clearer what's happening when one party plays politics rather than enlightening the public.

If you take a moment, you can probably think of other wedge issues — issues that one party uses as a bludgeon against the other, that persist partly because both would rather keep them politicized than try to solve them. Abortion has already been mentioned. Immigration is another such issue.

Thought leadership
Who are the main political thought leaders in today's America? In the distant past, we found many of them in Congress: influential statesmen like Henry Clay, Daniel Webster, and John C. Calhoun, the so-called Great Triumvirate of the 19th century. Before that, of course, were the first generation of leaders, including John Adams, Thomas Jefferson, Alexander Hamilton, and James Madison, who were even more famed for their political theories. In those days, theorists were also practitioners of democracy.

Nowadays, it seems that most politicians are too busy looking for donations, and too busy with team-oriented, partisan posturing, to engage in deep and nuanced thinking about political issues. Thought leadership seems largely to come from the media, where nationally known commentators set the pace of thinking about government policy. From columnists like David Brooks and E.J. Dionne to television hosts like Rachel Maddow, Sean Hannity and Anderson Cooper, media pundits fill in the gaps in how politics is understood, leading the public towards various ways of framing the issues — for both better and worse.

In other countries, it seems to me that people in government seem more able, and more inclined, to speak meaningfully about issues — whereas in America we often get platitudes instead of meaningful discourse. In other countries, prominent leaders such as prime ministers are expected to participate in "question time" on the floor of parliament, responding directly to questions from the opposition. I can imagine a world in which the Speaker of the House might have to be so responsive to other elected representatives, and it would be a healthy development for our democracy — but it's hard to imagine it happening under two-party duopoly.

To watch congressional hearings, for example, as many people did in September 2018 during the Brett Kavanaugh confirmation process, and again in February 2019 during Michael Cohen's testimony about President Trump, is to witness a show of partisanship elevated above material questions — not all of the time, but a lot of it. With a very restrictive five-minute rule in place, it's hard for representatives who want to get to the bottom of a question to really dig in. With every representative given equal time, many of them just use it to signal their own virtues to their base, instead of eliciting relevant information from the testifier.

I suspect that in a multiparty system, things would be organized in a more rational and productive way. There wouldn't likely be so much weight given to the idea of equal time for all sides when there are more than two sides. Perhaps instead of allowing equal time to a side that has little to no interest in the witness's testimony, more time could be given to those who want to use it. Maybe instead of settling on a vacuous "equal time" doctrine, there would be a tendency to follow processes that adhere to principles of competence and the gaining of knowledge — which is supposed to be the point of congressional hearings.

Our politics don't encourage smart, competent, ambitious people to seek elective office. Philosophers generally don't become politicians, anywhere. But in other democratic countries, where they have multiparty systems, the game of politics revolves more around issues and less around pandering, posturing, and seeking money from donors. Because a healthier party system promotes a stronger connection between the people and the government, and thus greater accountability, the work of being a politician gets more respect than in the U.S.

Women in leadership

The system isn't very friendly to women in politics, either — and this is an issue with important ramifications for democratic representation, considering that they are more than half the population. As of 2019, women occupy 23.6 percent of seats in the House, and 25 percent in the Senate. That's 78th in the world, ranked by percentage of seats in the lower house.[240]

Women have different interests than men, and differences of policy preference, on some issues. For example, 64 percent of women want stricter gun control, compared to 55 percent of men, according to the Pew Research Center.[241] Women are more likely to say that poverty is caused by circumstances beyond people's control — a belief held by 52 percent — than men, of whom only 39 percent agreed.[242] Of course, women have different views than men on issues such as reproductive rights and maternity. And there are many other differences. If we want truly representative democracy, it would help to have more women in elected office. Maybe it doesn't necessarily have to be fifty-fifty, but we can do better than one out of four.

PR systems tend to elect more women, as numerous studies have shown. The evidence is strong enough that as long ago as 1992, political scientists Wilma Rule and Pippa Norris could identify "the single-member district electoral system" as "largely responsible for limiting women's opportunity to serve in the Congress."[243] One of the main reasons, it appears, is that in a setting of multi-member districts, where parties put forward not just one candidate, but slates of several for each election, they tend to nominate more women. And when

---

[240] IPU 2019.
[241] Gramlich & Schaeffer 2019.
[242] NBC News 2014.
[243] Rule & Norris 1992, p. 41.

more women are nominated, more are elected. For more info on how PR helps women, see chapter 5 of Douglas Amy's book *Real Choices/New Voices* (2002).

Party system modifications

More parties will better allow for the electoral competition necessary to ensure that the government can be held accountable by the people. Thinking of party competition in terms analogous to those of markets, we see that monopolies don't serve customers very well. Duopolies don't either — and that's what we've had for the past century-plus (roughly since the Progressive Era — see figure 2.6). What these arrangements lack, for one thing, is responsiveness — so the remedy is for the system to be more fertile ground for innovation. In other words, it should both allow and promote political *entrepreneurship*. A more entrepreneurial system would do a better job channeling the real desires of the polity into representation in the halls of government, because parties would be freer to position themselves in the marketplace of ideas as they saw fit and as political demands shifted.

Our primary system contributes in a big way to political polarization. In recent decades, Republicans have increasingly had to move to the right to win primaries, and Democrats in many cases have had to move to the left. Then once the primaries are over, the major-party nominees tack towards the center to be competitive in the general election. That's assuming a diverse general electorate where it's advantageous to be not too far from the center. But in many cases, districts are not so centrist. The electorate has sorted itself into "red" and "blue" districts. In such districts, primaries only exacerbate polarization. Primary voters are partisan activists — so winning a primary depends on pleasing extremist voters.

Some democratic theorists, including Arend Lijphart[244] and Richard Pildes, have suggested abolishing primaries:

> [P]rimary elections have turned out to be one of the causes that contribute to the extreme polarization of politics today and it's

---

[244] Persily 2015, p. 74.

one of the few things that contributes to polarization in politics that we might actually be able to do something about by making an institutional change.[245]

Adopting a multiparty system would naturally tend to de-emphasize primaries because when a proportional system of voting is used, there is less need to narrow the field of candidates before the general election.

Such a system would probably have much shorter campaign seasons, because of the increase in predictability mentioned above, and the reduced significance of primaries. The United States has some of the most extended campaign cycles in the world. In the extreme case of the presidential race, it's nearly a two-year process. People from other countries marvel at this. In many democracies, election season only lasts for a few weeks. We could have that too (or at least something closer to it), with a different party system. Wouldn't that be nice? Not only for voters — it might also make a career as a politician a bit more attractive for good, talented people who would otherwise be repelled by the hardships of the campaign trail.

When parties are more clearly based on ideological differences, voters won't need to work so hard every election to figure out which way to vote. Instead of having to endure endless negative attacks by one side against the other, and having to weigh one candidate's character traits against another's, and considering to what degree the parties are hedging their bets on their ideological positioning, the most important thing for voters will be to figure out what their own ideological positions are, and which party best matches them. The parties would then function better as *channels* of political desires. That's not to say issues of character won't matter at all, but the process will put ideology more in the foreground of political debate. And that's where it should be, if we believe that democratic governance should be responsive to the will of the people.

If it sounds like I'm being naïve about how people come to identify with one party or another, let me reassure you. I understand that party identification is very complicated — that social factors make at

---

[245] Pildes 2010.

least as much difference as ideological ones.[246] Many people are Democrats or Republicans because their parents were that way, that's just how they grew up, and either they've never questioned it or their sociocultural biases stop them from seriously considering alternatives. These factors will continue to exist in a multiparty system — but I think they will diminish in power as this new political landscape sinks in.

What leads me to believe this? Consider that one of the social inhibitors to changing one's party affiliation is the air of betrayal that comes with "turning coat", with going to "the other side". When there are only two viable parties, switching from one to the other is seen by some as a kind of treason — in social terms, if not necessarily ideological ones. Switching from the Democratic to the Republican Party is comparable, for some people, to switching from the South to the North in the Civil War. (Or vice versa.)

In a multiparty system, voters would be encouraged to think about their partisan affiliations in ideological terms, and there wouldn't be such high costs associated with changing one's party. Of course, the change in attitudes won't happen overnight, and social group dynamics will still exert a strong influence. But more focused, coherent parties will allow for the kind of issue- and ideology-based discourse that democracies are supposed to have.

Realignments of the party system would be more fluid, and thus less disruptive, with a multiparty system than with just two parties. How does a party go from one end of an ideological spectrum to the opposite end, as the Democrats did on the issue of rights for ethnic minorities? The answer is: painfully, haltingly, confusingly, and not at all transparently. How does the Republican Party go from being the party that stands for free trade to the one standing for protectionism? Same answer. It muddies the waters for voters, who need to know what they are voting for. But in a system with more variety, where parties can take meaningful, ideologically coherent positions, they can rise and fall according to their success in the electoral marketplace of ideas. That's a more adaptive system, where changes in electoral

---

[246] Achen and Bartels 2016.

demands are reflected more transparently, and probably more gradually, in partisan positioning, than in the current system, where changing desires are submerged until eventually the tension boils over and causes turmoil and confusion.

Voter turnout

Something that doesn't seem to be considered often is the possible connection between a multiparty system and voter turnout. It's well-known that the United States has lower turnout than most other advanced democracies, as figure 4.3 shows. Could our two-party system be a contributing factor?

I think it is, for two main reasons. One, political parties are naturally good at rallying their voters to go to the polls. So, the more viable parties there are, the more likely voters will be to hear from one they sympathize with, urging them to vote. Perhaps they will also be more likely to heed the advice. When around a third of the population identify as independent, meaning they are "homeless" in terms of having a political party, we have a lot of people who would potentially be more engaged, given more choices. Political party "homelessness" contributes to disengagement.

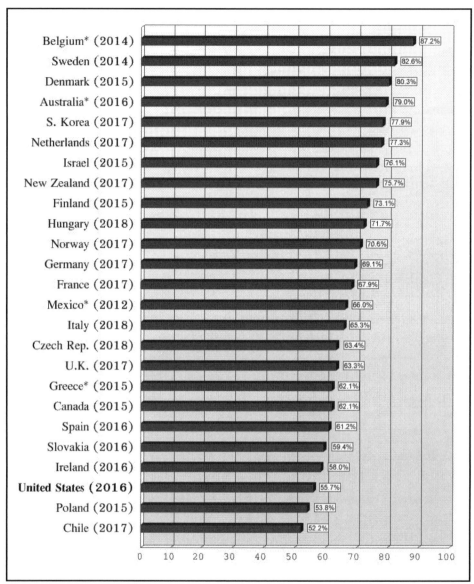

Figure 4.3. Votes cast in most recent national elections as % of voting-age population, selected countries

* Countries with compulsory voting

Source: Pew Research Center (DeSilver 2018).

In America, it's fairly common to hear about "get out the vote" (or GOTV) efforts, in which the rallying cry is something like, "It doesn't matter *how* you vote, just please vote!" It has always struck me that there's something odd about an exhortation like that. If you're an activist working to get out the vote, do you really not care how people are voting? For almost any citizen engaged in democracy, there are policy positions they care about — so there are better and worse ways to vote. Why would you want people to vote if they don't vote in a way you agree with?

Such efforts make ideological sense, however, if you have reason to think that more non-voters agree with your position than don't. Which brings us to voter suppression — the second reason our two-party system contributes to lower turnout than in other countries. As another symptom of the "seesaw", if high-likelihood voters favor one party more than low-likelihood voters, then it gives that party an incentive to keep turnout low, and the other an incentive to boost it. Voter turnout becomes a partisan battle. And this is a sad reflection on our aspirations as a democratic republic. Other democratic countries don't have such bitter fights over voter suppression. In a multiparty system with a healthy range of choices, when you have a party that wants voters to stay home, it tends to fare less well in the electoral marketplace.

In November 2018, Senator Cindy Hyde-Smith of Mississippi told a small crowd that she thought it was a "great idea" to "make it just a little more difficult" for some liberal college students in her state to vote.[247] That's a rare glimpse of the dynamic I'm talking about — not often spelled out so explicitly.

We are lagging behind other democratic countries in voting processes. Many of our voting machines are outdated and buggy. It's so bad, it's almost as if our leaders don't want us to have reliable elections. As one citizen posted on Twitter on election day of 2018:

> The US is full of clever people. If we wanted to make voting as easy as buying something on Amazon, we could. All of this hassle, all these long lines & broken machines & ID snafus, all

---

[247] Brice-Saddler 2018.

these lost votes — it's by design, by choice. It could be otherwise.[248]

Could this be a product of the two-party system — of the seesaw? Again I think the answer is "yes". If it serves a partisan interest that we cannot rely on election results, and the party it serves is one of only two major parties, then the system incentivizes weakness in voting procedures. But with more parties, I think we'd see more priority given to creating and maintaining a "level playing field" — including, of course, voting systems that we could have confidence in.

The U.S. is far outside the norm in many areas related to voter participation. In many democratic countries, elections happen on a weekend, rather than on a Tuesday as in our federal elections. In some, voting is mandatory; in many, voter registration is the government's responsibility, not individuals'.[249] There are plenty of things that could be done to improve voter participation in our country. Switching to a multiparty system would be a very effective one.[250]

Corruption

How does the problem of corruption fit into my high-level system diagram (figure 2.1)? And how would a change of party system affect it? Money in politics is a huge problem today, and has been for a while. Former president Jimmy Carter described the problem as giving "legal bribery the chance to prevail".[251] Convicted former super-lobbyist Jack Abramoff, who understands how things work better than almost anybody, summed it up by saying, "I think the great tragedy in American politics is what is legal, not what is illegal."[252]

As I said in chapter 2, I see the system depicted in the diagram as the "ship" of society and the state, traversing waters which include the power of money. The corruption of the system by money is like a

---

[248] D. Roberts 2018.

[249] Lijphart, in Persily 2015, p. 78.

[250] See Amy 2002, chapter 7.

[251] Weaver 2016.

[252] NPR News 2011.

"breach of the hull" — money having an improper influence on how democracy functions. If the ship were well-built, that is, if government effectively represented the people, in a responsive and responsible way, and had a well-functioning system of checks and balances, it would be more resistant to corruption. The problem is that the ship has lost structural integrity. The institutions designed to respond to the needs of the people are too weak, opening the door to the interests of big money getting their way at the people's expense.

A big part of the problem is that voters don't have defection options. As mentioned in chapter 3, many voters feel locked into a certain party because the other party stands for beliefs repugnant to them. So if a party becomes infected by corruption, what can these voters do about it? Not much, except decide to sit the next election out. In a competitive, multiparty system, by contrast, a corrupt party would fear voter defection and thus have good reason to avoid corruption.

With voters unable to hold representatives accountable for their failure to accurately represent, special interests are able to step into the gap. It's no wonder that the system functions much like an oligarchy, responding more to the interests of the wealthy (and big corporations) than of other Americans.[253] The two parties' duopoly over politics creates more space for special interests to get their way: Vote capture eases the process of regulatory capture.

The ideologically vague, big-tent nature of the major parties means it's not clear what voters are really asking for when they vote for one party or the other. Electoral mandates are subject to slippery interpretation, opening the door to special interests — which may be a bigger, more common problem than people realize. Consider, for example, the proliferation of unnecessary licensing requirements in many states:

> America is saturated with ridiculous licensing rules that do little to protect public health or safety. They exist mostly as a way to drive-up prices and restrict employment. Cosmetology licensing laws are some of the worst offenders of common sense, and Arizona's cosmetology licensing laws truly boggle

---

[253] See Gilens & Page 2014, 2016.

the mind. Doing something as simple as shampooing, drying, and styling hair requires a full-fledged cosmetology license, which includes years of training in hair and skin care, makeup application, and other un-related skills.[254]

This victory for special interests — established cosmetologists, in this case, and cosmetology schools — is a defeat for the general public of the state of Arizona, who would benefit from a more open, competitive landscape for suppliers of hair-care services. Yet the issue rarely even comes up in political debate. In a multiparty system, with more points of view represented, there would be more resistance to such special-interest hijackings of government power. The public interest would have more opportunities to be recognized in opposition to special interests.

One of the ways big money corrupts the system is through the "revolving door" between industry and the bureaucracy that is supposed to regulate it. Former representatives can make a lot of money after their political career ends, by working on behalf of industry interests — especially if they have shown themselves to be friendly during their time in office. Former senators Tom Daschle and Judd Gregg and former congressman Billy Tauzin are among those who earned millions of dollars following congressional careers, consulting or lobbying for industries with heavy involvement in national legislation.[255] Call it the "legislative-industrial complex".

(This connects to why term limits are not, in my view, a real answer to the problem of accountability. If implemented by themselves, they would do nothing about the revolving door and other vectors of excessive corporate influence. In fact, that door would probably just spin faster.)

In the broadest sense, corruption includes anything the government does to serve special interests at the expense of the public or national interest. Arms sales to other countries are a very consequential example. If not managed carefully, with strict attention to what's in

---

[254] Boehm 2017.
[255] J. Roberts 2014.

the best interests of the nation, they can cause harm by making wars more likely.

Naturally, companies want to maximize their profits. But their short-term gain isn't always in the public interest. In January 2015, on a conference call with investors, Lockheed Martin CEO Marillyn Hewson was asked whether the impending nuclear deal with Iran would reduce foreign income opportunities for the company. Hewson downplayed the potential impact, saying there was plenty of "instability" and "volatility" in the Middle East and Asia-Pacific regions, and that she saw both as "growth areas" for the company.[256]

Now, maybe Lockheed Martin only has the best interests of the United States at heart, and they only want to do their patriotic duty to keep the country peaceful and secure, in the face of threats that just happen to be good for their bottom line. But the conflict of interest is easy to see, even if only as a potential (and by Murphy's Law, what is potential will sooner or later become actual — and probably already has).

The point is that our major-party politicians benefit from the jobs and revenue generated by such foreign arms sales, and from the campaign support that big corporations like Lockheed Martin can give them. (According to OpenSecrets.org, in 2018 the company spent $4.7 million on political contributions, and $13.2 million on lobbying.) Meanwhile, these politicians don't pay much of a price for international conflicts encouraged by a flood of weapons sold by U.S. companies. In fact, the arrangement seems to promote a "vicious circle" where profit-seeking drives arms sales, which drive increased military tensions, which drive more arms sales. I think a multiparty system would have a better chance of bringing this arrangement to light, and managing it more critically, with more of an eye on whether it really serves the national interest.

Big-money donations are like a drug in our political system. Given just two major parties, it's hard for either of them to resist, when it knows that the other won't. It would be like unilateral disarmament. It would reduce a party's ability to compete effectively. Yet there is an

---

[256] Fang 2015.

appetite — or a *market* — for parties that resist the corrupting influence of money. In a multiparty system, parties would have more freedom to try out different formulas for success. Suppose that one of them declared it would not accept any large or corporate donations. Voters might respond very positively to that — and the more so the worse the perception of corruption became. The party might have a harder time at first getting the word out, because it wouldn't have millions of dollars to spend on advertising. But in the longer term, if it was responsible and well-run, people would hear about it. And even if it wasn't hugely successful, its example of integrity would help constrain the behavior of other parties.

The American electorate craves this kind of integrity. It's a huge unfed hunger, for parties that act on behalf of the people, not big corporations and other big-money special interests. They see both parties taking high-dollar donations, and they disapprove. But what option do they have?

Conclusion

The two-party system affects the overall system of American government in many ways. In this chapter I've tried to point out some, starting with the very important failure of checks and balances designed to stop any of the three branches from getting out of line. The failure to hold the executive branch accountable for misleading the country into the Iraq War is a classic example of the two-party system enabling the abuse of power.

Too often, parties put their own narrow interests — the interests of teamsmanship — ahead of their constitutional duties. As explained in the previous chapter, when Congress is controlled by a one-party Majority, accountability, responsiveness, and responsibility suffer. The legislative branch can become a rubber-stamping body for the executive branch, when the two branches are controlled by the same party, or conversely, can be overly obstructionist when they are controlled by opposite parties. A multiparty system would be "just right" — with enough variety to do the things voters want and to resist the things they don't.

A few decades ago, when we were still involved in the Cold War, our two major parties exercised restraint and accommodation in government. But since the early 1990s, things have gotten uglier. And the ugliness in party behavior extends beyond government into society as a whole, aided by partisan media, so that now we have become such a polarized nation we can barely talk to one another. Our dualistic party system rewards negativity, inviting voters to hate the other side more than choosing positive values to believe in.

In a multiparty system things wouldn't be so black and white. It wouldn't be so obvious to so many people that their side is "good" and the other side "evil". With more points of view visibly represented in society and the media, it would be harder to live in a one-party bubble where claims about reality can easily go unexamined. More parties means multi-sided fact-checking — and more prominence for objective reporting (because its value would be more evident).

In short, a seesaw isn't a very good model for politics — so the case for switching to multiparty is very strong. Now, having explained why we should switch, it's time to wrestle with the big problem — how to make it happen.

5. Overcoming Obstacles
or How, Part 2: The Politics

Now, finally, we come to the really hard question: How do we convince our elected officials, who are predominantly Democrats and Republicans, to pass the reforms we need to shift to a system in which those two parties will have to share power with others? We've defined where we want to go, and the steps needed to get there (chapter 1); we've seen how important the party system is, as a subsystem of representative democracy (chapter 2); and we've appreciated how high the costs of duopoly are and what we'd gain by having a multiparty system (chapters 3 and 4). But how do we actually get it done? How do we make it happen? A question of strategy, and tactics.

The point of this chapter is to answer that question. I'll begin with some thoughts about general strategy, then turn to some likely objections and how to answer them.

Getting lawmakers to act
The first thing to note is that most Americans don't fully appreciate how unusual our duopolistic system is in the democratic world, how simply we could adopt a multiparty system (without having to amend the Constitution), and how much difference this change would make to our dysfunctional politics. At least so it seems to me, and it's those gaps in understanding that I hope this book can help bridge.

So, education about the issue of our party system is very important. Spread the word. The more people there are who recognize the problem, the more there will be who are willing to demand that their elected representatives do something about it.

Although it's by no means easy, when awareness of a problem reaches a high enough level, and when voters demand changes from their elected leaders, a tipping point can be reached. Think of the Progressive Era, in which pressure was applied for changes to overcome the corruption of the patronage system and "back-room deals" among party leaders in choosing nominees for office. The reforms of this era were targeted in part against the excessive power of party "bosses", such as William M. "Boss" Tweed, the head of New York's Tammany Hall machine in the 1860s and beyond. Tweed used his position in New York City politics to enrich himself and his friends through corrupt means, fraudulently inflating costs of public projects so he could siphon some of the proceeds to himself and the Tammany machine. Progressive Era reforms, including party primaries, were intended to eliminate the "bossism" of the system.

The spoils system of the nineteenth century was another big problem. Winners of elective office used their power to give jobs to their supporters. As candidates, they used the promise of such "spoils" to win votes. This was a major feature of American politics until the Pendleton Act of 1883 shifted the civil service to be based on merit rather than political considerations.

Bossism and the spoils system were major problems that were deeply embedded in the structure of our political system in the 1800s. They gave advantages to incumbent politicians, who, I'm sure, felt reluctant to adopt reforms bringing them to an end. Yet eventually the reforms were adopted.

I think reforming our party system is similar. Yes, our elected leaders are almost exclusively Democrats and Republicans who won office under the conditions of two-party duopoly. This represents an obstacle to reform. (It's reminiscent of the quote by Upton Sinclair: "It is difficult to get a man to understand something, when his salary depends upon his not understanding it.") But given enough willpower, it can happen.

So far, so typical. Every reform movement depends on raising awareness among the population and asking elected representatives to act. But is there anything that can be done to make the issue more salient, or more urgent?

Yes, there definitely is. Consider: What do political candidates want from you? Your vote! So one way to apply pressure is to *refuse to give it to them.*

Voting against the two-party system

As a voter, you have options. There are often minor-party candidates running for office, who don't get much publicity. Seek out information about them. Learn what they stand for and what they would do if elected. Ask them what they would do to help end the two-party system. Share what you learn with friends and family. Maybe give them a campaign contribution. And maybe even *vote for them.*

Now, if you announce your intention to vote third-party, you'll get some pushback, not only from major-party candidates but also from their supporters. You'll be told not to "throw away" your vote, not to help a "spoiler" candidate. And such advice carries a certain amount of weight in many elections. But here's how to resist such pressure: Explain that not all voting systems are as vulnerable to the spoiler effect as plurality voting (or the two-round runoff system), that we could avoid such quandaries if we had a better system. Explain the alternatives to your friends.

Here's how the conversation might go:

"Hey Dan, are you planning to vote for X or Y in the upcoming election?"

"Actually, I'm thinking about voting for Z."

"What?! Z has no chance of winning! Why would you want to throw your vote away like that?"

"Well, I actually like what Z has been saying. I think he would be the best person for the job. And I don't appreciate being pressured into voting one way when my conscience tells me to vote another."

"But that's so idealistic. Sure, it would be nice if we could vote our conscience, but we have to be pragmatic, and understand how the system works. If you vote for Z you could very easily spoil it for the better of the two major-party candidates."

"True, I would prefer to see X elected than Y. But the difference between them is a little less than people think. And we could change our system so I don't have to worry about compromising like that. Do you know about ranked-choice voting?"

"No, what's that?"

"It's a voting system in which your ballot lists the candidates in order of preference. So, for instance, I could put Z as my #1 choice, and X as my #2. Tallying goes by rounds with the last-place candidate eliminated in each round. If Z gets eliminated, my vote transfers to X. This way, we voters can vote our true conscience without worrying about the spoiler effect."

"That sounds cool! But it's not the system we have. I would support adopting that system, but meanwhile, we have to recognize the limitations of the system we're actually using."

"Yeah, but how will we ever adopt that system unless there's pressure from voters? Our leaders are relying on our weak voting system to keep you from voting your conscience. It's kinda like being held hostage. Aren't you upset about that?"

"Well, ... I guess I haven't thought about it enough. I'm just hearing about this now for the first time."

"Time to start thinking about it. Our democracy is not working well enough. We need this kind of reform."

A conversation like this could be a good way to educate people about alternatives to our current system. It's a great time to introduce them to ranked-choice voting (and other voting methods), and proportional representation. If a candidate asks for your vote, tell them you'd be happy to rank them highly on your ballot — if not first, then second — if only the voting system supported ranked choices.

Voting for a minor party can be seen as a vote against the two-party system. Depending on state laws, if a party gets a certain amount — say 5 percent or so — of the vote in one year, it helps it qualify much more easily for the ballot in the next election. So giving them your vote is not just a protest against the two-party system, but also a substantive way to increase the number of parties on the ballot. That's not a change to the system, but it is a way to make the issue of party system more salient.

Of course, it's not always so easy to resist voting for one of the two major parties. The spoiler effect is real, and when a race is close and you have a strong preference for one candidate over the other, you may understandably decide to vote major-party. When a race is heavily lopsided, it means you can vote your conscience without much fear of spoiling the election. But this depends on being able to rely on polls. So as a strategy, it should be handled with care. If it catches on with a lot of people, it may make polls less reliable. Be careful not to trigger the spoiler effect if it could cause a lot of harm. When it's safe and when it's not is a matter of judgment.

There is one election in which many people's votes usually don't matter — the presidential election. Thanks to the misguided winner-take-all rule, many Americans' votes make a negligible difference to the outcome. For example, if you live in a deeply "red" (Republican) state and you prefer the Democratic candidate, you can predict (at least in normal circumstances) that your vote will be ignored — the Republican will get a majority of votes, and your state's electors will all vote for him. It will make no difference whether the winner gets 51 percent of the votes or 90 percent. Since your vote won't make a difference, you might as well vote third-party, if you are so inclined. Figure 5.1, below, illustrates how this works, in a state with 38 electors.

If your deep-red state is actually competitive in a certain election year, it probably means that the Republican candidate is weak, and that the Democrat is heading for a landslide victory. So in that case, your vote probably still won't matter to the outcome, because your state's electoral votes won't be needed for victory. (For the likelihood, based on state, that a voter can make a difference, see FiveThirtyEight's [2016] "tipping-point chance" and "voter power index" measures.)

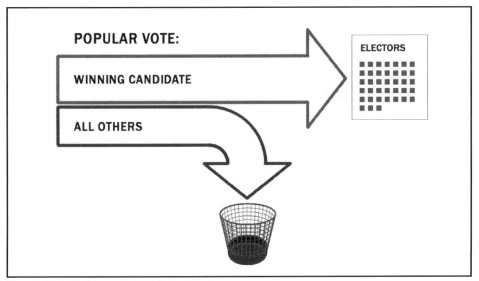

Figure 5.1. Winner-take-all example

What if you lean in the same direction as your state — for example, you lean Republican in a red state? In that case, your vote probably won't be needed. As long as the Republican wins more votes than the Democrat, all of the state's electors will vote for the Republican. So you can feel free to vote third-party if you want to.

In other words, every voter who doesn't live in one of the swing states (which usually number a dozen or so) can feel free to vote their conscience. This is a strategy that noted activist Noam Chomsky has recommended for voters on the left — in swing states, vote for the Democrat; otherwise, vote third-party.[257] It also applies to voters on the right, with respect to Republicans. And thanks to the inordinate amount of attention given to presidential elections, this can be a great way to stimulate discussion about the drawbacks of our party system and how it can be reformed. Left-leaning voters, imagine being at a left-wing social gathering, raising hackles with your third-party voting intentions, and then swooping in with the Chomsky reference upon meeting resistance.

---

[257] Halle and Chomsky 2016.

Of course, if we start electing presidents by popular vote, this logic would no longer apply, since every vote would count equally. Without the effects of state-by-state winner-take-all, every vote would matter.

Resonating with the electorate

Convincing others of the desirability of a multiparty system should be an easy "sell" in a free-enterprise-loving country like America. We understand the value of competition, how it helps ensure quality in the economic marketplace, by forcing producers to be responsive to consumer demands. Similarly, in the marketplace of ideas, it helps keep our leaders responsive to the demands of the people. This is an easy concept for most Americans to grasp.

Even elected officials should be able to see it. And this could be used to hold their feet to the fire — especially for Republicans, who pride themselves on their adherence to market principles and their recognition of the value of free enterprise. How can they claim to venerate the market and the benefits of competition, yet deny those benefits to voters in the political arena? This seems like a question to confront them with, if they resist reform.

The drive to adopt a multiparty system resonates deeply with American values. It's not just by analogy to the marketplace, either. As I've tried to make clear in this book, it also seems better aligned with the plan of our Founders, involving checks and balances within the structure of government. They did not foresee political parties as we know them today. But if they had, I think they would have preferred a multiparty system over the duopolistic one we have now.

Consider, once again, James Madison's words: "When a majority is included in a faction, the form of popular Government [...] enables it to sacrifice to its ruling passion or interest both the public good and the rights of other citizens."[258] A two-party system amounts to a prescription for "majority included in faction", and thus frequent hijackings and hostage-takings, as explained in chapter 3.

Another way to frame the need for reform is to think of it in technological terms: We haven't been keeping our systems of

---

[258] *Federalist* no. 10.

democracy up to date. Our "political infrastructure" is crumbling, and needs investment. As an Irish reporter told the U.S. radio program Radiolab in November 2018, American democracy is "kind of like a laptop from 1985."[259] This kind of message should resonate with people who believe, or would like to believe, that the U.S. can set an example for the rest of the world to follow. It's hard to be that "shining city on a hill" that so many politicians have spoken of when we refuse to upgrade our democracy from time to time. Do we or do we not want to form a more perfect union?

The Democracy Index (introduced in chapter 2) is a great tool for showing others how we stack up to the rest of the world. Understanding how much room for improvement we have, including specific ways of measuring it, may help to inspire a useful feeling of rivalry between our country and other democracies. An old adage of business management (attributed to Peter Drucker) is that "you can't manage what you can't measure". I think that's probably an overstatement, but there is truth in the idea that quantifying things often helps point us in the right direction for improvement. The Democracy Index serves well as a benchmark for how we're doing.

The problem can be seen as a conflict of interest between party in the electorate and party in government. In the electorate, the goal is for voters to be accurately represented, and for their ideas about policy preferences to be channelled into political parties that stand for coherent ideological programs. The market analogy applies very well here: We want competition to ensure accountability, and entrepreneurship to make sure that new ideas have a way into the political system. But there's a strong temptation for party in government to suppress competition and give itself an unfair advantage in the electorate.

To point this out, and frame it as a conflict of interest, is to put those who are suppressing competition on the defensive. Isn't it hypocritical for the parties in government to say they want the benefits of a competitive system, except when it comes to their own seats? The charge of hypocrisy resonates with people — so write about it in your

---

[259] Radiolab 2018, at 12:10 to 12:45.

blog, on your social-media feeds, maybe in a letter to the editor of your favorite newspaper.

The media seems to be more receptive to such ideas than in the past, because many intellectuals have noticed that things have become extremely dysfunctional. Prominent columnist David Brooks, for example, endorsed Rep. Don Beyer's Fair Representation Act, which would require multi-member districts and ranked-choice voting in all states.[260] In a *New York Times* editorial in May 2018, Brooks wrote:

> The good news is that we don't have to live with this system. There's nothing in the Constitution that says there have to be only two parties. There's nothing in the Constitution about parties at all. There's not even anything in the Constitution mandating that each congressional district have only one member and be represented by one party. We could have a much fairer and better system with the passage of a law.[261]

The Economist has also commented favorably on Rep. Beyer's proposal, saying that ranked-choice voting "might go some way to dampening down the dynamics that have made American politics so partisan", and noting how incompatible the two-party system is with the Founders' intentions:

> The first two presidents, George Washington and John Adams, both warned that a two-party system, in particular, would be anathema to the model of government they were trying to build.
>
> Aware that they could not solve the problem of parties altogether, the founders thought the constitution would at least ensure that they were reasonably numerous and ineffectual. But some of the features they built into it inadvertently encouraged politicians to concentrate themselves into just two blocs. And some of the mechanisms they put in place to guard against other concentrations of power went on to exacerbate the problems that such a two-party system can cause. [...]

---

[260] FairVote 2017.
[261] Brooks 2018.

Systems with elements of proportional representation, such as that sought by reformers of the electoral college or House districts, not only provide bulwarks against charges of illegitimacy. They also have a tendency towards consensus of the sort the founders wanted.[262]

Vox's Matthew Yglesias has also recognized the great things PR could do for this country:

> It would be better to have a country where everyone is voting for a party they are genuinely enthusiastic about, and then because no such party commands majority support, the leaders need to do some bargaining.[263]

When mainstream outlets like these recognize the problem, along with good ways of fixing it, that's cause for hope.

Change at what level?

Most of the legal changes needed to enable a multiparty system could happen at the state level — switching to multi-member districts, adopting the single transferable vote (STV) or another proportional voting method, revisiting laws concerning ballot access and party membership. The Constitution generally leaves the conduct of elections up to the states.

But Congress did pass a law in 1967 which requires that states use single-member districts. It was titled "An Act for the relief of Doctor Ricardo Vallejo Samala and to provide for congressional redistricting". (The first paragraph of this bill concerned an individual's immigration status and is not relevant to elections.) Before we could have proportional representation, we'd need to repeal this federal law (as the Fair Representation Act would).

Is that the only way to overcome this obstacle? Maybe not. It's interesting to note that in 1842, Congress also passed a law requiring the states to use single-member districts — but this requirement was not always observed. In fact, in the first election held after the law was enacted, four states continued to use at-large elections rather than

---

[262] "America's electoral system..." 2018.
[263] Yglesias 2018.

single-member districts. And their elected representatives were seated in the House despite this.[264] Had they not been seated, those states would not have been represented in the House, presumably, and that would obviously have run counter to the basic idea of representative democracy. It would probably have triggered a constitutional crisis — an opportunity for states to argue against the imposition of federal rules.

What lessons can we draw from that history today? Could a state simply ignore the 1967 mandate and use multi-member districts for its federal elections? And then, if their representatives were not seated, sue the federal government over the lack of representation? Or, should states challenge the law *before* holding elections? I don't know the answer — I'm not a lawyer. But it's worth keeping all options in mind.

Activism should focus on both the state and federal levels, when it comes to federal elections. We've seen the state of Maine adopt instant-runoff voting for federal elections. That's a step in the right direction, even if it isn't enough to give us the multiparty system we need. If every state did the same thing, we'd be well on our way. Aside from the U.S. Congress, there are plenty of other representative assemblies at all levels throughout the country — state, county, city, school board, and so on. The obstacles to making those proportionally elected will depend on the laws of each jurisdiction.

Some people think party reform needs to start on a local level before it gets to the higher levels of representation — especially the presidency. The columnist and activist Dan Savage colorfully expressed this sentiment in a May 2016 podcast, responding to a caller who supported Green Party presidential candidate Jill Stein:

> I have a problem with the Greens, I have a problem with the Libertarians. I have a problem with these fake, attention seeking, grandstanding Green/Libertarian party candidates who pop up every four years, like mushrooms in shit, saying that they're building a third party. And those of us who don't have a home in the Republican Party, don't have a home in the

---

[264] Mast 1995.

Democratic Party, can't get behind every Democratic position or Republican position, should gravitate toward these third parties. And help build a third party movement by every four fucking years voting for one of these assholes like Jill fucking Stein, who I'm sure is a lovely person, she's only an asshole in this aspect.

If you're interested in building a third party, a viable third party, you don't start with president. You don't start by running someone for fucking president.

Where are the Green Party candidates for city councils? For county councils? For state legislatures? For state assessor? For state insurance commissioner? For governor? For fucking dogcatcher? I would be so willing to vote for Green Party candidates who are starting at the bottom, grassroots, bottom up, building a third party, a viable third party.[265]

The trouble is, we can't afford to wait for party reform to happen on a local level, then gradually bubble up all the way to the top. We need accountability now, at all levels of government. And of course, the national level is the one with the greatest impact on the world, the only one where decisions to go to war or not are made. Minor-party candidacies, even when they can't win, are a way of challenging the existing structure and stimulating discussion about what kind of party system we should have — and the simple steps we could take to have it.

Many people who vote for third parties would otherwise not have voted at all. Providing more options on the ballot at least gives them a way to express themselves. It's not as clear as some would claim that a minor-party candidate deserves to be blamed for the outcome of an election. As Ralph Nader explained to journalist Amy Goodman in 2004, about the election of 2000:

[R]emember, Buchanan presumably cost four states for Bush. Such as New Mexico and Wisconsin. So, I mean, why are we even talking like this? Everyone has a right to run. There should be a level playing field. Should I complain that Gore

---

[265] Herz 2016.

spoiled it for me? Should I complain that they played dirty tricks in the last two weeks in some states with horrid telephone calls. The important thing here, Amy, is to get away from this two-party duopoly mindset which has to be broken if we are going to have more voices, more choices, more dissent.[266]

You might argue that Nader should have only run in "safe" states — i.e. non-swing states. But again, that deprives the voters of those states the full range of options. As Nader explains:

I run a 50-state campaign. I do not betray my volunteers. I'm not going to ever tell them that they worked their heads off to get me on the ballot, to mobilize forums, to spread the issues, and then say, sorry, there's a pullout here. No way that's going to happen. [...] [I]t's not my obligation to help other candidates get more votes. That's what has to be made very, very clear to the two parties who think this country belongs to them, and other parties who just stay away, not run, or pull out at the last moment.[267]

Voters can decide for themselves how to weigh the benefits of voting their conscience, and supporting reform of the system, versus the risks of triggering the spoiler effect. But let's not tell those who want to run for office that they shouldn't be giving people another option. If the idea is that two and only two candidates should ever run for a given office, how can that ever be implemented without violating people's freedoms? How feasible would it be to set such a limit? Americans value freedom of choice. There's no realistic way to stop people from running for office if that's what they are determined to do.

There's nothing wrong, of course, with working on the local level — in fact, spreading the word naturally happens most often at a small scale, between friends, family, and neighbors. And it need not be confined to politics — city councils, school boards, and the like. Are you a member of a club or church group? You may occasionally want

---

[266] Democracy Now 2004.
[267] Democracy Now 2004.

to make a collective decision, like what book to read next or what speaker to invite. Why not use the Condorcet IRV voting method? Or maybe you'll have occasion to select several winners out of a set of options. In that case, it would be a good opportunity to try STV, the single transferable vote. Or you could try approval voting or some other method. By using an alternative voting method, you'll help get people more familiar with it, which will help them see how it would apply in politics.

More strategery

No doubt there are many ways to bring about reform in society. Identifying and exploiting certain points of pressure is a good way to do it. For example, a nonpartisan organization known as Unite America is pushing what they call their "Fulcrum Strategy": Elect a handful of independent candidates to closely divided legislative bodies, who then will have enormous leverage to push for reform in a chamber in which no party has a majority of its own. They select certain races to endorse an independent candidate in, and support that candidate. Sounds like a good plan to me. They were the subject of an intriguing episode of Freakonomics Radio on Oct. 31, 2018.[268]

The metaphor of the fulcrum seems related to my idea of the seesaw. Think of a fulcrum as the pivot point of a seesaw — when it's moved left or right from the center, the result is that one side tends to go upward (and the other side downward) much more easily. You could think of a deep red or deep blue district as having a fulcrum that is off-center. What follows from such an image? One thing that occurs to me is that in such an uncompetitive district, people on the losing side may want to consider voting in the other side's primary — that is, if primaries are open. If they are closed, they may wish to consider joining the winning party and trying to change it from inside.

Another metaphor people have used to explain competitive systems involves a pair of ice cream vendors on a beach, each trying to attract as many customers as possible. They are selling their very similar

---

[268] "America's Hidden Duopoly" — Dubner 2018.

products out of a push-cart or something equally mobile, so the question they want to answer is, Where's the best place to set up shop? According to what's become known as *Hotelling's law*[269], assuming that potential customers are evenly distributed along the beach, and that they'll choose the vendor that minimizes how far they have to walk, the optimal strategy for the vendors is to set up right next to each other in the middle of the beach. That way, each will get 50 percent of the market, and there's no way for either to improve on that, given that their competitor stays in business. This economic tendency explains why traditionally, both parties were clustered near the political "center", and the fact that the electorate is *not* evenly distributed, but rather along a somewhat "normal" or "bell-curve" distribution, makes the center-clustering tendency even more significant for parties seeking to maximize their "market share".

Hotelling himself noted the applicability of this tendency to our party system, and how it helps explain the tendency of our politicians to hedge:

> The competition for votes between the Republican and Democratic parties does not lead to a clear drawing of issues, an adoption of two strongly contrasted positions between which the voter may choose. Instead, each party strives to make its platform as much like the other's as possible. Any radical departure would lose many votes [...] Each candidate "pussyfoots," replies ambiguously to questions, refuses to take a definite stand in any controversy for fear of losing votes. Real differences, if they ever exist, fade gradually with time though the issues may be as important as ever. The Democratic party, once opposed to protective tariffs, moves gradually to a position almost, but not quite, identical with that of the Republicans. It need have no fear of fanatical free-traders, since they will still prefer it to the Republican party, and its advocacy of a continued high tariff will bring it the money and votes of some intermediate groups.[270]

---

[269] Hotelling 1929.
[270] Hotelling 1929, pp. 54-55.

This needs some updating — there's a wrinkle that should be added for our more polarized times (aside from particular differences, concerning tariffs, in the partisan divide of 1929). What is not accounted for is a *two-tiered* competition where the first round is the primaries, now conducted among small minorities of party activists operating, often, in heavily gerrymandered districts. The two-tiered structure deprives the general public of the opportunity to choose freely.

In pushing for reform, it helps to keep small steps in mind, laying the groundwork for the future. Maybe people are not yet ready to see that it's time to abandon our two-party duopoly. But a tipping point may come, and it's very hard to predict what it will be, or when it will occur. Be ready to take advantage of opportunities whenever they arise.

Something for (almost) everyone

It's worth questioning the assumption that Democratic and Republican officials will always be opposed to changing the party system. Is the system we have what they would design if we were starting from scratch? Are they solidly in support of every one of its features? I doubt it, and I don't think they necessarily should be. Maybe part of the problem is a failure of imagination. So let's do some imagining right here — of how a multiparty system might actually be in their best interests.

If you're a candidate for public office, you face a very difficult road. Let's assume that you'll eventually be elected as either a Democrat or a Republican. Depending on the office, you may need to be on the campaign trail for more than a year, first winning your party's nomination, then the general election. (If you're running for president, it's more like two years — an extraordinary length of time compared to most countries.) You have to spend a lot of your time raising money, to get your message out to voters. You need to take positions on numerous issues and learn how to explain yourself without committing gaffes. You need to come up with a strategy to distinguish yourself from other candidates. In fact, you need to do that twice — once against your primary opponents, and again when you face a candidate from the other party — likely requiring a different strategy. This is all very taxing, requiring extraordinary tenacity and determination, not to mention lots and lots of time. No wonder so many of our representatives come from the upper ranges of income and wealth.

In a multiparty system things would be a lot different. Parties would be more coherent in their policy orientations, so candidates wouldn't have to spend so much time and effort developing their positions. Their membership of a particular party would indicate, to a large extent, their policy preferences. A party's choice of candidate for a given office would be more predictable, based more on their competence and character. The job of being a politician would be professionalized — meaning people who are interested in a political career would have a clearer path into the field. And this would make such a career more attractive to talented, intelligent, competent people.

More coherent parties, such as typically exist in multiparty parliamentary systems, mean voters have an easier time understanding what the parties represent, and thus can more durably identify with a party instead of having to evaluate candidates individually. The more party-centric the system, the more predictable the pattern of voter preferences:

> In presidential elections, there often is greater uncertainty over the identity of the candidates. Even to the extent the candidates are known, information about their attributes and policies often is not known until later still in the election cycle. By contrast, in parliamentary systems, parties tend to dominate. This is important because dispositions toward parties, while not fixed, are more durable than those toward candidates. Even to the extent party leaders are important to voters in parliamentary systems, their identities typically are known well in advance, earlier than presidential candidates.[271]

We should be wary of conflating the parliamentary-versus-presidential variable with the degree of party-centricity. But in this

---

[271] Jennings and Wlezien 2016; quoted in Friedman 2016.

case it's not a real problem: The first is a good proxy for the second, since most parliamentary systems are also highly party-centric. And in fact, it's party-centrism, as opposed to candidate-centrism, that Jennings and Wlezien find to be most significantly correlated with how highly structured voter preferences are[272] — and thus, I would say, with the typical length of campaign seasons.

In America, calling someone a "professional politician" is often intended as an insult. But that's a really weird thing — isn't it? Professionalism is good; amateurism is bad (this book being an exception, of course). I think in most democratic countries, a political career is not something that's regarded with disdain. Nor should it be. We want people who are capable and knowledgeable about how to perform public duties, including how to represent constituents. Those who use this term as an insult probably have in mind something related to corruption. To be a professional politician in America today is to be good at fundraising, at pandering to special interests. But that's because the party system is dysfunctional. If we fixed that, maybe "professional" wouldn't be viewed in such a negative way.

The main point is that having a more normal, predictable, professionalized party system would make being a politician more accessible to more people. (Maybe especially for women, and especially if they are mothers.[273]) So, this could be a good reason for politicians to support the switch to a multiparty system.

Besides politicians, there's a whole "political-industrial complex" of people who advise campaigns, lobbyists, and others, and writers and broadcasters who influence public opinion in relation to political leaders and parties. These people are often ideologues, or at least come at the issues they deal with from an ideological angle. So it seems to me that it would simplify their work, and make it more rewarding for them, to have a party system where parties are more clearly aligned with ideology.

Imagine for a moment that you're Karl Rove. You're a very savvy political operator who understands how politics and elections work,

---

[272] Jennings and Wlezien 2016, pp. 230-231.
[273] See chapter 5 of Amy 2002.

and what it takes to win them. But is winning the *only* thing you care about? No — if that were true, it wouldn't matter which side you were on. You're a conservative, and you work for candidates that pursue a conservative agenda. That's why you're a Republican. So, when your party nominates someone who is *not* a conservative, that's disorienting, right? Disappointing? Confusing? Maybe even *stressful*?

Here's what Rove wrote in April 2016, when it was fairly clear that Donald Trump would become the Republican Party nominee:

> Self-congratulations may make Mr. Trump feel good, but they do not bring together the party—his main task if he's to be the nominee.
>
> Mr. Trump fails to recognize that he has little of the moral capital of a typical nominee. A longtime Republican who has toiled in the vineyards can expect loyalty for having given it. Mr. Trump, on the other hand, has donated generously to Democrats and backed Sen. John Kerry in 2004. He has also savaged past Republican presidents, from Ronald Reagan to George W. Bush.
>
> Instead of seeking to build something new, Mr. Trump seems to aspire to blow up the GOP. He is graceless and divisive, denigrating the party he seeks to lead and his competitors. After Tuesday, Donald Trump may have a clearer path to the nomination. But his path to party unity remains dark, tangled and treacherous.[274]

Of course, as president, Trump has done a lot of favors for conservatives. But that still doesn't make him a poster-boy for conservatism. He is not the standard-bearer a guy like Karl Rove would hope for. In a multiparty system, the Republican party could be more consistently a conservative party. It would be harder for an outsider like Trump to come along and hijack it for his own populist interests.

Despite the above, however, Karl Rove prefers the two-party system over a multiparty one. Why that should be involves one of the major arguments against a multiparty system, to be addressed later in this

---

[274] Rove 2016.

chapter. But his thoughts on democratic theory are something different from his motivations as a principled ideologue, and the above was meant to show how the latter conflict with the dynamics of the two-party system. So, we can imagine a major political operator who is not Karl Rove, who would find a convincing case in the idea that multiparty politics would let them be truer to their ideological ideals. Or maybe a Karl Rove of the future would do so.

Before getting into those major objections to a multiparty system, let's consider one more group of powerful people who are interested in how the game of politics is played: the wealthy and big corporations. Suppose you're the chairman of the board of a large multinational corporation. Why would you want to change to a multiparty system — or at least not object to such a change?

The answer, I think, has to do with stability, in two senses. First, predictability: As a business leader, you want to know what the rules are likely to be in the future, so you can plan accordingly. On this score, what seems more stable? A system that alternates between two parties, often giving one or the other exclusive (or nearly exclusive) power over government policy? Or, a multiparty system in which no single party can govern on its own, but must aim for consensus and compromise, and is governed mostly from the middle? The latter seems much more stable in the long term. It is not as prone to extreme changes in policy as our seesaw two-party system is. Now, it may not be as likely for your favorite party to hold the reins of power in their hands for relatively brief periods of time, but the policies that are chosen by government would tend to be more lasting. And predictability is what you care about most of all, in business. Coping with regulations is not so hard; it's the constant changes that make life difficult for you.

Consider some of the ways the two-party system interferes with stability. There are frequent episodes of brinkmanship concerning default on the national debt. In a multiparty system this issue would be taken off the table instead of maintained as a political football used by one side against the other. Or consider foreign policy. We worked for years to strike a deal with Iran to curtail their nuclear weapons program and bring them into the fold of the global economic community — opening up a big new market for export and investment. But then, only a few years later, we withdrew from the pact. That's not a very predictable or stable business environment. You might even say politics has been *disruptive* to stable economic relations.

Second, a multiparty system will be more responsive and more responsible to the people that elect their governments, as I argued in chapter 3. That means voters will be more engaged with the system and generally more satisfied with government. Thus, they'll be less likely to turn things on their head. In a system with only two parties, it's difficult for changing demands of voters to be represented at the party level. The system tendency is for pressure to build up behind the scenes, along with increasing levels of cynicism and dissatisfaction, until eventually the pressure becomes so great that it cannot be ignored, and it bursts through into politics with very disruptive effects. The process of party realignment is painful and protracted — as Sundquist explained in great detail in *Dynamics of the Party System*. Simply put, the system lacks fluidity — and variety. But his analysis would've been a lot different given a multiparty system, in which changing demands and cleavages can be represented by new parties at a small scale before they become major political forces.

A government that fails to respond to the demands of its people runs the risk of eventually collapsing, or of becoming a tyranny, losing the public's confidence. Revolution then starts to be a possibility. If you're a business leader, that's the last thing you want (unless, perhaps, your business is in weapons or security). A stable, peaceful democracy with a strong middle class means happy, spending customers for business.

Also, a two-party system that's more prone to corruption than a multiparty system — because it offers fewer ways to hold elected leaders accountable — does not serve the interests of small businesses. Big, deep-pocketed corporations are more able to play the game of lobbying and political contributions to get favorable treatment from Congress. A 2012 poll found that "66 percent of small business owners agreed the *Citizens United* ruling was bad for small business because it gives big business unlimited political spending power".[275] A thriving, well-managed economy should put the interests of entrepreneurs and small businesses ahead of those of large, multinational crony capitalists.

Classic objections to a multiparty system: moderation, stability, accountability

It's time now to deal with some of the most significant arguments levelled against adopting a multiparty system. Advocates for such a system will be sure to encounter these, so it's important to be able to respond. The most "classic", perhaps, because of its long history, is the idea that the two-party system promotes stability (in contradiction to what I just claimed above). The system has "stood the test of time" and proven itself through the success of America compared to other countries of the world.

One of the main ways it promotes stability, according to supporters, is that it "forces diverse people to unite and work together".[276] The parties "have an incentive to moderate regional enthusiasms, to compromise ideological principles, and to unite voting blocs with very different cultural backgrounds and attitudes and very different economic interests and goals."[277] They "engage in cultural bridging that is crucial in a land as diverse as America".[278] Thus, the system fosters a spirit of tolerance and compromise in the interests of building and maintaining broad coalitions. The moderating force of the two-party system is claimed to be an important source of American exceptionalism — "the special character of the United States as a uniquely free nation based on democratic ideals and personal liberty"[279] — and credited for our historical good fortunes.

How should we respond to such claims? First of all, we can't really judge our success as a nation by our history, because we don't know what the history would have been under other circumstances —

---

[275] Arensmeyer 2015, Small Business Majority 2012.

[276] Lowi & Romance 1998, p. 71.

[277] Barone 2001.

[278] Lowi & Romance 1998, pp. 54-55.

[279] Tyrrell 2008.

under a multiparty system, for example. A "what if" question like this can't be definitively answered. But it's quite possible that we'd have been even more successful with more parties to represent the people. For one thing, black voters in the South might have had their rights guaranteed sooner than they did, because pro-civil-rights voters there would've had meaningful choices. As it was, the region was firmly under the grip of the Democratic Party for many decades; it was effectively a one-party system there. Monopoly conditions helped ensure that the government was not responsive enough to the people it was meant to serve.

Secondly, this spirit of "moderation" and "compromise" actually serves mostly to muddy the waters of what a party actually stands for. As I argued in chapter 2, voters have different views on different issues, and it's unrealistic to think that such a variety of viewpoints can be clumped into just two parties, if they stand for anything definite. Moderation and compromise are good things (much of the time), don't get me wrong. But why should they happen so much at the *intra*-party level? Wouldn't it make more sense to have parties that stand clearly for certain values, and then let compromises and moderation happen *between them*? I would say yes — this reflects what Schattschneider meant when he said that democracy is between the parties, not within them. And it lives up to (or, at least, more closely adheres to) the ideal expressed by John Adams that a representative assembly should be "an exact portrait of the people". If we're going to do representative democracy, but we're not interested in accurate representation, then what are we really doing?

As for American exceptionalism, it's noteworthy some of the ways our democracy really is exceptional. American voters are exceptionally ill-informed about politics. Voter turnout is exceptionally low compared to other democratic countries. For a country that's been practicing democracy for so long, it's exceptional that we rank so low on the Democracy Index. And we have an exceptionally restricted set of choices when it comes to political parties. Is that just a coincidence? No, I think we are exceptional — but not in a good way.

Another admired feature of the two-party system is that "the two parties make accountability easier" by making it "easier to assign blame".[280] This relates to the theory of responsible party government, which I discussed in chapter 3. As we've seen, the two-party system incentivizes negativity, because when one party makes the other look bad, it benefits because voters only have two choices. The game shifts from a question of understanding what voters want to a contest of getting them to hate one side or the other. We could call this "playing the seesaw". It's not a very good basis for responsive and responsible representative government.

That the structural dynamics of the party system are partly to blame for its dysfunction seems clear enough. Yet I think the seesaw tends to redirect blame to one side or the other — obscuring the fact that there's something wrong with the underlying structure. Many voters have unrealistic expectations that their party will be able to remake the government in their own image — which very rarely happens. These expectations are conditioned, to some extent, by responsible party theory — something our government was never set up to follow, that the Founders would never have countenanced, given their distrust of parties. The theory says that we can assign blame to the majority party if they fail to fully implement their program. But that's not how things actually work. So in the end, cynicism grows, people blame the other side for obstructionism, and the seesaw is reinforced. The system invites a game of blame — but the blame produced is in large part a fallacy, or misdirected.

A similar fallacy seems to lurk behind another argument, that the two-party system allows for more decisiveness in our elections. Often this argument focuses on how the electoral college is usually won by a much larger margin than the popular vote. The impression of a decisive victory enabled by the college's winner-take-all rule is lauded as an important source of a president's subsequent "mandate" to implement his policy proposals. But such "decisiveness" is an illusion: As is well-known, the balance of electors in the college does not reflect the votes of the people. In fact, it doesn't even always go the same way

---

[280] Lowi & Romance 1998, p. 38.

as the popular vote. It's hard to hold "decisiveness" in high esteem when it applies to decisions that actually reverse the majority choice of the people.

Beyond the electoral college, I suppose the argument about decisiveness is based on the way the two broad parties coalesce diverse opinions into a simplified one-or-the-other contest, in which one side "wins" — and the winner takes all (of a legislative body, or sometimes of a branch of government, or more than one). It looks more "decisive" but when the parties are so weakly based on principle, and when our standards of accurate representation are so impoverished, the impression of decisiveness is artificially manufactured.

Decisiveness can also be seen as the concentration of power in the hands of one party so that it may implement its policies without too much obstruction from others, and so that the electorate may judge simply on the basis of whether the policies "worked" or not. This sort of decisiveness brings to mind the hijackings that I mentioned in chapter 4 — it's the decisiveness of *disproportionate* concentration of power. But what if decisiveness means injustice? What if it means too much inclination to go to war, unnecessarily? — because I think it does. At the end of the day, I'll take justice over decisiveness.

Fragmentation and ungovernability

One of the most commonly heard arguments against adopting a multiparty system is that it would produce a very fragmented political landscape of parties, who would not be inclined to cooperate with each other. Without the aggregating influence of the large and loosely defined parties of the two-party system, we should "expect an outpouring of [splinter] parties—green parties, senior citizen parties, anti-immigration parties, right-to-life parties, pro-choice parties, anti-gun-control parties, homosexual rights parties, prohibition parties and so on down the single-issue line" and encouragement of "ideological and/or personalist parties".[281] The problem with such parties is that they are too narrowly defined: They don't have the

---

[281] Schlesinger 2000.

staying power of more broadly based parties. To accurately represent the diversity of issues and opinions in the country at such a low level would require a lot of them. The multiplicity of groups would make governing more difficult.

This issue is what convinces Karl Rove that a two-party system is best. Asked about tribalism in American politics, he replied:

> There's even more tribalism outside of a two-party system, and it is of a more destructive nature because it is oft-times based upon one simple issue or one personality. And that's one of the great things about our two-party system. Both parties tend to move away from their extremes in order to win elections. [...] imagine a system in which everybody could organize around personalities, single issues, and highly developed and very narrow ideologies. We'd get something like Italy. It's had 41 prime ministers and over 60 governments since World War II. Now maybe it's good that Italy topples its governments with great regularity, but I think it fundamentally undermines the confidence of the people in the system of government and in the system of democracy and in the system of the economy, as well. [...]
>
> [The two-party system] promotes stability by providing a barrier against multi-candidate races and the kind of disasters that we see in democracies in Western Europe and elsewhere, where the electorate is fragmented by a multi-party system with a wide range of parties, some of them based around personalities, some of them based around regional interests, some of them based around ideological constructs, others of them based around a single issue, some of them based simply around the idea of blowing up the existing system.[282]

Rove helpfully wraps a lot of meaningful complaints into a concise package here. Let's break it down in detail and address them one by one.

First, he brings up the instability of governments in Italy. It's important to notice, however, that Italy, along with many other

---

[282] Dubner 2016.

multiparty democracies, has a *parliamentary* system — which means there is no separate executive branch, as there is in presidential systems. Nor are there (usually) fixed terms of office. Rather, the party (or parties) that win an election get to choose the prime minister and other cabinet officers, a process known as "forming a government" — and these leaders can be replaced by a vote of no-confidence either from within their party or from the whole parliament.

This brings up a difference in word usage between America and countries with parliamentary systems. In our country, it's clear from the outcome of the election who will be in charge of the executive branch; the transfer of power is automatic and non-partisan. In parliamentary systems, by contrast, the outcome of the election is only the starting point for the formation of a governing administration. If one party wins a majority of legislative seats, the process is usually straightforward, perhaps only requiring the official approval of the head of state (for example, a monarch). But if no party controls a majority of seats, then negotiations are usually required. In this case, there can be a period of uncertainty following an election, while the composition of the administration is worked out — in other words, while a "government is formed".

I think this talk of *forming a government* may lead some people to misunderstand how the workings of other systems would apply to our case — by conflating the issue of party system with the one of parliamentary versus presidential systems. "Government" in a parliamentary context should often be translated as "administration" in a presidential context. With our presidential system and fixed terms of office, we needn't fear being *without a government*. Or at least, if there is any reason to worry about it, it wouldn't be because of our party system.

In short, comparing parliamentary to presidential systems is not comparing apples to apples. It's important to keep the differences in mind.

Probably the biggest chunk of the concern about government stability centers on the difficulties of multiple groups working together, especially if each of them is narrowly focused on its own agenda. Rove makes the point that the wider the range of interests, the more difficult it will be for the parties to agree on a common course of action. But as I argued earlier in the book, following majoritarian principles would actually be more common with more parties, as shifting majorities could be assembled issue by issue. And this would avoid the all-too-common hijackings, hostage-takings and obstructionism associated with the two-party system, where one party assumes the mantle of a lasting (at least for two years at a time) Majority that makes decisions on its own, at least for one legislative chamber if not for whole branches of government. There's more to this than just my opinion. In a study of 295 elections in 24 countries, political scientist Josep M. Colomer[283] found that "there is a strong negative correlation between the number of parties in government and the degree of policy change. The fewer parties in government the more changes, and vice versa."

It has often been observed that our Founders set up a system with very decentralized power, and that the party system helps bridge the divide between the legislative and executive branches. Joseph Romance[284] writes that the two-party system is laudable for allowing unified government at least some of the time, by "decreas[ing] the tendency of too much gridlock". But even under "unified" party control of government, things may not be so unified beneath the surface: When party labels don't actually represent shared values and policy goals, single-party control of both branches doesn't quite mean what it appears to. Single-party control of the legislative and executive branches in 2018 didn't prevent the government from shutting down, for example. So the two-party system doesn't solve the problem of how to have unified government.

Furthermore, a multiparty system clearly has the potential to be more representative of the people than a two-party system. This "higher fidelity" of representation promotes stability in the sense that the people will be more likely to get what they need from government. At the very least, they will have a greater sense that their voice is being heard.

---

[283] Colomer 2012.
[284] Romance 1998, p. 47.

Still, though, we can acknowledge that a system with more moving parts could be more difficult to manage in some respects. I'd respond to this worry in two ways. First, let's remember again that the executive branch is separate and that the presidency won't be multiparty, because it's occupied by just one person. If Congress can't agree on a new direction for public policy, the president will be there to implement current policies and to administer the government's operations. Presidential initiatives can set the agenda for Congress and spur action where necessary. And while Congress should assert its independence from the executive branch, that doesn't mean it has to ignore presidential leadership when it's responsive and responsible to the public interest. If the president is the type of person who understands the need for consensus (as he will tend to be if elected according to a Condorcet method, as recommended in this book), then his leadership could be very helpful in focusing minds and getting things done. The Speaker of the House, too, would tend to be more of a consensus-builder, working not just with his own party but across parties to forge legislation.

Before I come to the second response, I want to say a word or two more about stability in the law.

A brief digression on the purpose of a legislative body

Is it the main task of Congress to pass laws? Or is it to play the role of watchdog? Is it important to differentiate between the law, on the one hand, and bureaucracy, or governance, on the other? And if so, would a multiparty system do a better job maintaining the distinction?

It makes sense to me that the legislative branch was meant for passing changes to the law — which is meant to be (ideally) a stable, permanent or near-permanent thing. Conceivably, the law could be "perfected", in the sense that it has reached a balance of interests that can't be improved upon, given the political desires of the nation (at a particular moment in history). In that case, there wouldn't necessarily be much for Congress to do, aside from passing a budget each year — and this could be very similar to the previous year's budget, with just minor adjustments to deal with changing circumstances. There is no problem with this, if the main job of congressional representatives is to represent the people, and safeguard their interests, not necessarily to pass new laws.

If some people would call this situation "gridlock", maybe it's the *good* kind of gridlock — the kind that prevents bad laws and regulations from being passed. And meanwhile, a multiparty system would tend to avoid the *bad* kind of gridlock, the kind that is unresponsive to the demands of voters.

The system revolves more around money than around the public interest — with corporate lobbyists seeking, and getting, beneficial regulations. A lot of the "bloat" in federal regulations has mostly to do with industry loopholes and corporate welfare. Having a more representative Congress, with more variety, might very well lead to much of this bloat being eliminated, because a simpler and more comprehensive scheme would serve the country better. It might take a while to get there, but eventually I think there needs to be some streamlining of the law.

We have so many laws in this country that we can't even count them. A 2011 article in *The Wall Street Journal* found that the number of federal crimes had risen dramatically since the 1980s, especially regulatory crimes, and that:

> Estimates of the number of regulations range from 10,000 to 300,000. None of the legal groups who have studied the code have a firm number.
>
> "There is no one in the United States over the age of 18 who cannot be indicted for some federal crime," said John Baker, a retired Louisiana State University law professor who has also tried counting the number of new federal crimes created in recent years. "That is not an exaggeration."[285]

According to some judges and legal scholars, many Americans break the federal law every day without even realizing it.[286] That's not a good state of affairs: The law should be stable and predictable, so that reasonable people (and organizations) can know clearly how to avoid breaking it.

---

[285] Fields and Emshwiller 2011.
[286] Lynch 2009, Reynolds 2015.

Sartori remarked on this problem of "governing by legislating" in his 1987 book:

> There are many drawbacks — we are now discovering — in our legislative conception of law. In the first place, the rule of legislators is resulting in a real mania for lawmaking, a fearful inflation of laws. Leaving aside how posterity will be able to cope with hundreds of thousands of laws that increase, at times, at the rate of thousands per legislature, the fact is that the inflation of laws in itself discredits the law. This is not to say that governments should govern less. It is to say that it is both unnecessary and, in the longer run, counterproductive to *govern by legislating*, i.e., under the form and by means of laws. This is to confuse governing with lawmaking, and thus is a misconception of both.[287]

But how could it be otherwise? To legislate, after all, is to pass laws — isn't it? Well, originally, as envisioned by the founders of what Sartori calls "liberal constitutionalism", that was not really the main point of a legislative body. "Our conception of law," he says, "has changed"[288] over the centuries:

> The framers of liberal constitutions did not conceive of the state as being a *machine à faire lois*, a lawmaking machine, but conceived of the role of legislators as a complementary role according to which parliament was supposed to integrate, not replace, judicial law finding.[289]

Traditionally, law was conceived not only as something with the form of law, but also in terms of content: "that rule which embodies and expresses the community's sense of justice".[290] But liberal constitutionalism had to solve the problem of how society may be ruled by laws, not men — entailing that the lawmakers are also subject to the law. Who should make the law, and who should interpret it? The solution was to identify *the law* with *legislating* — so that law becomes equivalent to whatever the government proclaims, following

---

[287] Sartori 1987, pp. 324-5.
[288] Sartori 1987, p. 322.
[289] Sartori 1987, p. 308.
[290] Sartori 1987, p. 322.

its due process. This works well in many respects, but there is also something that gets lost: "In the formal conception, law is available to any content and a law without righteousness is nonetheless law."[291]

In the 1930s, Congress passed the Glass-Steagall act, which ran to 37 pages, to regulate the banking industry. The key provisions were repealed in 1999. In 2010, after the financial meltdown, it passed the Dodd-Frank law, regulating the same industry. The statute ran to over 800 pages, and mandated the creation of regulations that add up to over 22,000 pages.[292] I doubt that we have gained much, if anything, from such complexity. A big part of the reason for it, I think, is that our government is far too cozy with corporate interests. But another part of it is that the concept of law itself has been cheapened.

There is, or can be, a big difference between laws and rules, as the Dodd-Frank example illustrates. Laws should apply generally and be understandable to the people subject to them. Rules, on the other hand, may only apply to companies operating within certain industries. The power to make rules can be delegated by Congress to executive-branch agencies, as is often done. To those who say that the complexity of the modern world requires governing by legislating, this may be the answer: to better distinguish between laws and rules.

Executive orders are another kind of rule that may be considered something less than law. The authority of the president to issue them derives in part from the Constitution, which says that the president's duty is to make sure "that the Laws be faithfully executed". As long as the president acts according to the law, as passed by Congress, he is acting "faithfully", and the rules set may cover a lot of ground. If he exceeds what is allowed by the law, then he acts unfaithfully, and the order can be overturned by the judiciary.

These ideas have great bearing on modern-day debates about "legislating from the bench". When questions of jurisprudence no longer directly address legitimacy but merely a formal legality:

> judges cease to perceive themselves as law-finders (in the process of administering justice) and become more and more

---

[291] Sartori 1987, p. 323.
[292] Lux and Greene 2016, Greeley 2013.

judge-legislators in the manner of *politician-legislators*; both
categories increasingly take the law in their hand as if there
was nothing more to it than having a winning hand.[293]

What does all this have to do with our party system? The answer is
that more parties means more fairness and more accountability —
because of more accurate representation. Didn't John Adams have
exactly this in mind when he said that for a legislative assembly to "do
strict justice at all times, it should be an equal representation"?

Consider the effect our conception of law has on how we approach
issues of criminal behavior and punishment. There are some
important things to balance in this area — on the one hand, we want
to deter crime and ensure people's safety by not letting violent
criminals get off too easy. On the other hand, punishment that is too
severe or too rigid, i.e. not flexible enough to take account of unique
circumstances, can have undesirable consequences. Mandatory
minimums for non-violent offenses wreak havoc in impoverished
communities; rehabilitation is neglected as mass incarceration gets
higher priority and resources are stretched; prisons become sources
of gang membership and more violent crime.

At the party level, the need to balance such competing interests is
not recognized. Political leaders strive to appear tough on crime to
win swing voters. Meanwhile, many of the people most affected by
such policies are politically disengaged, or their votes are taken for
granted by one of the two major parties. So both parties end up taking
similar stances on the issue, and the result is a kind of societal
imbalance that takes a long-term toll on our political well-being, on
justice and how it is perceived. Eventually, after decades, leaders of
both parties may realize that things are out-of-balance, and reform
the system. But perhaps later, the cycle repeats, as the lessons of
imbalance are forgotten and the parties succumb to the same political
pressures.

It's easy for people to look at such a cycle and conclude that the
problem was mostly short-sightedness on the part of our elected
leaders. And no doubt that had something to do with it. But if we look

---

[293] Sartori 1987, p. 326.

beyond that to the structure of our system of representation, and ask whether it could have offered more resistance to this short-sightedness, or whether the premise of governing by legislating opened the door to it, I'd say that the answer is yes, to both questions. Seesaw politics entails parties exploiting the low fidelity of our representation for partisan ends (i.e., teamsmanship), by passing legislation — but in the process they often undermine justice, and thereby cheapen the law.

More parties would mean a more complete consideration given to changes in law, thus more stability — and thus, I think, a better chance in the long term for law to be simplified, and to regain some of its old prestige of durability and justice.

More about ungovernability

Getting back to Rove and his concern that too many parties in Congress would make government unworkable — that is, would make the nation *ungovernable* — the first response, then, is that by improving the fidelity of representation, the quality of legislation should improve due to a truer majoritarianism based on shifting majorities instead of a hijacking-prone Majority faction — with the quantity of legislation, and more importantly the complexity of the law, eventually decreasing. And that where a spur to action is needed (that is, when Congress needs a "kick in the ass"), the president may provide it, as she also ensures that day-to-day operations continue while Congress figures out what it wants to do and how to do it.

The second response is far simpler to express: *alliances*. Parties can agree publicly to cooperate with each other to push through a common agenda. This happens all over the world in various countries. It's very common in parliamentary systems when parties have to collaborate on selecting a prime minister, as we've already covered above. It can also take a more lasting form, such as in Australia, where the Liberal Party and National Party have an alliance with roots going back to the 1920s; it apparently has been a stable marriage since the 1940s.

Alliances between parties also appear in presidential systems. Take Chile as an example. The country has many parties — in the elections of November 2017, 16 won seats in the Chamber of Deputies, the lower house of the national congress. But most of these are members of some larger coalition. One of the earliest alliances was the *Concertación* ("coalition"), which came together in the late 1980s to oppose the continued rule of General Augusto Pinochet. The main constituents of this coalition were the Christian Democratic Party, the Socialist Party, the Party for Democracy, and the Radical Party, all center-left parties. The other main coalition of parties in Chile was the right-wing Alliance, which included the National Renewal party and the Independent Democratic Union, among others.

The composition and names of each of these two major coalitions have changed over the years. Bachelet regained the presidency in the 2013 election, with her Socialist Party now a member of the New Majority coalition, which replaced the *Concertación* in 2013. Piñera won again in 2017 as a candidate endorsed by several parties, most of them members of *Chile Vamos* ("Let's Go Chile"), a center-right coalition that replaced the Alliance in 2015. These two major coalitions have been key forces in Chilean politics since the end of the Pinochet regime. They help to ameliorate the negative effects of fragmentation.

Figure 5.2, below, shows the composition of Chile's main national legislative body, the Chamber of Deputies, as elected in 2017. As in the party history charts I've showed earlier (figures 2.4 and 2.6), the full width of this chart represents 100 percent of the seats in the chamber. The colored rectangles running horizontally across the middle represent parties, with width proportional to the percentage of seats occupied. The parties are shown here on top of taller colored rectangles, which represent the coalitions they belong to — again with width proportional to the percentage of seats. Party labels appear in the top part of the chart, coalition labels in the bottom part.

As you can see, while there are many parties (and one independent legislator, shown on the far right), the number of coalitions is considerably smaller. There are four major ones represented in the chamber as currently seated, along with a couple of small ones — and in the past there have typically been only two major ones.[294]

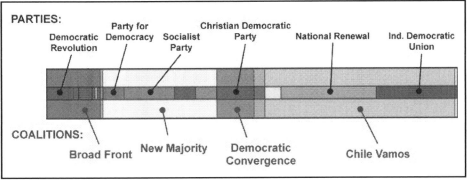

Figure 5.2. Parties and coalitions in Chile's Chamber of Deputies, as elected in 2017 (Full-color version: daneckam.com/book/btp/figures.)

What's the difference between having a multiparty system with, say, two big alliances of parties, and having a two-party system consisting of big-tent parties that amalgamate different interests under their banner? The answer to this question is more clarity for voters and the signals they are transmitting with their votes. A voter who has a clear idea of what his party stands for, as well as how it intends to use whatever power it gains, is in a better position (relative to self-government) than a voter who only has a vague idea of what his party stands for and how it will use power. And the parties understand voter's interests better by considering how the vote is composed. For example, if an alliance consisting of party *A* and party *B* gets two-thirds of its votes from *A*, it means something different than if two-thirds of the votes come from *B*.

---

[294] Note: only parties that won seats are shown; the chart does not include those that stood for election but failed to win. So although it looks like the Democratic Convergence coalition consists of a single party, in fact it includes other parties that won no seats.

More parties, more fairness

Let's look more deeply into the idea that with more parties in Congress, setting the rules will tend to be more fair. The rules that the House and Senate follow are, of course, very important in the process of legislating. They help determine who sets the agenda and which bills get scheduled for a vote — and these can be very powerful tools of obstruction. So it makes a big difference how this works.

It seems intuitive, to me, that when you have more players at the table, it's less likely that some part of them will be able to bend the rules to their own narrow interests. With only two, it's not that hard to rig something up that would allow both sides opportunities to have their way (perhaps alternating, according to which one has a majority). But the more players are involved, the more complicated such rigging becomes. Trading favors between two groups can happen along a single dimension — left vs. right, for example, or just team "A" vs. team "B". Add a team "C", though, and suddenly we need two dimensions to represent their positions. And if we add a team "D" or beyond, we need three dimensions. The possibilities for trading favors or privileges between different groups become so numerous that negotiations based on narrow, outcome-focused interests are very difficult to navigate in such a way as to leave most parties satisfied. Given such complexity, it's a lot easier to fall back on basic principles, like fairness, to guide the negotiations.

As game theorist H. Peyton Young writes:

> By appealing to standards of fairness, the negotiators increase the likelihood of an agreement by narrowing the range of possible disagreement. A further benefit of relying on standards of fairness is that it relieves the bargainers of responsibility for having "given in." It converts what might otherwise degenerate into an arbitrary contest of wills into a "principled" or "objective" solution that can be justified—both to the bargainers themselves and to their constituents (Fisher and Ury 1981).[295]

---

[295] Young 1991, pp. 4-5.

Remember that we're talking about rules of procedure here, which are used to determine how political issues will be decided. So it's a "meta" thing: a game that sets up the game. It seems to me that fairness is clearly desirable in this context. Players don't want to be seen as rigging the game — that would devalue whatever victories they manage to achieve in playing it. When competitors agree to an athletic contest, they implicitly agree that the goal of the contest is to let the best player win. Deciding on the rules of the competition is simplified because everyone sees the value of fairness.

In politics it's analogous, insofar as a basic democratic principle says that a majority should prevail over a minority. We should be able to agree that we want a fair procedure for identifying such majorities. The "real" (substantive) contest is the vote on policy; the procedural rules are just designed to bring us to that point of decision.

Using a principled approach can help with this in several ways, as Young explains:

> [F]raming negotiations in terms of fairness principles represents an advance over mere haggling for several reasons. First, there are relatively few concepts of fair treatment that are credible in any given situation, and this fact helps to focus the negotiations. Second, an agreement based on fairness principles is not likely to generate grudges. The outcome does not rest on the cleverness of the parties, their bargaining ability, or their willpower, so it is unlikely that anyone feels bested or "had." This enhances the durability of the agreement. Third, a negotiation based on explicitly formulated principles can serve as a guide to future negotiators in similar situations. It establishes a precedent, and this in itself has significant social value.[296]

These rules are not formulated in a vacuum. At the beginning of every new Congress, before each chamber adopts its rules, standard parliamentary procedure is in effect. So any change to that default would have to improve on it for a majority of those negotiating. This means there's already a foundation of basic fairness in the way things

---

[296] Young 1991, p. 43.

are structured, which can be built upon to create rules that are both efficient and fair.

In case this still isn't quite enough to be fully convincing, it would be nice to prove somehow, with game theory or perhaps some other form of economic theory, that a system with more parties tends towards more fairness. Unfortunately, I'm not that well-versed in such subjects. But it would seem that the concept of the *core* (introduced in chapter 3, in the context of policymaking) is useful here. It's the set of policy positions that cannot be defeated, given some decision rule, in this case the default parliamentary procedure rules. If the core exists in a particular scenario, then it would save the parties a lot of time and effort to acknowledge that their negotiations should probably converge on it. But this isn't quite the strong, theoretical proof I'm looking for.

However, I have found something almost as convincing in empirical findings from comparative political science. In a 2006 paper published in *Legislative Studies Quarterly*, Royce Carroll, Gary W. Cox and Mónica Pachón studied the allocation of what they call "mega-seats" in the national democratic assemblies of 57 countries. Mega-seats are positions of importance such as cabinet posts and committee chairs. The authors define the "majoritarian bonus" of an assembly as the difference between a party's share of the available mega-seats and its share of seats. Thus it is a way of measuring disproportionality in the allocation of governing powers and responsibilities.

The authors note that in newer, less-established democracies, "the interaction between parties and rules may be hard to predict". There is an extended process of parties adapting to the rules and figuring out how to best change them in their own interests. But they do find that:

> [T]he majoritarian bonus in the allocation of mega-seats tends to be larger in systems with a smaller effective number of parties. This correlation may arise because larger parties engineer larger majoritarian bonuses, because larger majoritarian bonuses drive smaller parties out of business, or both

In other words, the fewer the parties, the more the allocation of mega-seats tends to be disproportional to parties' overall seat shares.

They also find that "older democracies tend to have larger majoritarian bonuses than younger ones", and that the more a country has experience of democracy, the more its intra-legislative majoritarian bonuses tend "to approximate those awarded in general elections."

Essentially, this paper seems to establish that systems with more parties tend to be more proportional in the allocation of mega-seats. If we can agree that proportionality is a kind of fairness, or that it's a proxy for fairness, then this amounts to strong support of what I've been claiming.

The rules that govern procedures in the House and Senate are very difficult for average citizens to understand. When an important bill is referred out of committee, its next step (in the House) is often the Rules Committee, where a so-called "special rule" is created to govern its passage on the floor. This practice began in 1883 — before then, the Rules Committee primarily focused on considering changes to the House's permanent rules.[297]

When bills are regularly passed using custom rules that override the standing rules, that's not exactly what I'd call a rule-based system. Rules are supposed to be general — applying to all, or almost all, business. The Rules Committee, through many ups and downs over the decades, is to a large extent a tool of the majority party for controlling the legislative agenda. It's not a structure friendly to the "republican principle", that is, the majority rule for decision-making. It is friendly to the interests of obstructionism.

I don't think other democracies do things in such a complicated way. Unfortunately, I don't know how to precisely compare the structure and procedures of the U.S. House with those of the legislative assemblies of other countries — because it's rather technical, and because I don't read any foreign languages well enough to comprehend the relevant documents (which are not the sort of things that are often translated). I looked up the standing rules for New Zealand's House of Representatives, and they seem very straightforward, fair and reasonable — but then, it might be said that

---

[297] Schickler 2005.

that's because it's a parliamentary system. Well, I don't think it would hurt if we were more like a parliamentary system in terms of rules and procedures. It would surely be easier for the average person to understand. Maybe it would help the Congress function more like a deliberative body and less like a trough for special interests.

Overbearing personalities vs. structured party systems

Getting back to Karl Rove's complaint against multiparty systems — another part of it is that parties are sometimes formed simply on the basis of one strong individual — they are little more than a vehicle for that person to gain power. It's true that this is a real problem in some countries. For example, look at Brazil's party system. In 1989, Fernando Collor de Mello formed the National Reconstruction Party to back his bid for the presidency, which he won; he served as president from 1990-92, resigning the office as impeachment proceedings were under way.[298]

Switching parties is also very common in Brazil. For example, Jair Bolsonaro left the Social Christian Party to join the Social Liberal Party in 2018, the year he was elected president.

Brazil has a weak, fragmented party system. It's typical for more than 20 parties to have seats in Congress. This is partly a result of how the system is set up:

> Brazil's electoral rules encourage voters to focus on individual candidates more than parties. The large number of parties and frequent mergers and splits make it harder to grasp what the parties represent than is the case in most democracies, and the large number of candidates also might place comparatively high informational demands on voters. In terms of voter range of choice, both among and within parties, the system has a lot to offer. On the other hand, the electoral system makes it comparatively difficult for voters to develop attachments to parties.[299]

---

[298] Ames 1994.
[299] Mainwaring 1999, p. 278.

With changes to its system, the country could develop stronger parties and be less susceptible to this tendency towards "personalism". The issue is whether party labels actually represent something connected to ideology and public policy, or whether they are merely vehicles for electing power-seeking individuals. This is known in political science as the "structuring" of a party system — as I mentioned in chapter 2 in discussing the emergence in the 1820s of the Second Party System. A structured party system features mass, organized parties that represent abstract images relating to ideology or policy program, for example — whose leaders associate themselves with it because they agree with what it stands for. By contrast, in a party system that is not structured, "the leaders stand above the party" — that is, the leaders come first, the party second.[300]

We should ask how resistant our own party system is to this phenomenon. Is it only in multiparty systems that parties can be used as vehicles for one person's political agenda? I think not. Donald Trump is a strong personality who has bent the Republican Party to his will. Its image — what it stands for — after 2016 is different than it was before. In some ways, this is even worse than what we see in personality-driven parties within multiparty systems: The Republican Party is well-established and very powerful as an institution, allowing him to skip past much of the work of party-building that individuals must carry out in other countries.

Personalism enters the two-party system through the inherent ideological weakness of its "big-tent" structural dynamics — a problem that has been recognized for a long time:

> [E]ach party has sought winning coalitions by attempting accommodations among competing interests it hopes will appeal to more contributors and voters than will the rival accommodations offered by the opposition party. This strategy, it is conceded, has resulted in vague, ambiguous, and overlapping party programs and in elections that offer the voters choices between personalities and, at most, general

---

[300] Sartori 1968, pp. 292-3.

programmatic tendencies, certainly not unequivocal choices between sharply different programs.[301]

Things don't have to be this way. In most advanced democracies, we see some familiar patterns of party ideology. There are conservative parties, social-democratic parties, liberal parties, and socialist parties. In recent times we often find anti-immigration parties, as this issue has become more salient. Where ethnic divisions are important, there are often parties that appeal to an ethnic minority — for example, in Israel there are Arab parties. This is how a party system is supposed to function — channeling the interests of the electorate, making sure that all voters (or at least all reasonable ones) can be represented.

Now, you may well find it undesirable that anti-immigration parties, or "extremist" parties, will win seats in a multiparty system, given enough traction in the electorate. I understand that. But denying representation to citizens who hold such views is not the best way to handle the problem. Better that such views are channelled through the party system and dealt with openly:

> When [an extremist] party threatens to develop enough power to influence the direction of policy, it then behooves those who find its point of view repugnant to develop opposing arguments and educate the electorate. Seeking to escape the tougher challenges of democracy by denying fundamental freedoms has the result of seriously weakening democracy itself.[302]

Is it actually helpful to the practice of democracy to deny representation to extremist views? It makes it easier to avoid certain challenges, to be sure. But excluding such views from the halls of government doesn't make them go away. They continue to exist on the sidelines of politics, exerting influence on it both through the corrosive effects of disengagement and by pulling parties in their direction. They act as factions within the two major parties, trying to "capture" it, to remake it in their own image. Occasionally, their attempts succeed.

---

[301] Ranney 1975, p. 201.
[302] Lawson 1997, p. 63.

When extremist views are channelled, though, into party and even (if popular enough) into seats, they become visible to all, including the mass media, who are then forced to reckon with them. Assuming that the extremist party offers nothing of merit, it can be dismissed, derided, or satirized more definitively. And if it has, in some way, a meritorious message, then it can be recognized more clearly. In short, there are benefits to democracy when political viewpoints are channelled through a healthy party system — even for viewpoints we don't like.

Some people claim that the rise of the Nazis in Germany had a lot to do with the Weimar Republic's system of proportional representation. But this is not accurate, as Douglas Amy explains:

> The rapid growth of the Nazi party in the 1930s is widely acknowledged to have been due to a complex combination of factors, primary among them the economic depression of that time and the association of the Weimar Republic with Germany's defeat in World War I. Given these conditions, the appeal of the Nazi party was strong, and its power would probably have grown irrespective of the electoral system in place. Indeed, if Germany had had single-member plurality elections in 1932, Hitler probably would have taken power a year earlier than he did under PR.[303]

At the Nuremberg trials, Hermann Göring (one of the highest-ranking Nazis) elaborated this point about how Germany's PR elections delayed the Nazis' takeover:

> Had the democratic election system of England or the United States of America existed in Germany, then the National Socialist German Workers Party would, at the end of 1931 already, have legally possessed all seats in the Reichstag, without exception. For in every electoral district in Germany at that time, or at the beginning of 1932 at the latest, [...] the NSDAP was the strongest party; that is to say, given an electoral system as it is in Great Britain or in the United States all these weaker parties would have failed to gain any seats and

---

[303] Amy 2002, pp. 206-7.

from this time on we would have had only National Socialists in the Reich, in a perfectly legal way according to the democratic principles of these two great democracies.[304]

Amy also points out that the vast majority of proportional representation (PR) systems *did not* descend into tyranny, as happened in 1930s Germany. One case does not establish a rule, or even a tendency. The historical record shows that PR systems have generally produced moderate governments, "despite the presence in several countries of small extremist groups".[305]

In America, we're used to the idea of parties as vehicles of ideology or program. It's deeply ingrained in the mythology of our party system — for example, the (debatable) idea that one party stands for small government and the other for activist government. Even though, thanks to the "big tents" that our two major parties function as, this is sometimes more advertising than reality, we understand that parties are supposed to be identified with different viewpoints. We understand the value of party channelization, even if we don't speak of it in such terms. Or, at least, we're used to political discourse being structured by such an understanding.

A multiparty system would be even more strongly channelized than our two-party system, because party ideology would be clearer and more coherent. So it would do a better job resisting the pull of "personalism".

Anti-system parties

The last piece of Rove's objection I want to deal with is how to handle anti-system parties, which are based on "the idea of blowing up the existing system". A good example might be a communist party, which stands for the idea of communist revolution — that is, a party representing the view that the basic structure and processes of our government are corrupt and deserve to be sabotaged. Any party that refuses to reject the use of violence for political ends, such as a fascist party or an anarchist party, would also qualify.

---

[304] Avalon Project; Bogdanor 1984, p. 123.
[305] Amy 2002, p. 207.

This is indeed a serious concern. Such anti-system parties are usually unwilling to cooperate with others to do the things that government needs to do. So they can severely "gum up the works". What can be done about this problem?

First, I would say (echoing Kay Lawson's quote above) that democracy takes work. If you have neighbors who like to vote for an anti-system party, talk to them. Try to convince them that their approach is problematic. Ask them what system they'd substitute — complaining is easy, coming up with a workable solution is harder. Convince them to change their mind. With the increased number of choices in a multiparty system, there will be more options — including, with luck, at least one that makes sense to such people. The fact that a multiparty system will include a wider range of perspectives will tend to reduce the level of anti-system feeling among the disillusioned:

> [T]he ability of such groups to have a political voice through the electoral system could decrease their sense of political frustration and make them less likely to employ violence or other undesirable means to attract attention to their views.[306]

But this may not solve the whole problem. What else can be done? There are some systemic adjustments that can be made, some engineering that can be done, to make it harder for extremist anti-system parties to win seats. One way is to have a fairly low district magnitude, say five. This would mean an effective election threshold of around 20 percent of the vote — parties that didn't meet or exceed this wouldn't win seats (see chapter 1). Or there could be a higher district magnitude with an artificially imposed threshold of 10 percent or more. Both approaches would help keep fringe parties out of power.

It could be helpful for the government to refuse to recognize parties that won't agree to some basic tenets of representative democracy. For example, if a party won't sign a pledge to work within the law to achieve its political goals, then I think the government (either state or federal) would be justified in refusing to acknowledge its legitimacy.

---

[306] Amy 2002, p. 210.

While parties are essentially private organizations, they do rely on the state to include their names on ballot papers (or electronic voting machines) and for other kinds of recognition. This kind of thing could be denied to anti-system parties. While freedom of association is an important principle, it's okay, at least in my view, to make some compromises for the good of society — for example, I don't think that parties should be allowed to exclude members on the basis of race or sex. And I think a party that advocates extra-legal means of taking power (such as terrorism) can and should be similarly regulated.

It's even possible to ban parties. To be sure, this is an extreme step — sort of like "going nuclear". It's not a step that should be taken lightly: If abused, it could be a major conflict of interest, with parties in power unfairly insulating themselves against competition. It also conflicts with freedom of association. But many democracies have found ways to exclude anti-system parties, without losing the essential elements of representation and accountability needed for a healthy political system. Examples include extremist parties associated with the Basque separatist movement in Spain (Batasuna, Euskal Herritarrok, and Askatasuna), Sinn Féin between 1956 and 1974 in Northern Ireland, and the Socialist Reich Party and Communist Party of Germany, banned in 1952 and 1956, respectively.

There are also steps that can be taken to isolate extremist and anti-system parties short of banning them. The term *cordon sanitaire* (French for "sanitary cordon") is used in political science to refer to a kind of quarantine of parties, such that all other parties represented in a legislative body refuse to cooperate with them in any sort of coalition. It's kind of like a political boycott.

In short, anti-system parties can be a significant challenge, but there are ways to deal with them.

The difficult combination?

Next, I want to consider an argument put forward by political scientist Scott Mainwaring, in an influential 1993 article titled "Presidentialism, Multipartism, and Democracy: The Difficult Combination". In it, he made the case that a multiparty system works better in parliamentary systems than in presidential ones, and that a two-party system tends to work better in presidential settings. This argument seems to have gotten quite a bit of traction in the 1990s.

One of Mainwaring's points is that presidentialism has some disadvantages compared to parliamentary systems — for example, when a president is at severe loggerheads with the legislative branch of government, he cannot easily be replaced before the next election. (Impeachment is a difficult thing to accomplish.) In parliamentary systems, by contrast, the head of government can usually be deposed through particular mechanisms such as a vote of no confidence, which may trigger a new election. Or, if a prime minister falls out of favor within her own party, the party can vote to replace her. This makes for a more responsive and accountable system. Another issue is that because the executive and legislative branches are elected separately, a situation of deadlock is more likely than in parliamentary systems, where the PM is almost always drawn from the party that wins the most seats.

I don't dispute that parliamentary systems have some advantages — while also having some relative disadvantages. But if we're being realistic, I think we have to understand that we're not very likely to switch from a presidential to a parliamentary system any time in the foreseeable future. It would require not just a constitutional amendment, but a whole new constitution. So the question is, can we make our presidential system work, and improve on it with changes to the party system?

I would mention that if we used a Condorcet voting method, or perhaps another solid method (see chapter 1), to elect our presidents, it would make them more likely to be consensus-oriented and thus have a better chance to work with the legislative branch. As for impeachment, it shouldn't be easy, but it should be an effective deterrent to presidential misbehavior — and a multiparty system would at least be a major step away from what has sometimes functioned as near immunity from it, as I argued in chapter 4.

But Mainwaring's main thrust is that there's something about the *combination* of presidentialism and multiparty democracy that is especially troublesome. He argues that there are three reasons for this: (1) that it increases the likelihood of deadlock between the executive and legislative branches of government, (2) that it tends to increase ideological polarization, and (3) that interparty coalition-building, which is generally more important in a multiparty system, is more difficult in presidential than in parliamentary systems.

On the first point, he explains that it is more likely in a two-party system for a president to have a majority or something close to it in the legislative branch, which naturally eases the task of carrying out a legislative agenda. And "[w]hen incentives for legislative support break down, parliamentary systems have institutionalized mechanisms for dealing with the problem; presidential systems do not."[307] He also says that when a president reaches a point of deadlock with the legislature, he lacks tools for pushing through his program.

On the second point, Mainwaring argues (citing Downs 1957) that ideological polarization is less likely in a two-party system: "Competition tends to be centripetal [i.e. center-seeking] because to win a majority, the parties must win votes from the center of the political spectrum."[308] Intense ideological divisions, he says, "are unlikely in the context of a two-party system."[309]

Let me respond to these two points before turning to the third. With regard to intense ideological division, I suppose this essay is showing signs of its age. American politics has become more polarized since 1993, as politicians have gained in both skill and willingness to put teamsmanship over the public interest — to "play the seesaw". It seems pretty clear that a two-party system is no guarantee of moderate, center-seeking political competition. That's not to say that polarization is something we can afford to ignore; it is indeed something to be concerned about. But I think with greater variety would come a greater inclination to mix elements of what today we consider "left" and "right", and a better chance of seeing Downs's classic "bell-curve" model of voter distribution realized in practice. And again, a good choice of voting method can help ameliorate the problem.

---

[307] Mainwaring 1993, p. 217.
[308] Mainwaring 1993, p. 219.
[309] Mainwaring 1993, p. 220.

As for the president's ability to push through a legislative agenda, in the American system, this is supposed to be the job of Congress, not the president. I know that the president can be an important instigator of congressional action, and a multiparty system would by no means eliminate that function. But he *shouldn't* be able to push through an agenda that is out of line with what voters want. With Congress constituted as a more accurate representation of the people, it's a *good* thing that the power of passing legislation should reside with it, as our Founders of course intended. If the president has a worthy legislative agenda, Congress should take it up and pass it. Yes, partisan disagreements may interfere to some extent, but the American people are pragmatic — they want things that make sense to be done. Representatives who engage in obstruction will have to face voters and explain why.

I suspect that many political scientists, including Mainwaring, take government by legislating as a premise, an immutable fact of political-system functioning. He says as much when he says[310] that "it is difficult to govern effectively without passing laws". But I don't think the Founders saw things that way. I think when they separated the executive from the legislative branch, they expected the executive to govern under the current laws of the land. As I sketched out above, we may someday return to a simpler, more elegant view of law which makes a stronger distinction between it and mere administration. In fact, the American separation-of-powers design may be friendlier to such a view than a parliamentary system, as Sartori suggests[311]:

> English constitutionalism separated the power to rule from the power to ascertain and apply the law, but hardly separated the exercise of power between parliament and government. The latter is a distinctive feature of the American presidential system only.

Imagine a world in which the law has been streamlined and stabilized because it reflects a simple, compromise consensus about what it should be. Imagine that the budget is similarly stabilized, with

---

[310] Mainwaring 1993, p. 215.
[311] Sartori 1987, p. 336.

built-in adjustments based on demographic and cost-of-living formulas — so passing a new budget would mostly be about affirming the same revenues and expenditures as in the previous year, with perhaps just a few tweaks. And suppose Congress has given the executive branch a reasonable amount of leeway to administer government as it sees fit, within prescribed parameters. Legislation is mostly concerned with reform of the law, wherever it is found to no longer fit the times.

Now, this idealized picture will probably never be exactly realized, but it illustrates the point that legislation doesn't have to be so identified with governing. We should keep in mind, too, that we have a federal system in which a lot of law is (and was meant to be) the purview of the states. So let the states handle those responsibilities as they will. Maybe some state could even try out a parliamentary form of government, offering maximum responsiveness to the will of its residents. That would be an enlightening experiment, both for that state's residents and for the rest of the nation as it observes the effect on governance.

Am I being unrealistic here? I don't think so — though I am thinking about this in a very long term way. As I said, I think Americans are pragmatic people. How many of us want our government to continue to pass thousands of laws every year? Do we want to keep governing by legislating forever, or do we recognize a need to get back to a more comprehensible view of the law? If the latter, I hope we can see how a multiparty system can help, by ensuring that we have requisite variety — that is, variety which reflects the diversity of the people — in Congress, and by offering more resistance to special interests.

The third problem with the combination of presidentialism and multipartism, Mainwaring writes, is that it's more difficult to build "stable interparty legislative coalitions".[312] Whereas in coalition parliamentary governments, the parties in the coalition must cohere in their support of the government, or see it toppled, in a presidential system the administration does not depend directly on party support for its power. The president, Mainwaring argues, chooses her own

---

[312] Mainwaring 1993, p. 220.

cabinet (subject to advice and consent), instead of the cabinet being largely the result of inter-party deals that help keep the coalition parties invested in the administration's leadership. Party discipline tends to be lower in presidential systems. And parties have an incentive to oppose government policy when the president is not of their party:

> [A]s new presidential elections appear on the horizon, party leaders generally feel a need to distance themselves from the president in office. By remaining a silent partner in a governing coalition, party leaders fear they will lose their own identity [...] [and] bear the electoral costs usually associated with incumbency without enjoying the benefits.[313]

He makes a good point here. The often cynical posturing of parties against a president's policies, even when their leaders understand the need for them, creates challenges for the smooth operation of government.

But some later scholarship on these questions has found that presidents actually have a wide range of techniques for handling the problem, and that the earlier view of a "difficult combination" was too pessimistic:

> A broader comparative focus suggests that presidents tend to overcompensate for the anticipated perils of separated powers by utilizing a diverse set of tools, which they deploy in many different combinations. This toolbox makes the task of predicting *a priori* the dynamics of coalitional presidentialism much more complicated, and may explain why presidentialism has not had the destabilizing effects that were anticipated by the first wave of presidential scholars.[314]

Presidents can use the power of cabinet appointments and other favors, along with "pork", meaning support for projects that help individual legislators in particular ways. Along with the power to help set the agenda for legislative action, and powers of party leadership, these are the main components of what has been called the "executive

---

[313] Mainwaring 1993, p. 222.
[314] Chaisty, Cheeseman, and Power 2012.

toolbox".[315] And, of course, the power of the presidential veto is very considerable.

(Note: pork is ugly and inefficient, it's true — not really an intended part of the design of a democratic system. But maybe a little of it isn't all that bad, compared to the alternatives.)

So while challenges do exist, I don't think they are show-stoppers. I think if we're aware of these pitfalls and stay attuned to their potential for disruption, we'll be able to avoid them. We can hope for help from a more diverse media to educate the public about what to realistically expect. Political experts will be more sought-after to explain how the system actually works, as opposed to the unrealistic promises made by parties during campaign season. In a multiparty system, with more perspectives on the table for the public's consideration, expertise and realism will be more highly valued than in the seesaw system we now have.

The debate about presidentialism will surely continue in the domain of comparative politics. But it's clear, at least, that there are arguments on both sides.

It seems like a lot hinges on how well-established institutions are — both governmental and party-system institutions. The United States has one of the most well-established constitutions in the world, and stable institutions to go with it — a very different case from most other presidential democracies of the world, which have stable regimes dating back only a few decades. Unlike the party systems of some countries, such as Brazil's, which is largely based on personality, ours is structured by ideology, though not very coherently or consistently.

A structured system for realists

In their book *Democracy for Realists: Why Elections Do Not Produce Responsive Government* (2016), Achen and Bartels argue that the "folk theory of democracy" has been taken too seriously in many analyses of American democracy. This folk theory says that democracy works by the people deciding what their preferences are for public policy,

---

[315] Raile, Pereira, and Power 2011.

then making rational choices in voting based on those preferences. But this is mostly mythology; most voters, in reality, don't have time to be well-informed on issues, and they are not so rational:

> People tend to adopt beliefs, attitudes, and values that reinforce and rationalize their partisan loyalties. But those loyalties, not beliefs or ideologies or policy commitments, are fundamental to understanding how they think and act.[316]

In a somewhat more realistic theory of voter behavior, voters are ignorant of ideology and its implications for policy, but they at least know how the conditions of their lives have improved or worsened during a political cycle, and they vote by applying a retrospective judgment on the performance of elected leaders. However, Achen and Bartels point out, they are myopic: They put disproportionate emphasis on how they feel at voting time, forgetting "how they have felt over the course of the incumbents' term in office"[317]:

> The voters, not knowing what the best policies are, content themselves with asking at election time whether events have gone well or badly lately. Then they vote that myopic judgment.[318]

In this book, I've complained at length about the big-tentism of the two major parties, the fact that they aren't truly as committed to a coherent ideology as they pretend to be, the fact that they form electoral coalitions between groups that have different interests and then often take some of those groups for granted. I have emphasized the idea of a party system as a way to channelize the various leading ideologies of pluralistic liberal democracy. I may have seemed, at times, to assume that voters think about politics in a rational, ideological, policy-oriented way, which guides their decision-making at election time.

In fact, I have not suggested that all voters behave in such a way, or even that most of them do. I hope I have not implied it, either — my argument doesn't depend on such a claim. I've acknowledged that people have a variety of social reasons for identifying with the

---

[316] Achen & Bartels 2016, p. 296.
[317] Achen & Bartels 2016, p. 175.
[318] Achen & Bartels 2016, p. 211.

political party of their choice — for example, maybe they're a Democrat because their parents are. I appreciate what Achen and Bartels write about the need to be realistic about party identification.

But the fact remains that some people do think of party as a vehicle for achieving policy goals. Well-educated people who pay attention to political and cultural news — that is, the intellectual (and "pseudo-intellectual") — tend to think of it this way. Those people are often influential with their friends and family. The media, too, if they're serious about political issues, tend to view parties with an understanding of their place in the theory of representative democracy — as a connection between the demands of voters and the policies that government follows.

These forces nudge society towards an ideological understanding of parties. After all, policies and their implementation are the ultimate "products" of government — where the rubber meets the road, so to speak — and political ideology is what primarily shapes policy. That's why we consistently see, in well-established multiparty democracies around the world, that the parties primarily distinguish themselves by ideology.

In some measure, the problems with voter behavior pointed out by Achen and Bartels are fundamental, perhaps inherent, problems of democracy. A self-governing system is not a simple thing to achieve. It requires expertise; I fully agree with them when they say:

> [E]ffective democracy requires an appropriate balance between popular preferences and elite expertise. The point of reform should not simply be to maximize popular influence in the political process, but to facilitate *more effective* popular influence. We need to learn to let political parties and political leaders do their jobs, too. Simple-minded attempts to thwart or control political elites through initiatives, direct primaries, and term limits will often be counterproductive.[319]

Yet I get the feeling that some of the authors' analysis may be conditioned by the two-party system. For one thing, duopolistic politics feeds the idea that voters' myopic, retrospective judgment

---

[319] Achen & Bartels 2016, p. 303.

might just be enough to make democracy work, even if they are ignorant of policy and ideology. In an "us versus them" world, voters lack defection options. They are encouraged simply to ask themselves if they are better or worse off at election time than they were two or four years prior. "Responsible party" theory has also encouraged this. Duopoly promotes voter disengagement.

It also encourages "scapegoating impulses of democratic electorates".[320] In some ways, such impulses tend to be worse under duopolistic conditions, because of a "seesaw" dynamic which rewards negative campaigning, and also tends to promote hijacking and hostage-taking by majority factions — as explained earlier in this book. Achen and Bartels acknowledge that a "healthy democratic culture among political elites" can help constrain such scapegoating impulses.[321] I'd add that if the elites were less polarized into two "us versus them" camps — if they more accurately reflected the true variety of political opinion, and along with this variety an increased alertness to the need for consensus and compromise where possible — we'd have the makings of a healthier democratic culture. In short, I don't think the case for a multiparty system is really in conflict with the authors' arguments for a more realistic theory of democracy.

Remember that party in government exists alongside party in the electorate — and people in government, because their jobs are centered on policy, understand the value of party's connection to policy, and behave accordingly (at least some of the time). That is, they want party reality to align with party image (all other things being equal).

Madison was the opposite of a populist; he believed that worthy men of virtue were best-suited to representing the people in government. He would have fully understood and appreciated the need for thought leadership, as I've called it, and he might have been able to see, given the course of American history since his time, that a healthy party system can be the vehicle for promoting such leadership. After all, parties are organizations, and any well-run

---

[320] Achen & Bartels 2016, p. 144.
[321] Achen & Bartels 2016, p. 144.

organization recognizes and promotes quality within its own ranks. And at their best, they are organizations focused on pursuing the public good; when they fail at that, they are subject to voters for accountability. So their structure gives them a tendency to incentivize integrity, public service, and thought leadership — or *worthiness*, in Madisonian lingo. And thought leadership, like a catalyst added to a solution, organizes its environment — meaning it frames the discussion, showing the leading ways to understand and analyze political questions — and does this despite being (initially) a small part of the discourse.

So, it's not required that the whole electorate behave rationally, with primary regard for policy preferences, in order for the party system to be structured along policy-oriented, ideological lines. Party leaders and thought leaders see things that way, and that's enough, especially given some time for a new "ecosystem" of parties to develop and be reflected in political media. Some people may still inherit their party identification from their parents. But others will notice that the new party system offers more choices and more possibilities to support what they really believe in, and be encouraged to consider policy preferences first. Over time, this pattern will tend to be normalized.

I don't think there's anything unrealistic at all about the idea of having a multiparty system in America. It would be more in line with what our Founders would have expected, had they known that political parties were unavoidable, because it resists the problem of hijacking via a faction that includes a majority. It would align much better with avowed American values concerning entrepreneurship, innovation, and competition in a free marketplace of ideas. It would give us the variety of representation that we need in order to truly consider ourselves a representative democracy.

6. Answering Misconceptions

"Voting, like any other process, is subject to scientific treatment; there is one right method of voting which automatically destroys bilaterality, and there is a considerable variety of wrong methods amenable to manipulation and fruitful of corruption and enfeebling complications. The sane method of voting is known as Proportional Representation with large constituencies and the single transferable vote and it is as reasonable and necessary that the country should adopt it as soon as possible as that it should adopt the right types of aeroplane and the best sorts of gun." — H. G. Wells, The Elements Of Reconstruction (1916)

There's a long list of misunderstandings, misconceptions, and ill-informed or misguided objections to some of the ideas put forward in this book — so many that I figured I should take another chapter to deal with them.

Criticisms of ranked-choice voting
In this section, I'll deal with some complaints that have popped up from time to time in debates over ranked-choice voting.

Complaint: "It's too complicated."

Some critics complain that voting in a ranked-choice election, such as instant-runoff voting (IRV) or the single transferable vote (STV), is too difficult for voters to understand. But most people have everyday experience with ranking preferences. Ask someone to list their top three favorite flavors of ice cream, for example. There isn't much chance they would fail to understand the request, even if they really only like two kinds of ice cream. In that case, they could imagine picking a third flavor, if they had to — even if they weren't really committed to their selection. And in fact, ranked-choice voting doesn't usually require voters to rank more than one option.

It can be seen as a user experience (UX) problem. We tend to think of ballots as static things: Voters are asked to place a "1" next to their first choice, a "2" next to their second choice, and so on. It's their responsibility, in many systems, to make sure their markings make sense. This is where a lot of confusion can arise. But things don't have to be so static — and as technology progresses, more sophistication will become the norm. Imagine a system that interacts with the voter in an intelligent way — maybe an artificial intelligence that asks them directly, "Who is your first choice in this election?" Then, upon receiving that input: "OK, got it! Now, in case your first choice doesn't win, do you have a second choice?" If so, then it goes on to record each choice in order of preference; if not, then: "OK, I have all of your selections for this office. Now let's move on to the next election." If this sounds far-fetched now, it won't in the future.

Studies have found that most voters do not have a hard time understanding ranked-choice voting, especially after trying it out:

> As part of the two surveys conducted by the Eagleton Poll with Professors Tolbert and Donovan, likely voters in cities using RCV were asked :"When you voted in the recent election, how easy was it to understand the voting instructions?". In the 2013 survey, an overwhelming majority (90%) of respondents in RCV cities found the RCV ballot easy to understand. Similarly, 89% of respondents in RCV cities in California found the RCV ballot easy to understand.[322]

Apart from the process voters go through to cast a ballot, there is also the tallying process, after all ballots have been cast. It's true that this process can be a little complicated and difficult to explain to people, especially in the case of STV for multi-seat elections. But voters actually don't need to understand this part of the electoral process, as long as they can have confidence that it is working reliably and fairly. Video animations are a great way of explaining these

---

[322] FairVote, d.u.

processes. I've seen some videos that take just a few minutes to explain STV with an example, and being able to visualize it makes it very clear how it works.

This is another area where technology can help. It would not be a difficult thing to create a computer program to dynamically generate a video animation showing how the tallying went, round by round, for a particular election. It would actually be a fun video to watch — seeing how each round went, who was eliminated, how their votes were transferred to the other candidates, and so on, would make the tallying process very tangible and comprehensible for voters. Such a video could be released at the time of announcing the election results.

Who would create such technology? I don't think we need worry too much about that. As capabilities progress it will get simpler and simpler to create. As demand for better voting systems grows, interest in such systems will naturally grow at the same time. Where there's a will, there's a way.

Even without such intelligent technology, it's really not rocket science to list a few options in order of preference. "It's as easy as 1-2-3," as former Vermont governor Howard Dean says.[323]

Complaint: *"It doesn't guarantee that the winner has a majority of votes."*

One of the selling points of ranked-choice voting is that it doesn't prematurely award victory to a candidate who has less than a majority of votes — it requires additional rounds of tallying in such cases. Thus, it deals with the concern expressed by Alexander Hamilton (in *Federalist* no. 68) that it's "unsafe to permit less than a majority to be conclusive". But some people misunderstand how this works.

For example, the town of Cary, North Carolina tried instant-runoff voting in 2007 for their city council elections. In one district with a three-way race, the leading candidate got 38.1 percent of first-preference votes — 1,151 out of 3,022. After eliminating the third-place finisher, along with three write-in votes, that candidate won with 50.9 percent of votes counted in the final round — 1,401 out of

---

[323] Dean 2016.

2,754. Yet an anti-instant-runoff-voting activist complained that the 1,401 votes that won the election were only 46.4 percent — less than a majority — of the total number of ballots cast — 3,022 — and thus that the claim that IRV ensures a majority winner is a "lie".[324]

But that only makes sense according to the wrong calculation: If you divide the winner's votes in the final round by the total number of votes cast in the *first* round, then yes, it may be less than 50 percent. But that's the wrong choice of denominator. Percentages need to be calculated using the figures from the current round of tallying — and if we're talking about the final result, that means the final round.

Keep in mind that we don't have compulsory voting in the U.S. In other words, we allow people to abstain. Some voters did not express a preference between the two finalists in this election — that's why the number of voters dropped from 3,022 in the first round to 2,754 in the second. Should they have been required to choose, even if they had no preference? No. In traditional runoff elections, we don't require everyone who voted in the first round to go back to the polling station for round two. And when the turnout for the second round is a fraction of the first-round turnout, we don't divide the winner's vote tally in the second round by the total number of votes cast in the first round. It would seem quite absurd to do it that way. So why treat final-round results in an IRV election like that? It's simply not what is meant by "majority winner".[325]

Complaint: *"It gives some people more votes than others."*

In 2011, the United Kingdom held a referendum on whether to use instant-runoff voting, or the "alternative vote" (AV), as it is known there. Conservative Prime Minister David Cameron argued that the method is unfair because it gives some people more votes than others:

> There's an inherent unfairness under AV. Supporters of unpopular parties end up having their votes counted a number of times, potentially deciding the outcome of an election, while

---

[324] IRV in the US 2010.
[325] See Slatky 2010.

people who back more popular parties only get one vote. Why? Because if you vote for a mainstream candidate who is top of the ballot in the first round, your other preferences will never be counted. But if you vote for a fringe party who gets knocked out, your other preferences will be counted. In other words, you get another bite of the cherry.[326]

This is a misleading argument, as explained by the director of political analysis for U.K. market research firm Ipsos MORI:

> [C]ontrary to the arguments of some opponents of AV, **this system does not involve some people getting more votes than others**. Every voter gets just *one* vote, which is counted several times. Your second preference is not a second vote, it is an instruction about how you want your (only) vote to be used if it would be wasted because your first choice candidate can't win. Each vote is counted in each round of voting: the only difference is that if your candidate still has a chance of winning it will be counted for the same candidate each time, whereas if your candidate has dropped out it will be counted for a different candidate.[327] [emphasis in the original]

Again, if we just think of a standard runoff situation, and think of IRV as a compressed version of that, it becomes clear that this argument makes no sense. Every voter gets the same, single vote per round.

Complaint: *"We can't know who won until all the votes, from all precincts, are tallied."*

This one is absolutely true. But so what? I guess some people are used to watching election-night coverage, and seeing results come in from a certain number of precincts; when that number reaches, say, 80 percent (it's often far less), and one candidate has a solid lead, the media go ahead and report the winner. If the winner's lead is big enough, it's not just projected, it is a mathematical certainty.

---

[326] Cameron 2011.
[327] Mortimore 2011.

With ranked-choice voting, it's a little more complicated because, if no one wins in the first round, the next round will depend on who comes in last, thereby being eliminated, and how their votes are redistributed to other candidates. So it's harder to know how the tallying will go until you have all the ballots in. In the general case, you can't calculate it.

So, in a multiparty system we might have to get used to a different kind of election night. We might have to wait a few more hours to know the results of our elections. (In the future, with more advanced technology, this could be reduced to minutes.) I really don't think this is a big demand to make, considering the benefits of upgrading our electoral and party systems. I suppose the people who have the most to lose are the news media, who love to devote endless hours of coverage to a "horse-race" version of political competition. Well, I don't mind if they have to change their ways. They are very adaptable. Let's stay focused on creating a more perfect union, and not give this concern any more time than it deserves.

The imperfections of single-winner ranked-choice

One criticism of IRV is true, and useful to keep in mind: It's not what we should really be aiming for. Because it's a single-winner voting method, it's a winner-take-all system, which doesn't support proportionality in representation. (There's no way to split a person into parts, while expecting those parts to fulfill the task of representing voters.) So it's not the best solution for multi-seat representative assemblies. It's more suitable for singular offices, like president, vice president, governor, mayor, etc.

Even for elections like those, IRV has some shortcomings, such as the "center squeeze" pathology and failure of the Condorcet criterion, as discussed in chapter 1. That's why I recommend Condorcet IRV for single-winner elections.

As Douglas Amy points out, reformers who advocate for IRV without acknowledging its imperfections risk boxing themselves in when it comes time to go further:

> [I]t is unclear how reformers would be able to easily shift
> political gears after the adoption of IRV and begin to promote

a change to PR. They would have to turn from enthusiastic supporters of IRV to severe critics of that system—an inconsistency that would surely not go unnoticed by the public, the media, and policymakers.[328]

Think of IRV as a stepping stone to a better system — a compromise, where fully proportional representation is beyond reach for the short term — not the ultimate goal.

Geographic representation

Many people are troubled by the idea of congressional districts getting larger to support multiple seats per district (assuming we keep the number of House representatives fixed at 435). They are used to the idea of *constituent services* — the casework that congressional offices carry out to help local constituents — and of having just one person to make demands of when they have a problem, not several people. Under multi-member districting with proportional representation, each district would have several reps, and contain several times more people than do our current, single-member districts. If there were five reps for a given district, for example, it would mean five times as many people in that district.

There are a couple of reasons I'd say this concern is misguided. For one thing, given the population of the United States, there are already a lot of people in every district — around 750,000, in fact. So how much of a personal connection can really exist, in our current system? Do we really believe that the people who represent a district can be responsive to the demands of so many people, when they call or write to the rep's office? I think this is largely a fantasy, a product of a kind of democratic mythology we like to tell ourselves. It's not really true. Representatives love to act as if they are listening, and are devoted to serving their local constituents. But much of it is just that: an act. When push comes to shove — I mean, when you ask your rep to vote a certain way on a matter of policy, and he has a different opinion on the issue — your opinion will be ignored. At bottom, we live in a representative democracy, not a direct democracy. While people who

---

[328] Amy 2002, p. 219.

invest a lot of time lobbying their rep may be rewarded to some degree for their efforts, in a representative democracy it's the electoral process that mainly guides policy, at a high level.

Secondly, I'd say we probably have too much "localism" at the national level of our politics. If representatives are really supposed to pursue the interests of their local district, who is supposed to be mindful of national interests? The idea of federalism is that we have separate levels of government — local, state, and federal. Each of those levels should be focused on its own problems. If there are local or regional issues that need attention from elected officials, shouldn't it be the local or state leaders whose job it is to address them? As James Madison wrote in *Federalist* no. 10, the federal nature of our Constitution happily refers "the great and aggregate interests [...] to the National, the local and particular to the State Legislatures".

In some ways, national divisions of interest find proxies in the local interests of different regions, as expressed here in a mid-20th-century book:

> The Congressman from New Mexico is also Congressman of the Mexican-Spanish stock; the member from Boston, of the urban Irish, as the New Yorker of the urban Jews. The gentleman from Montana, Nevada and Colorado can speak for the mining industry. Through the Cleveland or Pittsburgh or Gary member, Congress hears the voice of the steel mills. The auto workers can send their ambassadors from Detroit or Flint. The tall corn and fat hogs are not forgotten by the Congressmen from Iowa.[329]

But this is hardly a reliable way of making sure the people, in all their diversity and variety, are represented in government, proportionally. Yes, in the 1950s a representative from the Pittsburgh area probably represented the interests of steel mill workers — to the extent that such workers shared interests. But where one works is not determinative of one's political views, and this way of representing variety depends on differentiation between cities and regions. There's another way these divisions can be represented, and it's much more

---

[329] Burnham 1959, p. 328.

direct — on the basis of party, the natural way democracies connect voters with government officials. The way that would naturally evolve from using proportional representation.

Some places, including my hometown of Austin, Texas, have been moving towards single-member districts for representative assemblies. In 2012, the city voted to adopt a system with a mayor (elected citywide) and ten council members, each elected from one of ten geographically defined districts, which were mapped out by a citizens' commission. Previously, there had been six council members, each elected citywide in separate "by place" elections. Since such at-large elections were recognized as tending to favor (i.e. overrepresent) the majority, two of the places were informally reserved for ethnic minorities: place 6 for an African-American council member, place 2 for a Hispanic member, in an arrangement known as the "gentleman's agreement". The goal of adopting single-member districts (SMDs) was to "provide neighborhoods with greater accountability and deliver more equitable representation to minority populations".[330] Certainly a very worthy goal. But the adoption of SMDs brings with it a risk of "ward-style" politics in which council members elected from separate neighborhoods have less incentive to think about the interests of the whole city, worrying instead only about their own area. So far, Austin has seemed to avoid the worst of such "ward politics", but will that continue on a permanent basis, when the structure of the system rewards it?

Ensuring minority representation in an SMD system requires carefully considering demographic data and drawing "majority-minority" districts to ensure that minority groups can elect a representative of their choosing. As I pointed out in chapter 1, this works better for groups that are geographically concentrated than for those who are dispersed — creating a problem for the movement away from segregated housing. If we someday manage to fully integrate all races, how will it be possible to draw single-member districts so that minorities have a chance at representation?

---

[330] Samuels 2008.

"Representational equity" is the principle at stake here, and it applies to partisan divides as well. On this score, too, single-member districts don't necessarily serve Austin very well — while it's generally considered a left-leaning, progressive city, its city council is not just left-leaning, but disproportionately dominated by left-leaners.[331] Political minorities don't have representation in proportion to their numbers. By contrast:

> Proportional representation meets this criterion [of representational equity] by ensuring majority rule while guaranteeing minority representation. PR is based on the recognition that there are numerous factional divisions in a city and that it is essential to make it impossible for any faction or political party with a slight electoral majority to elect all members of a city council or school board. In the first election after the abandonment of PR by New York City, Democrats won 24 of the 25 city council seats in 1949, although they polled only 52.6 percent of the votes cast. Had PR been in effect, the party division would have been 13 Democrats, six Republicans, three Liberals, and three American Labor Party members.[332]

Coming from an at-large voting system, it's understandable that the citizens of Austin wanted something better. It's too bad, though, that they didn't (or couldn't) seriously consider a proportional representation system like STV, which has been used in Cambridge, Massachusetts for its city council since the 1940s, and was used in many other American cities during the first half of the 20th century.[333] STV allows voters to choose representatives based on distinctions that matter to them. If racial and ethnic differences are important in the politics of the community, STV will allow them to elect people who embody those differences — regardless of how geographically concentrated or integrated minority voters are. If other differences — economic or cultural ones, for example, or

---

[331] Findell 2018.

[332] Zimmerman 1992, p. 215.

[333] See Appendix C of Amy 2002 — "The Forgotten History of Proportional Representation in the United States".

geographic ones — are more important than racial and ethnic ones, then voters can choose representatives based on those distinctions. Proportional representation adjusts itself to the differences voters consider important.

As Douglas Amy writes, by allowing "various racial and ethnic groups [...] to elect representatives to the city council and school committee [...] PR attempts to build consensus not by excluding some interests and parties from the legislature but by including as many as possible. In the long run, there is a better chance of resolving conflicts if all political groups participate in the governing process."[334] Cambridge has regularly elected ethnic minorities to its city council, and relations between ethnic groups have been smoother than in many cities. "It's the reason Cambridge didn't burn during the years of the demonstrations, the reason desegregation of the schools was achieved without any significant community disruption," according to a former member of the school committee.[335]

What we should strive for is accurate representation according to the issues and divisions that people care about. That implies proportionality, which means that for councils and other legislative bodies, we should use multi-member districts (or no districts), not SMDs. Yes, we want geographic representation, but the geographic area should be neither too big nor too small. Too big would be a district that includes more than one city, for local government, or more than one state, for federal representatives — something we don't need to worry about, because no one is asking for it, and which would be impossible without a constitutional amendment anyway. Too small would be districts that divide up a coherent political community (such as a city) into geographic chunks. They don't allow, at least not in the best and most flexible way, for accurate representation of the whole community.

Another reasonable alternative would be to go with a mixed-member proportional (MMP) system, as is used in Germany and New Zealand — I briefly described it in chapter 2. This would preserve

---

[334] Amy 2002, pp. 202-3.
[335] "After the Vote is Cast..." 1987.

single-member districts while also allowing for some proportionality of representation on a partisan level.

Voting for individuals vs. voting for parties

I've often heard people say that they vote for the individual candidate, not the party. I suppose they might well object to the argument of this book, noting that the plan proposed is a party-centric one. "Dan," they'd say, "Don't you realize that by adopting proportional representation, we'll be giving parties a lot more power?"

It's true that this is a more party-centric plan than some people would like. But every advanced democracy in the world is party-centric. That's not a coincidence: Parties are the institutional linkage between citizens and their government. We need to embrace this as the fact of life it is. It's a necessary part of representative democracy.

The criticism of a party-centric vision seems to be largely based on the idea that representatives should think for themselves and not fall into line with their peers because of partisan affiliation — in other words, a rejection of *party discipline* as a valid force in legislative negotiations. I would agree that groupthink can often be a problem when humans get together. But the idea of treating legislators as atomized individuals, with no group-level associations, doesn't work very well.

Just as it's hard to herd cats, it's hard to get hundreds of legislators to agree on an agenda and to follow through on it consistently. Hierarchical structures of leadership are therefore very useful. There's a need to reduce large numbers to smaller, more manageable numbers.

What's more, the vision of individual legislator responsibility is idealized and not very accurate. Parties already exert influence over elected representatives, and, especially in recent times, the influence has been very considerable. So we already have a lot of the party discipline that some think of as a problem.

But, in contrast to other democracies, where party discipline is exercised on behalf of parties that represent points of view based coherently on ideology, in ours the parties are too big to be that coherent or consistent. So, we get teamsmanship without the benefit of having teams that stand clearly for something.

Governing requires negotiation and compromise. There's a balance to be found between too few sides of a negotiation and too many. A well-structured system of parties avoids both extremes, helping to keep attention focused on the public interest while avoiding the risk of one side hijacking the system to serve its own narrow or special interests. If individual responsibility is the norm, there are many sides to placate, and there's a high chance that one, or a few, of the crucial votes may demand something special for their own constituents. Such a situation leads to pork-barrel politics — not the best way for a nation to manage competing interests.

When "bridges to nowhere" are built, or when we need to close some military bases and can't, because of political considerations, the idea of the individually responsible legislator lies near the heart of the problem. To have an effective, functional democracy at the national level, we need to think in terms of parties, not individuals.

This doesn't mean that there's no place at all for individual responsibility. Parties will be able to hold their members responsible, even to the point of expelling them if necessary. Those who act irresponsibly, or bring discredit to their party, will be unlikely to move upward in the party's organizational hierarchy. And if the electoral method is the single transferable vote (STV), or open-list PR, voters will still be voting for people, alongside parties.

Are minor parties too "fringey"?

Today, the leading minor parties in America are the Libertarians and the Greens. Some of their ideas strike a lot of Americans as well outside the mainstream. And there are smaller parties with even more marginal viewpoints. I'm not saying that all third-party ideas are fringey, or that being outside the mainstream is necessarily a good indicator of unworthiness — but sometimes it is. Some people are concerned that a multiparty system would strengthen such extreme politics.

It's true that proportional representation would broaden the range of views represented in government. But this isn't a bad thing. Since it would be a more accurate, higher-fidelity form of representation, more people would be engaged in politics and feel that their voices were being heard. Instead of dissenters shooed off into the shadows, where they may grow cynical and resentful, their views will be out in the open. And maybe bringing them out of the shadows and into the light would help some realize how they fit in (or fail to fit in) to a bigger picture of how our republic is meant to function, democratically — involving negotiation and compromise.

Furthermore, the parties themselves would change — becoming more pragmatic, less "fringey" as they become more viable vehicles of professional politics. We have to keep in mind that it's a very different thing to be a third party under duopolistic conditions, systematically denied seats and essentially confined to acting as a protest group, and being a minor party in a system that is more open and competitive, a system that gives a fair shot to a new party that has its act together. By "act" I mean a compelling line of thinking about policy, competent and strong leadership, and a commitment to responsive and responsible government. In a proportionally elected multiparty system, minor parties will see that they have a shot at becoming major parties, and respond accordingly, by making their platforms more coherent and more likely to attract a mass following.

In short, context makes a big difference here — the rules of the game have an effect on the character of the players. Today's minor parties are not the parties of tomorrow's reformed system.

The Australian experience
One occasionally hears some grumblings about Australia's use of ranked-choice voting — that some people there are not happy with it. I think there are two main complaints that have some validity. The first is that for their lower house of parliament, they use instant-runoff voting and single-member districts, and most of the seats go to one of two big parties: Labor and the Lib-Nats, i.e. the Liberal-National coalition, which is actually two different parties that have a more-or-less permanent alliance. Well, counting the Liberal Nationals of Queensland, the coalition is actually made up of *three* parties. Actually, come to think of it, the Country Liberals of the Northern

Territory are also part of the coalition, so there are really *four* parties that belong to it (or, at least, four different party labels). But it's true that the Australian House has a dichotomous character, with two main groups dominating politics — though not in the same duopolistic way as in the American system.

This is not that surprising, in light of the point made earlier in this chapter that single-winner ranked-choice voting should not be the ultimate goal of reform, because it does not implement proportional representation. It is a winner-take-all method, because it elects one single person to represent a whole district. It does tend to disadvantage minor parties somewhat, though not as much as plurality voting. So Australia is not the perfect model of where we should want to go.

Nevertheless, I think Australia has a much healthier party system than the United States. The country comes ninth in the Democracy Index, compared to 25th for the U.S. Surely the less duopolistic nature of their party system — allowing voters more options, thus securing greater accountability of the government to the people — plays a part in this.

The other problem with Australia's voting system, in my opinion, is the use of what they call the "group voting ticket". For a long time in Australia, voters were required to specify a complete list of ranked preferences. So if there were six candidates running for a single seat, say, voters were asked to list all six in order of preference — even if they only knew their top two or three preferences. This was complicated and led to a lot of ballots being filled out incorrectly; so a custom developed whereby the parties would give advice to their voters on how to rank not just themselves (top of the list, of course) but also all the other parties competing in the election. And the parties registered their recommended orderings with the government, which allowed voters to check one simple box to use their favorite party's recommendations. (This is known as voting "above the line".)

Now, we know that instant-runoff voting is sensitive to the order in which candidates are eliminated. This fact makes tactical voting a significant issue in IRV — again, not as bad as in plurality voting, where the spoiler effect is huge, but still significant. But it's hard for individual voters to know how to "game" the system — i.e. how to take advantage of IRV's sensitivity to help their preferred party. It's easier for the parties, with their polling data and greater expertise, to know how various ways of ranking other parties could help them. So I suspect that the use of the group voting ticket has increased the scope for tactical voting and allowed parties to be effective in gaming the system. It has now been abolished in many jurisdictions.[336]

In my view, we should not allow devices like the group voting ticket in our elections. Let's make it *optional* for voters to choose second, third, fourth, and lower preferences. For those who choose to rank multiple candidates, let's encourage them to make their choices for themselves. This should help reduce the tendency towards two-party domination.

Transitional problems

Some people are concerned about the transition from our current system to a multiparty one. What if one of the two major parties — the one you hate, let's say — is slower to fragment than the one you prefer? After all, when we implement a major change in electoral rules, it will take a while for the effects of that change to be fully absorbed. It will put us on the path to a competitive multiparty system, but it won't instantly take us there. What if, in the transitional period, the "other side" manages to hold onto its legislative majority or near-majority?

The answer to this problem lies in alliances between parties. To stop a large faction from taking too much power, smaller factions can team up with each other, like the Liberals and Nationals in Australia — or on a less permanent basis. It might be uncomfortable, during this period, to recognize that differing factions still need to cooperate with each other — *we were promised multipartyism!* — but it can be done.

Whatever party remains, in this new multiparty system, a vague, big-tent party, including several factions, will be working at a competitive disadvantage to parties that can stand for a coherently focused platform — or set of values. In the long term, world

---

[336] See "Why you should vote below the line today" 2018.

experience seems to show that in proportionally elected systems, the trend is against parties that purport to represent half the electorate, or that typically win half or more of the votes. Voters see the advantages of truer representation over a system that suppresses variety.

What about the Senate? How can it be proportional?

Because every senator is elected statewide in staggered elections — that is, one at a time — we can't have multi-member districts or proportional representation for the U.S. Senate without amending the Constitution. This means we'll have to use a single-winner voting method, which tends to be less friendly to new and minor parties.

However, they can be much friendlier than the plurality system we use today, as we've seen. Instant-runoff voting eliminates the worst, at least, of the spoiler effect, and thus allows voters to vote their conscience, including voting for a minor-party candidate or an independent. If we use Condorcet IRV, the system will promote centrism and consensus-building. Maybe that will help make sure that the biggest parties will be clustered around the political center.

At the same time, the changes in political culture brought about by a multiparty system, with House elections leading the way, will encourage voters to take minor parties more seriously. Such parties may begin to gain traction in national conversations about politics — and, after a while, be confident enough to take on a Senate race, and eventually, perhaps, to win a few.

Even if the Senate continued to be somewhat dominated by two major parties, we'd be a lot better off than we are now. We'd have left behind duopoly, the systematic exclusion of alternative voices, which would mean that the two major parties would no longer be safe and secure in their dominance — they could be replaced if they fail to perform well in the eyes of voters.

The Senate has been thought of as a "saucer", into which House legislation is poured and allowed to cool — in other words, a moderating filter. James Madison termed it a "necessary fence" against the dangers of "fickleness and passion". The Founders thought that those elected to the Senate would be among the greatest and most enlightened citizens. There may be some value in thinking of it this way. Maybe the bicameral structure of our legislative branch, and the smaller number and longer terms of senators, serve a useful function.

In the long term, we may want to reform the Senate. If this "cooling" or moderating function seems to be more important than we realized, we could (though I'm not saying we should) return to letting state legislators choose senators (as was the norm before 1913). That probably sounds outlandish to some, but if we (in the *very* long term, say) manage to reform state-level government, maybe it won't seem so unfair, because more diverse state-level party systems will more accurately represent the interests of the people. Or, we could decide that the Senate has outlived its usefulness and should be abolished, by a constitutional amendment. I'm not taking a position, I'm just saying there are options.

But what does seem clear to me is that today's Senate is more like a deep-freeze experimental cryo-weapon than a cooling saucer. Through its obstructionist rules and the stranglehold of the party duopoly, the political realities of the Senate are responsible for much of the dysfunction we see in government. Ending the duopoly and creating a more competitive party system would, I believe, reduce the obstructionism that has become commonplace in the Senate by pushing it (slowly) towards fairer rules.

Conclusion

People can come up with a lot of objections to something, when they're afraid of change. Some of these complaints have real substance; others don't. With some fact-checking and further investigation of the objections, along with the general principles by which electoral methods affect the party system, it's not that hard to answer the objections.

7. Summarizing the Argument

Can a multiparty system fit into American democracy? The answer to that question is clearly yes. With just a few significant changes to how we run our elections and how we regulate our political parties, we would see a much higher level of competitiveness between them, giving voters more choices and thus more power to hold elected leaders to account. This healthier party system would resonate deeply with treasured American values concerning free enterprise and opportunity. A more open party system would better align its incentives with the interests of voters, because a party that failed to perform well could be gradually replaced with a newer, better-performing party — i.e. one that delivers more responsible, more responsive, higher-fidelity representation.

The recipe consists of the following structural changes. First, we need to get over our aversion to multi-member districts, by realizing that they don't necessarily mean the horrible system of plurality at-large voting that was historically used in this country. What they should mean is the opportunity for proportional representation. We should have a larger district magnitude (and larger districts) by electing several members to represent each district. This will also enable a multiparty system to thrive, if we use a voting method friendly to it. So the second change is to switch to such a system.

A good proportional method for multi-member districts is the single transferable vote (STV). There may be other good ones, not to mention better ones (perhaps some kind of Condorcet STV, or a hybrid of ranked-choice and approval voting). But STV would be a fine place to start, and has been tested and used in many other countries and localities for a long time.

These two changes — to districting and to our voting method — would give us a multiparty House of Representatives, and set us on the way to a somewhat more diverse Senate, although Senate races are single-winner and thus can't be proportionally elected without amending the Constitution. For single-winner races, I would recommend an expressive system that escapes the worst of the spoiler effect, like Condorcet IRV. This would be a good system for the presidency, but we might need to amend the Constitution to implement it. Meanwhile, the National Popular Vote Interstate Compact would be a big step in the right direction.

Similar changes can be implemented for state-level governments. I've focused in this book on the national level of politics, but that's mostly because of space and time limitations. Most of the arguments I've made, if not all, could apply equally to any democratically governed jurisdiction afflicted by a two-party system.

How parties fit into the constitutional design of our government

Our country's founders would, I believe, have preferred a multiparty system to a two-party duopoly, had they known that parties were such an inevitable part of democratic politics. No democratic country can do without parties: They perform a key function, in the theory of democracy, of channelizing the various ideologies that exist in a polity into groups of representatives who can then bargain with each other in government. Political parties are an essential part of the "steering" mechanism by which a society is able to govern itself.

Problems arise, however, when a party has too much power — as when, for example, it has a majority of seats in both houses of Congress. Then it is able to hijack the system and run the whole show on its own, assuming that its members cohere well enough in voting together — which in recent decades they have, as teamsmanship has increased along with more polarization and negative campaigning. We've increasingly experienced a politics based on seesaw dynamics, in which winning has become more a matter of vilifying the other side than of advancing a sensible program.

The Founders devised a system of checks and balances between the various branches of the federal government, in order to prevent any form of tyranny from taking over. They also instituted, or recognized and validated, federalism, which further divides power between the states and the federal government. They thus dispersed the powers of government both "horizontally" and "vertically". They were acutely aware that historically, republics had not survived, that democracy on its own is not safe from becoming tyranny. Having rebelled against the King — that is, against a tyranny of the minority — they turned to the opposite problem: tyranny of the majority. How, they asked, could this be prevented?

James Madison, especially, considered this problem carefully. He thought that guarding against the danger of a faction (read "party") that includes a majority was "the great desideratum, by which this form of Government can be rescued from the opprobrium under which it has so long labored, and be recommended to the esteem and adoption of mankind".[337] To meet this demand, he answered that by extending the size of a republic, a greater variety of parties would be included, and this would afford "greater security [...] against the event of any one party being able to outnumber and oppress the rest". As I explained in chapter 3, though he wrote about this in geographic terms, he understood that it's the variety of interests that is the key to preventing tyranny. Geography was simply the main source, for him, of varied interests.

We do have an extended republic, both geographically and in terms of ideological viewpoints. Yet in our current system, with its duopoly of parties, we constantly see one of the two main parties outnumbering and oppressing the other: Hijacking control of the legislature to pursue their own partisan interests. Taking the government hostage to get their way. Refusing to hold the executive accountable when he happens to be of their own party. It's true that control changes hands from time to time, from one party to the other. But within each congressional term, we have a Majority faction. We see this reflected in the way the Speaker of the House is selected, for example — with no input expected from those who are not members of the majority party — whereas our founders expected the whole House to choose its speaker.

---

[337] *Federalist* no. 10.

We have, to a large degree, exactly what Madison feared, and what he would have predicted, given a two-party system:

> the fewer the distinct parties and interests, the more frequently will a majority be found of the same party; and the smaller the number of individuals composing a majority, and the smaller the compass within which they are placed, the more easily will they concert and execute their plans of oppression.[338]

By extension of this logic, when the number of parties composing a majority is just one, they'll have an easier time of "execut[ing] their plans of oppression".

But Madison understood the difficulties of self-government better, perhaps, than any of the other Founders, noting the strong "propensity of mankind to fall into animosities". As Achen and Bartels write in *Democracy for Realists*, he "anticipated the experimental finding of 20th-century psychologists that group attachments are easily generated and profoundly felt."[339] They hope for:

> a framework for thinking about voters that escapes from the populist liberalism that has constrained so much recent thought. Madison pointed the way [...] It is time to set Jeremy Bentham [i.e. the populist ideal of democracy] aside and bring James Madison back in.[340]

I share this appreciation for Madison's genius. He seemed to have a natural understanding of how systems work, how their structure makes a big difference, how they are composed of sub-systems, and how those fit together and interact. So I think he would have appreciated the ways our duopolistic party system interferes with the proper functioning of our government, for the reasons I've pointed out in this book.

We should, generally speaking, make decisions according to the majority principle — which Madison referred to as the "republican principle". When a majority does not get its way, it means that a *minority* effectively rules. As I explained in chapter 3, the majority principle is the fairest way to make collective decisions. In certain

---

[338] *Federalist* no. 10.
[339] Achen and Bartels 2016, p. 215.
[340] Achen and Bartels 2016, p. 230.

exceptional cases, such as for passing a constitutional amendment, a super-majority may make sense; but for the most part, legislative decision-making should follow the majority principle. This is not the "tyranny of the majority" that the Founders feared. True tyranny of the majority occurs at the hands of a *faction* with the power of a majority — or a "Majority", as I've been calling it (following Guinier 1994) — i.e. a party that rules on its own. What Madison and the other Founders would want for the country is less of that, and more of decision-making by *shifting majorities* — majorities formed in order to deal with particular issues, case by case. This is something a multiparty system would do a better job delivering.

System modifications

We haven't always had the duopolistic, two-party system we have today. As figure 2.6 shows, in the 19th century it was not at all uncommon for minor parties to have footholds in Congress — and despite their small numbers, to use these footholds to influence policy. Many people have the feeling that the two-party system is the natural and eternal state of affairs in American political history. It isn't. This idea is part of a mythology that we should question.

   Let's take a closer look at how the changes proposed in this book would affect the overall system of self-governance we use, by referring to the high-level system diagram I included in chapter 2. I reproduce part of it below:

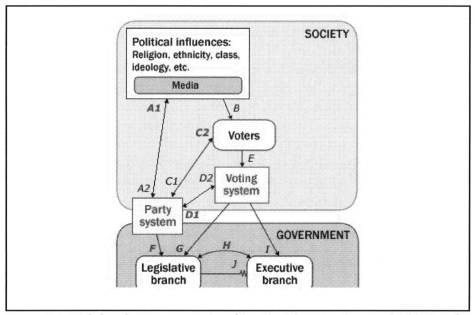

Figure 7.1. High-level system overview (detail with main changes highlighted)
(Full-color version: daneckam.com/book/btp/figures.)

Of course, the main changes proposed would be to the "voting system" block — the adoption of multi-member districts and proportional representation. This would profoundly change the party system through arc *D1*. Parties as organizations would become stronger — more ideologically coherent, more in control of their positioning within the political landscape, more professionalized. But they would be weaker in terms of their freedom to ignore voters, through their power to rig the system (e.g. through gerrymandering and unfair rules for ballot access). A healthy republic requires that parties respond to voters. Voters are supposed to choose leaders, not the other way around. That means we should want a competitive environment for parties, where good performance and innovation are rewarded, and bad performance, irresponsibility and stagnation are punished through a loss of votes. We need to maintain a level playing field, where the referees don't share the interests of players.

Party in government would also be weakened. It would no longer be the norm for a single party to rule on its own (either the whole legislative branch or one of its two chambers). Negotiation and compromise between parties would be necessary for Congress to do its job, and thus would be recognized and more highly valued. This is how the Founders imagined the legislative branch working. The Hastert rule, and other devices that obstruct the will of a majority, would become a thing of the past. Hijacking and hostage-taking by party leaders would cease to be standard operating procedure.

The party system's effect on the legislative branch, represented by arc *F*, would change quite a bit. There would still be a major influence, but in different ways. Congress would develop different ways of organizing its efforts. It would also be more representative of the people, due to the effects of proportional voting on seat distribution (arc *G*). The party system would become a more effective linkage between the demands of voters and the performance of government in translating those demands into policy. While the major parties individually would become weaker, the party *system* itself would become stronger — if by "stronger" we mean more capable of performing its function of channelizing the interests of voters.

These changes would, in turn, affect arc *H* profoundly. The president shares a party with members of Congress — and this is good, to a certain extent, because it helps bridge the gap between two branches of government that need to cooperate to implement government policy. But when the president has the unquestioning, uncritical support of too many representatives — and especially when he has it from a majority — accountability suffers, as I explained in chapter 4. Presidents effectively have license to abuse their power. Congress becomes unable to effectively check the executive branch, which is one of its most important functions. So, more variety in the parties represented in Congress would make it a more effective balance against the executive.

Changes to the party system wouldn't just affect government; they would also have major effects on our society, via arcs *A1* and *C2*. The media would have to get more sophisticated, and present more sides of an argument, as the party system became more capable of representing nuance. In time, traditional journalistic values such as objectivity would be strengthened, as the best way to approach a more varied world of ideas and opinions. This would affect the way voters thought about the world; more variety of ideas would nudge them away from insular "bubbles" of perception, because they'd have a greater exposure to, and awareness of, alternate ways of thinking (arc *B*). By stepping off of the seesaw, perhaps they'd be less prone to "us vs. them" thinking, and seek out basic values and ideals that Americans have in common, even while we disagree about how to achieve them. In short, we'd see things less in black and white, and more in shades of gray — that is, more accurately.

I think Madison and most other Founders would agree, if they were living today, that such changes would help us live up to their expectations for the republic they founded. They would realize that we can't avoid parties altogether. They would notice that we're the only major democratic country with a duopoly of parties in the system, and that the two major parties we have are far too vague and "big-tent" to be effective in accurately representing the views of voters.

Why have I been talking so much about the Founders? Is it because I think they were perfect, their opinions infallible? No — of course not. But I do think they came up with a pretty solid design for how a democratic republic could function. Of course, many of them owned slaves, and they didn't deal with that massive problem, but as amended by the 13th, 14th and 15th amendments, the Constitution seems to provide a workable framework for a fair and just society. That is, just governance is possible — not that it's guaranteed. It's up to elected representatives, in this framework, to implement just policies. Considering the time in which it was written, it's an impressive piece of constitutional engineering — i.e. setting up a structure within which self-government can occur in a sustainable way.

I've tried, in this book, to explain both how and why we should switch to a multiparty system in the United States. The mechanics of how — that is, the structural changes to the system — are pretty straightforward to explain. The more challenging part of how is in convincing people, especially influential people, including partisan activists, that the change would benefit our country, and being able to counter objections and answer questions. By connecting my argument to the designs of the Founders, as well as to the concept of a marketplace of ideas, which can assist with ensuring accountability to the "consumers" — that is, voters — I hope I've provided some useful lines of reasoning that will make the shift easier.

Some objections to a multiparty system are misconceived or not very well-founded, and can be answered fairly easily, given enough knowledge. Others are not quite so easy to overcome — some of them are tied closely to the difficulties inherent to democracy. Self-government is inherently not easy. But there are answers for them, and there are tools the engineer can employ, such as restructuring and making minor tweaks, to adjust things in such a way as to minimize the problems. And, crucially, we need to keep in mind the costs of the party system we currently have. Many of these costs are not widely understood, largely because we take the two-party system so much for granted. I think if we take a long-term perspective, including an understanding that no other advanced democracy has a duopoly for its party system, we'll see that the benefits of the changes I've been promoting would far outweigh the costs.

Bibliography

Abramowitz, Alan I. (2015), "Beyond Confrontation and Gridlock: Making Democracy Work for the American People", chapter 14 of Persily 2015: pp. 197-207.

Achen, Christopher H., and Larry M. Bartels (2016), *Democracy for Realists: Why Elections Do Not Produce Responsive Government*, Princeton University Press.

Adams, John (1776), *Thoughts on Government, Applicable to the Present State of the American Colonies*. URL: http://origin.heritage.org/initiatives/first-principles/primary-sources/john-adams-thoughts-on-government

Adams, John (1780), Letter to Jonathan Jackson, October 2. *The Works of John Adams*, vol. 9, p. 511. URL: https://books.google.com/books?id=j9NKAAAAYAAJ&dq=John%20Adams%20works&pg=PA511#v=onepage&q&f=false

Adler, Jonathan H. (2016), "No, President Obama CANNOT appoint Merrick Garland to the Supreme Court if the Senate does nothing", *The Washington Post*, April 11. URL: https://www.washingtonpost.com/news/volokh-conspiracy/wp/2016/04/11/no-president-obama-cannot-appoint-merrick-garland-to-the-supreme-court-if-the-senate-does-nothing/

"After Mueller, what next?" (2019), *The Economist*, April 27. URL: https://www.economist.com/leaders/2019/04/27/after-mueller-what-next

"After the Vote is Cast, Where Does It Land?" (1987), *The New York Times*, Nov. 4. URL: https://www.nytimes.com/1987/11/04/us/cambridge-journal-after-the-vote-is-cast-where-does-it-land.html

Alden, Edward (2005), "'Cheney cabal hijacked US foreign policy'", *Financial Times*, October 19. URL: https://www.ft.com/content/afdb7b0c-40f3-11da-b3f9-00000e2511c8

"A majority of Americans want abortion to be legal in the first two trimesters" (2019), *The Economist*, May 16. URL: https://www.economist.com/leaders/2019/05/18/a-majority-of-americans-want-abortion-to-be-legal-in-the-first-two-trimesters

"America's electoral system gives the Republicans advantages over Democrats" (2018), *The Economist*, July 12. URL: https://www.economist.com/briefing/2018/07/12/americas-electoral-system-gives-the-republicans-advantages-over-democrats

Ames, Barry (1994), "The Reverse Coattails Effect: Local Party Organization in the 1989 Brazilian Presidential Election", *The American Political Science Review*, Vol. 88, No. 1 (March), pp. 95-111. URL: https://www.jstor.org/stable/2944884

Amy, Douglas J. (2002), *Real Choices/New Voices: How Proportional Representation Elections Could Revitalize American Democracy*, second edition, Columbia University Press.

Andris C, Lee D, Hamilton MJ, Martino M, Gunning CE, Selden JA (2015), "The Rise of Partisanship and Super-Cooperators in the U.S. House of Representatives". PLoS ONE 10(4): e0123507. https://doi.org/10.1371/journal.pone.0123507 See also high-resolution network graphs at http://www.mamartino.com/projects/rise_of_partisanship/

"Are women paid less than men for the same work?" (2017), *The Economist*, Aug. 1. URL: https://www.economist.com/graphic-detail/2017/08/01/are-women-paid-less-than-men-for-the-same-work

Arensmeyer, John (2015), "Citizens United ruling hurts small business", *The Hill*, Jan. 16. URL: https://thehill.com/blogs/ballot-box/229690-citizens-united-ruling-hurts-small-business

Argersinger, Peter H. (1980), "'A Place on the Ballot': Fusion Politics and Antifusion Laws", *The American Historical Review*, vol. 85, no. 2, April, pp. 287-306. URL: http://www.jstor.org/stable/1860557

Arkin, James (2017), "The Budget Process Is Failing. Can Anyone Fix It?", *RealClearPolitics*, July 12. URL: https://www.realclearpolitics.com/articles/2017/07/12/the_budget_process_is_failing_can_anyone_fix_it_134438.html

Arrow, Kenneth J. (1963), *Social Choice and Individual Values*, 2nd ed., Yale University Press.

Arrow, Kenneth J. (2008), "Arrow's theorem", *The New Palgrave Dictionary of Economics (2nd edition)*, edited by Steven N. Durlauf and Lawrence E. Blume, Macmillan Publishers.

The Avalon Project, Nuremberg Trial Proceedings Vol. 9, Yale Law School. URL: http://avalon.law.yale.edu/imt/03-13-46.asp#Goering1

Babington, Charles (2006), "Democrats Won't Try To Impeach President", *The Washington Post*, May 12. URL: http://www.washingtonpost.com/wp-dyn/content/article/2006/05/11/AR2006051101950.html

Bailey, F.G. (1970), *Strategems and Spoils: A Social Anthropology of Politics*, Basil Blackwell.

Barone, Michael (2001), "The Electoral College and the Future of American Political Parties", in Gregg 2001, pp. 79-86.

Barrett, Ted, and Deirdre Walsh (2016), "Congress suddenly has buyer's remorse for overriding Obama's veto", CNN, Sept. 29. URL: http://www.cnn.com/2016/09/29/politics/obama-911-veto-congressional-concerns/

Benham, Chris, and Warren D. Smith, "Woodall's 'Smith,IRV' Condorcet voting method", RangeVoting.org. URL: http://rangevoting.org/SmithIRV.html

Bennett, Robert W. (2001), "Popular Election of the President Without a Constitutional Amendment", *The Green Bag*, vol. 4, no. 3 (Spring), pp. 241-246. URL: http://www.greenbag.org/v4n3/v4n3_articles_bennett.pdf

Berlau, John, Chris Chocola, Burton Folsom, and others (2011), "Down on the Downgrade?", *National Review*, August 9. URL: https://www.nationalreview.com/2011/08/down-downgrade-nro-symposium/

Berman, Ari (2015), *Give Us the Ballot: The Modern Struggle for Voting Rights in America*, Farrar, Straus and Giroux.

Binder, Sarah A. (2010), "The History of the Filibuster", The Brookings Institution, April 22. URL: https://www.brookings.edu/testimonies/the-history-of-the-filibuster/

Binder, Sarah (2014), "How we count Senate filibusters and why it matters", *The Washington Post*, May 15. URL: http://www.washingtonpost.com/blogs/monkey-cage/wp/2014/05/15/how-we-count-senate-filibusters-and-why-it-matters/

Binder, Sarah A., and Steven S. Smith (1997), *Politics or Principle? Filibustering in the United States Senate*, Brookings Institution Press.

Boehm, Eric (2017), "Why Does Blow-Drying Hair in Arizona Require 1,000 Hours of Training?", *Reason*, Dec. 27. URL: http://reason.com/blog/2017/12/27/blow-drying-hair-in-arizona-requires-100

Bogdanor, Vernon (1984), *What Is Proportional Representation: A Guide to the Issues*, Martin Robertson & Company.

Bolotnikova, Marina N. (2016), "Reassessing the Gender Wage Gap", *Harvard Magazine*, May-June. URL:

https://harvardmagazine.com/2016/05/reassessing-the-gender-wage-gap

Bordes, Georges, and Nicolaus Tideman (1991), "Independence of Irrelevant Alternatives in the Theory of Voting", *Theory and Decision*, vol. 30, pp. 163-186.

Bostrom, Nick (2018), "The Vulnerable World Hypothesis", nickbostrom.com, Nov. 4(?). URL: https://nickbostrom.com/papers/vulnerable.pdf

Brams, Steven J., and M. Remzi Sanver (2006), "Voting Systems That Combine Approval and Preference", New York University, March. URL: http://www.nyu.edu/gsas/dept/politics/faculty/brams/approval_preference.pdf

Brennan, John O. (2016), "Statement from Director Brennan on Justice Against Sponsors of Terrorism Act", Central Intelligence Agency, Sept. 28. URL: https://www.cia.gov/news-information/press-releases-statements/2016-press-releases-statements/statement-from-director-brennan-on-justice-against-sponsors-of-terrorism-act.html

Brice-Saddler, Michael (2018), "GOP senator: It's a 'great idea' to make it harder for 'liberal folks' to vote", *The Washington Post*, Nov. 16. URL: https://www.washingtonpost.com/politics/2018/11/16/cindy-hyde-smith-its-great-idea-make-it-harder-liberal-folks-vote/

Brooks, David (2018), "One Reform to Save America", *The New York Times*, May 31. URL: https://www.nytimes.com/2018/05/31/opinion/voting-reform-partisanship-congress.html

Browder, Cullen, and Matthew Burns (2017), "Senate OKs election changes", WRAL.com (Raleigh, NC), April 26. URL: http://www.wral.com/senate-oks-elections-changes/16666800/

Brownstein, Ronald (2007), *The Second Civil War: How Extreme Partisanship Has Paralyzed Washington and Polarized America*, The Penguin Press.

Burden, Barry (2005), "Ralph Nader's Campaign Strategy in the 2000 U.S. Presidential Election", *American Politics Research*, vol. 33 no. 5, September, pp. 672-699.

Burnham, James (1959), *Congress and the American Tradition*, Henry Regnery Company.

Calhoun, John C. (1851), *A Disquisition on Government*.

Cameron, David (2011), "Votes referendum: Cameron speech in full", BBC, Feb. 18. URL: https://www.bbc.com/news/uk-politics-12504935

Campbell, Colin (2017), "Before leaving office, McCrory protected 908 state jobs from political firings", *The News & Observer*, Feb. 23. URL:

http://www.newsobserver.com/news/politics-government/state-politics/article134611879.html

Capehart, Jonathan (2012), "Republicans had it in for Obama before Day 1", *The Washington Post*, Aug. 10. URL: https://www.washingtonpost.com/blogs/post-partisan/post/republicans-had-it-in-for-obama-before-day-1/2012/08/10/0c96c7c8-e31f-11e1-ae7f-d2a13e249eb2_blog.html?utm_term=.0844e32a2915

Carroll, Royce, Gary W. Cox, and Mónica Pachón (2006), "How Parties Create Electoral Democracy, Chapter 2", *Legislative Studies Quarterly*, vol. 31, no. 2, May, pp. 153-174.

Chambers, William Nisbet, and Walter Dean Burnham, eds. (1967), *The American Party Systems: Stages of Political Development*, Oxford University Press.

Chafetz, Josh (2011), "The Unconstitutionality of the Filibuster", *Cornell Law Faculty Publications*, Paper 181. URL: http://scholarship.law.cornell.edu/facpub/181

Chaisty, Paul, Nic Cheeseman, and Timothy J. Power (2012), "Rethinking the 'Presidentialism Debate': Conceptualizing Coalitional Politics in Cross-Regional Perspective", Paper prepared for the 22nd IPSA World Congress, Madrid.

Chantrill, Christopher (date unknown), "Federal Deficit Since the Founding", USGovernmentSpending.com. URL: https://www.usgovernmentdebt.us/spending_chart_1792_2020USp_X Xs2li1l1tcn_G0f_Federal_Deficit_Since_the_Founding

Chideya, Farai (2016), "Black Voters Are So Loyal That Their Issues Get Ignored", *FiveThirtyEight*, Sept. 9. URL: https://fivethirtyeight.com/features/black-voters-are-so-loyal-that-their-issues-get-ignored/

Coaston, Jane (2018), "Self-described Nazis and white supremacists are running as Republicans across the country. The GOP is terrified.", July 9. URL: https://www.vox.com/2018/7/9/17525860/nazis-russell-walker-arthur-jones-republicans-illinois-north-carolina-virginia

Colomer, Josep M. (2012), "The More Parties, the Greater Policy Stability", *European Political Science*, Volume 11, Issue 2, June, pp. 229-243. URL: https://link.springer.com/article/10.1057/eps.2011.34

Colomer, Josep M., and Iain McLean (1998), "Electing Popes: Approval Balloting and Qualified-Majority Rule", *Journal of Interdisciplinary History*, vol. 29, no. 1 (Summer), pp. 1-22.

Committee on Political Parties (American Political Science Association) (1950), "Toward a More Responsible Two-Party System", *American Political Science Review*, vol. 44, no. 3, part 2, supplement, September.

Congressional Digest (1940), "The Practical Operation of the Federal Budget System" vol. 19, no. 2, February.

Conyers, John, Jr. (2006); compiled by the House Judiciary Committee Democratic staff, edited by Anita Miller. *George W. Bush versus the U.S. Constitution: The Downing Street Memos and Deception, Manipulation, Torture, Retribution, and Cover-ups in the Iraq War and Illegal Domestic Spying*, Academy Chicago Publishers.

Cooper, John Milton, Jr. (2009), *Woodrow Wilson: A Biography*, Alfred A. Knopf.

Cox, Gary W., and Mathew D. McCubbins (1993), *Legislative Leviathan: Party Government in the House*, University of California Press.

CQ Almanac (1970), "Electoral College Reform Victim of Senate Filibuster", CQ Press. URL: https://library.cqpress.com/cqalmanac/document.php?id=cqal70-1291702

Cuellar, Henry (2001), Letter to John Steiner (of the City of Austin Law Dept.), Texas Secretary of State Elections Division, July 23. URL: https://www.sos.state.tx.us/elections/elo/hc1.html

Dean, Howard (2016), "Howard Dean: How to Move Beyond the Two-Party System", *The New York Times*, Oct. 7, URL: https://www.nytimes.com/2016/10/08/opinion/howard-dean-how-to-move-beyond-the-two-party-system.html

Democracy Now (2004), "Spoiler or Exposer of a Spoiled System: Nader Announces Presidential Bid", *Democracy Now*, Feb. 23. URL: https://www.democracynow.org/2004/2/23/spoiler_or_exposer_of_a_spoiled

DeSilver, Drew (2018), "U.S. trails most developed countries in voter turnout", Pew Research Center, May 21. URL: http://www.pewresearch.org/fact-tank/2018/05/21/u-s-voter-turnout-trails-most-developed-countries/

Dewar, Helen (1995a), "Flag Amendment Blocked in Senate; Democrat Tries to Force Helms to Act on Treaty, 18 Nominations", *The Washington Post*, December 7. Accessed through Factiva.

Dewar, Helen (1995b), "Senate Sends Ambassadors to Work", *The Washington Post*, December 15. URL: https://www.washingtonpost.com/archive/politics/1995/12/15/senate-sends-ambassadors-to-work/a45bde61-827a-42fd-9ad0-28fc677e4093/?utm_term=.c30a5850aca9

Dews, Fred (2016), "Brookings's role in 'the greatest reformation in governmental practices'—the 1921 budget reform", The Brookings Institution, October 12. URL: https://www.brookings.edu/blog/brookings-now/2016/10/12/brookings-role-in-1921-budget-reform/

Dimond, Diane (2014), "A Republic or a Democracy — Let's Get This Straight", *The Huffington Post*, Dec. 11. URL: https://www.huffingtonpost.com/diane-dimond/a-republic-or-a-democracy_b_6306120.html

Dionne, E. J. (1991), *Why Americans Hate Politics*, Simon & Schuster.

Disch, Lisa Jane (2002), *The Tyranny of the Two-Party System*, Columbia University Press (paperback edition).

Diskant, Gregory L. (2016), "Obama can appoint Merrick Garland to the Supreme Court if the Senate does nothing", *The Washington Post*, April 8. URL: https://www.washingtonpost.com/opinions/obama-can-appoint-merrick-garland-to-the-supreme-court-if-the-senate-does-nothing/2016/04/08/4a696700-fcf1-11e5-886f-a037dba38301_story.html

Downs, Anthony (1957), *An Economic Theory of Democracy*, Harper and Row.

Dreyfuss, Ben (2015), "A Republican Senator Just Sent Out a Tweet So Stupid Our Children Will Learn About It in Stories", *Mother Jones*, June 8. URL: https://www.motherjones.com/politics/2015/06/apple-just-announced-oh-wait-that-is-a-different-post/

Dubner, Stephen J. (2016), "Ten Ideas to Make Politics Less Rotten", Freakonomics Radio, July 27. URL: http://freakonomics.com/podcast/idea-must-die-election-edition/

Dubner, Stephen J. (2018), "America's Hidden Duopoly", Freakonomics Radio, Oct. 31. URL: http://freakonomics.com/podcast/politics-industry/

Dunleavy, Patrick, and Françoise Boucek (2003), "Constructing the Number of Parties", *Party Politics*, vol. 9, no. 3, pp. 291-315.

Duverger, Maurice (1954), *Les Partis Politiques*, 2nd edition, Colin.

Ecarma, Caleb (2017), "Senator Bob Corker Didn't Read the GOP Tax Bill He's Voting For: 'I Never Saw the Text'", *Mediaite*, December 16. URL: https://www.mediaite.com/online/senator-bob-corker-didnt-read-the-gop-tax-bill-hes-voting-for-i-never-saw-the-text/

Eckam, Dan (2016a), "Multimember District Representation in the US and in the States", DanEckam.com, April 20. URL: https://www.daneckam.com/?p=165

Eckam, Dan (2016b), "Evolution of the Two-Party System", DanEckam.com, Oct. 17. URL: https://www.daneckam.com/?p=314

Eckam, Dan (2017), "New Zealand's Party System History", DanEckam.com, Sept. 17. URL: https://www.daneckam.com/?p=392

Eckam, Dan (2019), "What's the Best Way to Deal With Gerrymandering?", DanEckam.com, July 4. URL: https://www.daneckam.com/?p=458

[EIU] The Economist Intelligence Unit (2019), "Democracy Index 2018: Me too?", *The Economist*. URL: http://www.eiu.com/Handlers/WhitepaperHandler.ashx?fi=Democracy_Index_2018.pdf&mode=wp&campaignid=Democracy2018 and interactive chart at https://www.economist.com/graphic-detail/2019/01/08/the-retreat-of-global-democracy-stopped-in-2018

Edwards, George C. III (2011), *Why the Electoral College Is Bad for America: Second Edition*, Yale University Press.

Electoral Reform Society, "What Is STV?". URL: https://www.electoral-reform.org.uk/sites/default/files/What-is-STV.pdf

Elliott, Philip and Nash Jenkins (2018), "How the Government Broke Down", *Time*, January 20. URL: http://time.com/5110952/government-shutdown-donald-trump/

Epstein, Leon (1986), *Political Parties in the American Mold*, University of Wisconsin Press.

Everett, Burgess (2015), "How Planned Parenthood could shut down the government", *Politico*, July 29. URL: https://www.politico.com/story/2015/07/government-shut-down-planned-parenthood-120787

Everett, Burgess (2016), "McConnell throws down the gauntlet: No Scalia replacement under Obama", *Politico*, Feb. 13. URL: https://www.politico.com/story/2016/02/mitch-mcconnell-antonin-scalia-supreme-court-nomination-219248

FairVote (2009), "Michael Steele's RNC Win Helps Show how Instant Runoff Voting Works: Ranked voting methods abound in America culture", Feb. 4. URL: http://www.fairvote.org/michael_steele_s_rnc_win_helps_show_how_instant_runoff_voting_works_ranked_voting_methods_abound_in_america_culture

FairVote (2017), "The Fair Representation Act". URL: https://www.fairvote.org/fair_rep_in_congress#why_we_need_the_fair_representation_act

FairVote (date unknown), "Data on Ranked Choice Voting: Ranked choice voting and voter turnout, participation and understanding". URL: https://www.fairvote.org/data_on_rcv#research_rcvvoterturnout

Fang, Lee (2015), "Big Bank's Analyst Worries that Iran Deal Could Depress Weapons Sales", *The Intercept*, March 20. URL: https://theintercept.com/2015/03/20/asked-iran-deal-potentially-slowing-military-sales-lockheed-martin-ceo-says-volatility-brings-growth/

Farrell, Jane, and Sarah Jane Glynn (2013), "What Causes the Gender Wage Gap", Center for American Progress, April 9. URL: https://www.americanprogress.org/issues/economy/news/2013/04/09/59658/what-causes-the-gender-wage-gap/

Farrington, Dana (2017), "Watch: Sen. McCain Calls for Compromise in Return to Senate Floor", NPR, July 25. URL: https://www.npr.org/2017/07/25/539323689/watch-sen-mccain-calls-for-compromise-in-return-to-senate-floor

Fields, Gary, and John R. Emshwiller (2011), "Many Failed Efforts to Count Nation's Federal Criminal Laws", *The Wall Street Journal*, July 23. URL: https://www.wsj.com/articles/SB10001424052702304319804576389601079728920

Findell, Elizabeth (2018), "Election might signal end to left-right diversity on Austin council", *Austin American-Statesman*, Oct. 7. URL: https://www.statesman.com/news/20181007/election-might-signal-end-to-left-right-diversity-on-austin-council

Fisher, Roger, and William L. Ury (1981), *Getting to Yes: Negotiating Agreement without Giving In*, Little, Brown.

FiveThirtyEight (2016), "Who will win the presidency?". URL: https://projects.fivethirtyeight.com/2016-election-forecast/?ex_cid=rrpromo#tipping-point

Flores, Nicolas (1999), *A History of One-Winner Districts for Congress*, undergraduate thesis, Stanford University. URL: http://archive.fairvote.org/library/history/flores/index.html

Ford, Lacy K., Jr. (1994) "Inventing the Concurrent Majority: Madison, Calhoun, and the Problem of Majoritarianism in American Political Thought", *The Journal of Southern History*, vol. 60, no. 1 (Feb.), pp. 19-58.

Friedman, Uri (2016), "American Elections: How Long Is Too Long?", *The Atlantic*, Oct. 5. URL:

https://www.theatlantic.com/international/archive/2016/10/us-election-longest-world/501680/

Friedrich, Carl Joachim (1937), *Constitutional Government And Politics, Nature And Development*, Harper & Brothers.

Gaines, Brian J. (2001), "Popular Myths about Popular Vote-Electoral College Splits", *PS: Political Science and Politics*, v. 34, no. 1, Mar., pp. 70-75. URL: http://www.jstor.org/stable/1350312

Gierzynski, Anthony, Wes Hamilton, and Warren D. Smith (2009), "Burlington Vermont 2009 IRV mayor election", RangeVoting.org. URL: http://rangevoting.org/Burlington.html

Gilens, Martin (2012), "Under the Influence", *Boston Review*, July 1. URL: http://bostonreview.net/forum/lead-essay-under-influence-martin-gilens

Gilens, Martin, and Benjamin I. Page (2014), "Testing Theories of American Politics: Elites, Interest Groups, and Average Citizens", *Perspectives on Politics*, 12(3), 564-581.

Gilens, Martin, and Benjamin I. Page (2016), "Critics argued with our analysis of U.S. political inequality. Here are 5 ways they're wrong.", *The Washington Post*, May 23. URL: https://www.washingtonpost.com/news/monkey-cage/wp/2016/05/23/critics-challenge-our-portrait-of-americas-political-inequality-heres-5-ways-they-are-wrong/

Golosov, Grigorii V. (2010), "The Effective Number of Parties: A New Approach", *Party Politics*, vol. 16, no. 2, pp. 171-192.

Goodman, H.A. (2016), "Debbie Wasserman Schultz And The DNC Favored Hillary Clinton Over Bernie Sanders. Where's The Outrage?", *The Huffington Post*, August 16. URL: https://www.huffingtonpost.com/entry/debbie-wasserman-schultz-and-the-dnc-favored-hillary_us_57b365a4e4b0b3bb4b0800bd

Goodman, Josh (2011), "The Disappearance of Multi-Member Constituencies", *Governing*, July 7. URL: http://www.governing.com/blogs/politics/The-Disappearance-of-Multi-Member-Constituencies.html

"The Governing Trap" (2014), *National Review*, Nov. 5. URL: http://www.nationalreview.com/article/392082/governing-trap-editors

[GPO] Government Publishing Office (1967), Public Law 90-196 (H. R. 2275). URL: https://www.gpo.gov/fdsys/pkg/STATUTE-81/pdf/STATUTE-81-Pg581-2.pdf

Gramlich, John, and Katherine Schaeffer (2019), "7 facts about guns in the U.S.", Pew Research Center, October 22. URL:

https://www.pewresearch.org/fact-tank/2019/10/22/facts-about-guns-in-united-states/

Greeley, Brendan (2013), "In Financial Reform, Keep It Simple Like Glass-Steagall", Bloomberg Businessweek, April 12. URL: https://www.bloomberg.com/news/articles/2013-04-12/in-financial-reform-keep-it-simple-like-glass-steagall

Green, Joshua (2011), "Strict Obstructionist", *The Atlantic*, January/February. URL: https://www.theatlantic.com/magazine/archive/2011/01/strict-obstructionist/308344/?single_page=true

Green-Armytage, James (2011), "Four Condorcet-Hare Hybrid Methods for Single-Winner Elections", *Voting matters*, Issue 29, October; published by McDougall Trust. URL: http://www.votingmatters.org.uk/ISSUE29/I29P1.pdf

Gregg, Gary L. II (ed.) (2001), *Securing Democracy: Why We Have an Electoral College*, ISI Books.

Grieder, Erica (2016), "The Conservative Case for Hillary Clinton", *Texas Monthly*, June 6. URL: https://www.texasmonthly.com/burka-blog/conservative-case-hillary-clinton/

Griffiths, Shawn M. (2018), "Revolutionary New Voting Method Bolstered By over 16,000 Voters in Oregon County", *The Independent Voter Network*, July 9. URL: https://ivn.us/2018/07/09/revolutionary-new-voting-method-bolstered-16000-voters-oregon-county/

Groeger, Lena, Olga Pierce, Justin Elliott and Theodoric Meyer (2012), "House Seats vs. Popular Vote", ProPublica, Dec. 21. URL: https://projects.propublica.org/graphics/seats-vs-votes

Grunwald, Michael (2012), "The Party of No: New Details on the GOP Plot to Obstruct Obama", *Time*, Aug. 23. URL: http://swampland.time.com/2012/08/23/the-party-of-no-new-details-on-the-gop-plot-to-obstruct-obama/

Guinier, Lani (1994), *The Tyranny of the Majority: Fundamental Fairness in Representative Democracy*, The Free Press.

Hacker, Jacob S. and Paul Pierson (2015), "Confronting Asymmetric Polarization", chapter 3 of Persily 2015: pp. 59-70.

Hakim, Catherine (2011), "Feminist myths and magic medicine: the flawed thinking behind calls for further equality legislation", Centre for Policy Studies, June 3. URL: http://eprints.lse.ac.uk/36488/

Halle, John and Noam Chomsky (2016), "An Eight Point Brief for LEV (Lesser Evil Voting)", JohnHalle.com, June 15. URL:

https://johnhalle.com/hallechomsky-an-eight-point-brief-for-lev-lesser-evil-voting/

Hanchett, Ian (2016), "Cuccinelli: RNC 'Cheated,' 'Violated Their Own Rules'", *Breitbart*, July 18. URL: http://www.breitbart.com/video/2016/07/18/cuccinelli-rnc-cheated-violated-their-own-rules/

Harris, Sam (2018), "Waking Up Podcast #114 - Politics and Sanity: A Conversation with David Frum and Andrew Sullivan", SamHarris.org, January 22. URL: https://samharris.org/podcasts/114-politics-and-sanity/

Harris, Sam (2019), "Waking Up Podcast #160 - The Revenge of History: A Conversation with Michael Weiss and Yascha Mounk", SamHarris.org, June 17. URL: https://samharris.org/podcasts/the-revenge-of-history/

Haydar, Nour, and Nick Sas (2018), "National Party pledges to expel 'hate and racism' as four more Young Nats resign over alt-right connection", The Australian Broadcasting Corporation (ABC), Nov. 2. URL: https://www.abc.net.au/news/2018-11-02/more-young-nationals-resignations-party-vows-to-expel-alt-right/10461228

Herrnson, Paul S., and John C. Green, ed. (1997), *Multiparty Politics in America*, Rowman & Littlefield Publishers.

Herz, Ansel (2016), "Dan Savage on Jill Stein: Just No", The Stranger, July 19. URL: https://www.thestranger.com/slog/2016/07/19/24362128/dan-savage-on-jill-stein-just-no

Hiaasen, Scott, Gary Kane, and Elliot Jaspin (2001), "Felon Purge Sacrificed Innocent Voters", *Palm Beach Post*, May 27.

Hickey, Walter (2013), "The Longest Filibuster In History Lasted More Than a Day—Here's How It Went Down", *Business Insider*, March 6. URL: http://www.businessinsider.com/longest-filibuster-in-history-strom-thurmond-rand-paul-2013-3

Hill, I. D. (1988), "Some Aspects of Elections — to Fill One Seat or Many", *Journal of the Royal Statistical Society. Series A (Statistics in Society)*, Vol. 151, No. 2, pp. 243-275.

Hoff Sommers, Christina (2012), "Wage Gap Myth Exposed — By Feminists", *The Huffington Post*, Nov. 4. URL: https://www.huffingtonpost.com/christina-hoff-sommers/wage-gap_b_2073804.html

Hofstadter, Richard (1948), *The American Political Tradition and the Men Who Made It*, 1973 edition, Vintage Books (originally published in 1948 by Knopf).

Hofstadter, Richard (1969), *The Idea of a Party System: The Rise of Legitimate Opposition in the United States, 1780-1840*, University of California Press.

Holcombe, A. N. (1911), "Direct Primaries and the Second Ballot", *American Political Science Review*, vol. 5, no. 4 (Nov.), pp. 535-552. URL: http://www.jstor.org/stable/1945022

Hollandsworth, James G., Jr. (1998), *Pretense of Glory: The Life of General Nathaniel P. Banks*, LSU Press.

Hotelling, Harold (1929), "Stability in Competition", *The Economic Journal*, vol. 39, no. 153, March, pp. 41-57.

Huckabee, David C. (1995), "Reelection Rates of House Incumbents, 1790-1994", Congressional Research Service, March 8.

Huder, Josh (2018), Tweet at 10:32 AM, 7 Feb 2018: "In short, the Pelosi filibuster continues because of politics, not procedure. The GOP has all the procedural tools they need to stop it. Pelosi wants them to cut her off. And if they do, expect a fun show." Twitter.com. URL: https://twitter.com/joshHuder/status/961276571335233539

Huntington, Samuel P. (1991), "Democracy's Third Wave", *Journal of Democracy*, vol. 2, no. 2, Spring.

Icsman, Marilyn (2018), "John Boehner slams Republicans: 'There is no Republican Party. There's a Trump party'", *USA Today*, May 31. URL: https://www.usatoday.com/story/news/politics/onpolitics/2018/05/31/former-speaker-john-boehner-criticizes-republican-party/661544002/

Illing, Sean (2016), "The real reason we have an Electoral College: to protect slave states", Vox, Nov. 12. URL: https://www.vox.com/policy-and-politics/2016/11/12/13598316/donald-trump-electoral-college-slavery-akhil-reed-amar

[ILSR] Institute for Local Self-Reliance (2008), "Cumulative Voting – Amarillo", ILSR.org, Nov. 26. URL: https://ilsr.org/rule/voting-systems/2167-2/

[IPU] Inter-Parliamentary Union (2019), "Percentage of women in national parliaments", IPU.org. URL: https://data.ipu.org/women-ranking?month=9&year=2019

[IRV in the US] Instant Runoff Voting in the United States (2010), "The Instant Runoff Voting Lie, as told to Cary, North Carolina", Instantrunoff.blogspot.com, July 8. URL: http://instantrunoff.blogspot.com/2010/07/instant-runoff-voting-lie-as-told-to.html

Jacobs, Ben (2015), "On the Iraq war, Jeb Bush had a terrible, horrible, no good, very bad week", *The Guardian*, May 15. URL:

https://www.theguardian.com/us-news/2015/may/15/jeb-bush-iraq-war-ivy-zietrich-isis-george-w-bush

Jacobson, Louis (2012), "Barack Obama ad says women are paid '77 cents on the dollar for doing the same work as men'", *PolitiFact*, June 21. URL: https://www.politifact.com/truth-o-meter/statements/2012/jun/21/barack-obama/barack-obama-ad-says-women-are-paid-77-cents-dolla/

Jacobson, Louis (2014), "Congress has 11% approval ratings but 96% incumbent reelection rate, meme says", *PolitiFact*, Nov. 11. URL: http://www.politifact.com/truth-o-meter/statements/2014/nov/11/facebook-posts/congress-has-11-approval-ratings-96-incumbent-re-e/

Jennings, Will and Christopher Wlezien (2016), "The Timeline of Elections: A Comparative Perspective", *American Journal of Political Science*, vol. 60, no. 1, Jan., pp. 219-233.

Johnson, Jenna (2014), "Is this how Maryland's 3rd Congressional district is supposed to look?", *The Washington Post*, Sept. 21. URL: https://www.washingtonpost.com/local/md-politics/in-maryland-anti-gerrymandering-activists-take-message-to-their-target/2014/09/21/2f3dce36-4180-11e4-9a15-137aa0153527_story.html

Jussim, Lee (2017), "Why Brilliant Girls Tend to Favor Non-STEM Careers", *Psychology Today*, July 20. URL: https://www.psychologytoday.com/us/blog/rabble-rouser/201707/why-brilliant-girls-tend-favor-non-stem-careers

Kammen, Michael, ed. (1986), *The Origins of the American Constitution: A Documentary History*, Penguin Books.

Kar, Robin Bradley & Jason Mazzone (2016), "The Garland Affair: What History and the Constitution *Really* Say About President Obama's Powers to Appoint a Replacement for Justice Scalia", *New York University Law Review Online*, vol. 91, May, pp. 53-114. URL: http://www.nyulawreview.org/online-features/garland-affair-what-history-and-constitution-really-say-about-president-obamas

Kessler, Glenn (2011), "Lessons from the great government shutdown of 1995-1996", *The Washington Post*, Feb. 25. URL: http://voices.washingtonpost.com/fact-checker/2011/02/lessons_from_the_great_governm.html

Klein, Ezra (2017), "This is not how the Senate is supposed to work", *Vox*, September 29. URL: https://www.vox.com/policy-and-politics/2017/9/29/16373460/senate-budget-reconciliation-filibuster

Koger, Gregory (2010), *Filibustering: A Political History of Obstruction in the House and Senate*, The University of Chicago Press.

Kondik, Kyle, and Geoffrey Skelley (2016), "Incumbent Reelection Rates Higher Than Average in 2016", *Sabato's Crystal Ball*, Dec. 15. URL: http://www.centerforpolitics.org/crystalball/articles/incumbent-reelection-rates-higher-than-average-in-2016/

Kurtzleben, Danielle (2013), "The Federal Budget Is Not a Household Budget", *U.S. News & World Report*, March 5. URL: https://www.usnews.com/news/articles/2013/03/05/the-federal-budget-is-not-a-household-budget

Laakso, M., and R. Taagepera (1979), "'Effective' Number of Parties: A Measure with Application to West Europe", *Comparative Political Studies* 12: 3–27.

Lawson, Kay (1997), "The Case for a Multiparty System", chapter 3 of Herrnson and Green 1997 (pp. 59-72).

Lee, Frances E. (2009), *Beyond Ideology: Politics, Principles, and Partisanship in the U. S. Senate*, University of Chicago Press.

Lee, Mike (2016), "The Case for Congressional Empowerment", lee.senate.gov. URL: https://www.lee.senate.gov/public/index.cfm?p=article1project

Leip, Dave, Dave Leip's Atlas of U.S. Presidential Elections. URL: http://uselectionatlas.org/

Lessig, Lawrence (2011), *Republic, Lost: How Money Corrupts Congress—and a Plan to Stop It*, Twelve.

Levitsky, Steven and Daniel Ziblatt (2018), *How Democracies Die*, Crown.

Lijphart, Arend and Bernard Grofman (1984), *Choosing an Electoral System: Issues and Alternatives*, Praeger.

LoGiurato, Brett, and Grace Wyler (2012), "Ron Paul Supporters Disrupt The Republican National Convention", *Business Insider*, August 28. URL: http://www.businessinsider.com/republican-national-convention-floor-dissent-from-ron-paul-supporters-2012-8

Lovegrove, Jamie (2016), "Independent presidential candidate Rocky de la Fuente sues Texas over ballot access", *Dallas News*, Sept. 19. URL: https://www.dallasnews.com/news/politics/2016/09/19/independent-presidential-candidate-rocky-de-la-fuente-sues-texas-ballot-access

Lowi, Theodore J., and Joseph Romance (1998), *A Republic of Parties?: Debating the Two-Party System*, Rowman and Littlefield Publishers.

Lux, Marshall, and Robert Greene (2016), "Dodd-Frank Is Hurting Community Banks", *The New York Times*, April 14. URL: https://www.nytimes.com/roomfordebate/2016/04/14/has-dodd-frank-eliminated-the-dangers-in-the-banking-system/dodd-frank-is-hurting-community-banks

[LWV] League of Women Voters (1988), "League Refuses to 'Help Perpetrate a Fraud'", October 3. URL: http://lwv.org/press-releases/league-refuses-help-perpetrate-fraud

Lynch, Tim (2009), "Are You a Criminal? Maybe You Are and Don't Know It", Cato Institute, December 9. URL: https://www.cato.org/blog/are-you-criminal-maybe-you-are-dont-know-it

Madison, James (1787), Letter to Thomas Jefferson, Oct. 24. URL: http://press-pubs.uchicago.edu/founders/documents/v1ch17s22.html

Madison, James (1830), Letter to Robert Young Hayne, April 3.

Mainwaring, Scott (1993), "Presidentialism, Multipartism, and Democracy: The Difficult Combination", *Comparative Political Studies* 26: 198-228. URL: http://cps.sagepub.com/content/26/2/198

Mainwaring, Scott P. (1999), *Rethinking Party Systems in the Third Wave of Democratization: The Case of Brazil*, Stanford University Press.

Mann, Thomas E. & Norman J. Ornstein (2012), *It's Even Worse Than It Looks: How the American Constitutional System Collided With the New Politics of Extremism*, Basic Books.

Martis, Kenneth C. (1982), *The Historical Atlas of United States Congressional Districts, 1789-1983*, The Free Press.

Martis, Kenneth C. (1989), *The Historical Atlas of Political Parties in the United States Congress: 1789-1989*, Macmillan.

Mast, Tory (1995), "The History of Single-Member Districts for Congress: Seeking Fair Representation Before Full Representation", FairVote. URL: http://archive.fairvote.org/index.php?page=526

Matthews, Dylan (2013), "Voting Rights Act ruling: Here's what you need to know", *The Washington Post*, June 25. URL: https://www.washingtonpost.com/news/wonk/wp/2013/06/25/voting-rights-act-ruling-heres-what-you-need-to-know/?utm_term=.decb9b45a54c

Matthews, Dylan (2016), "An ex-senator called Trump backers 'brownshirts,' in case you wondered how the RNC's going", *Vox*, July 18. URL: https://www.vox.com/2016/7/18/12217300/gordon-humphrey-nevertrump-fascists-brown-shirts

McCarthy, Devin (2012), "How the Electoral College Became Winner-Take-All", FairVote, August 21. URL: http://www.fairvote.org/how-the-electoral-college-became-winner-take-all

McConnell, Mitch (2019), "The Filibuster Plays a Crucial Role in Our Constitutional Order", *The New York Times*, August 22. URL:

https://www.nytimes.com/2019/08/22/opinion/mitch-mcconnell-senate-filibuster.html

McCormack, John, and Michael Warren (2016), "Mike Lee Fights the RNC Machine", *The Weekly Standard*, July 18. URL: http://www.weeklystandard.com/mike-lee-fights-the-rnc-machine/article/2003368

McGann, Anthony J. (2002), "The Tyranny of the Super-Majority: How Majority Rule Protects Minorities", Center for the Study of Democracy (UC Irvine): CSD Working Papers, Oct. 1. URL: http://escholarship.org/uc/item/18b448r6

McLean, Iain, and Arnold B. Urken (1992), "Did Jefferson or Madison Understand Condorcet's Theory of Social Choice?", *Public Choice*, vol. 73, no. 4, June, pp. 445-457.

Medina, Eden (2015), "Rethinking algorithmic regulation", *Kybernetes*, vol. 44, no. 6/7, pp. 1005-1019.

Michaels, Samantha (2018), "Wisconsin's GOP Aims to Strip Power From the Incoming Democratic Governor", *Mother Jones*, Dec. 2. URL: https://www.motherjones.com/politics/2018/12/wisconsin-gop-scott-walker-tony-evers/

Mikkelson, David (2015), "Obama on the Debt Limit", *Snopes.com*, April 18. URL: https://www.snopes.com/politics/obama/debtlimit.asp

Mill, John Stuart (1859), *On Liberty*.

Miller, Nicholas R. (1983), "Pluralism and Social Choice", *The American Political Science Review*, vol. 77, no. 3, Sept., pp. 734-747. URL: http://www.jstor.org/stable/1957271

Millhiser, Ian (2015), "Senator Unveils New Obamacare Attack, Immediately Becomes A Laughingstock", *ThinkProgress*, June 8. URL: https://thinkprogress.org/senator-unveils-new-obamacare-attack-immediately-becomes-a-laughingstock-7444818262b0/

Mock, Jamie (2010), "District 22 Candidate Calls For Impeachment Of President Obama", FortBendNow.com, Feb. 19. URL (archived version): https://web.archive.org/web/20110725002425/http://www.fortbendnow.com/2010/02/19/44085

Montgomery, Horace (1954), "The South Between Two Political Parties", *The Georgia Review*, Vol. 8, No. 1 (Spring), pp. 90-96. URL: https://www.jstor.org/stable/41380638

Morse, Yonatan L. (2012), "The Era of Electoral Authoritarianism", *World Politics* 64, no. 1, January, pp. 161–98.

Mortimore, Roger (2011), "A Guide to the Alternative Vote", Ipsos MORI Social Research Institute, Feb. 7. URL:

https://www.ipsos.com/sites/default/files/publication/1970-01/RM-AVarticle.PDF

NBC News (2014), "Poll: Fewer Americans Blame Poverty on the Poor", NBCNews.com, June 20. URL: https://www.nbcnews.com/feature/in-plain-sight/poll-fewer-americans-blame-poverty-poor-n136051

Needham, Lindsey (2012), "Election Wonk: Growing trend of plurality wins in governors' races", FairVote, May 4. URL: http://www.fairvote.org/election-wonk-growing-trend-of-plurality-wins-in-governors-races

Niemi, Richard G. and William H. Riker (1976), "The Choice of Voting Systems", *Scientific American*, v. 234, no. 6 (June), pp. 21-27.

NPR News (2011), "Jack Abramoff Calls D.C. Politics Dirty As Ever", *Tell Me More*, Nov. 18. URL: https://www.npr.org/2011/11/18/142506539/jack-abramoff-calls-d-c-politics-dirty-as-ever

PBS NewsHour (2015), "Shields and Brooks on the Senate's trade battle, train safety funding", PBS, May 15. URL: https://www.pbs.org/newshour/show/shields-brooks-senates-trade-battle-train-safety-funding

Persily, Nathan, ed. (2015), *Solutions to Political Polarization in America*, Cambridge University Press.

Pildes, Richard (2010), "Abolish Primary Elections", *Big Think*, August 23. URL: https://bigthink.com/videos/abolish-primary-elections

Poundstone, William (2008), *Gaming the Vote: Why Elections Aren't Fair (and What We Can Do About It)*, Hill and Wang.

Priest, Dana, and William M. Arkin (2010), "Top Secret America", *The Washington Post*, July 19-21. URL: http://projects.washingtonpost.com/top-secret-america/article-index/

Quinnipiac (2013), "Background Checks Could Lead To Gun Confiscation, Many Voters Tell Quinnipiac University National Poll; But 91 Percent Want Universal Gun Checks", April 4. URL: https://poll.qu.edu/national/release-detail?ReleaseID=1877

Radiolab (2018), "Tweak the Vote", WNYC Studios, Nov. 4. URL: https://www.wnycstudios.org/story/tweak-vote

Raile, Eric D., Carlos Pereira, and Timothy J. Power (2011), "The Executive Toolbox: Building Legislative Support in a Multiparty Presidential Regime", *Political Research Quarterly*, Vol. 64, No. 2, pp. 323-334, June. URL: https://www.jstor.org/stable/23056394

Ranney, Austin (1951), "Toward A More Responsible Two-Party System: A Commentary", *American Political Science Review*, Vol. 45, No. 2 (June), pp. 488-499.

Ranney, Austin (1962), *The Doctrine of Responsible Party Government: Its Origins and Present State*, University of Illinois Press.

Ranney, Austin (1975), *Curing the Mischiefs of Faction: Party Reform in America*, University of California Press.

Reagan, Ronald (1988), "Remarks to State and Local Republican Officials on Federalism and Aid to the Nicaraguan Democratic Resistance", American Presidency Project. URL: http://www.presidency.ucsb.edu/ws/?pid=35584

Real News Network (2017), "Clinton Democrats Hate the Left - RAI with Thomas Frank (4/6)", Real News Network, September 12. URL: https://www.youtube.com/watch?v=RMNYaRQ-MqY

Reilly, Benjamin (2004), "The Global Spread of Preferential Voting: Australian Institutional Imperialism?", *Australian Journal of Political Science*, vol. 39, no. 2 (July), pp. 253-266. URL: https://crawford.anu.edu.au/pdf/staff/ben_reilly/breilly8.pdf

"The Republican Crisis" (2016), *National Review*, Oct. 10. URL: http://www.nationalreview.com/article/440924/donald-trumps-access-hollywood-tape-republican-partys-crisis

Resnick, Gideon (2016), "Bernie Sanders: From the Guys Who Brought You George W. Bush", *The Daily Beast*, April 5. URL: http://www.thedailybeast.com/articles/2016/04/05/bernie-sanders-from-the-guys-who-brought-you-george-w-bush.html

Reynolds, Glenn Harlan (2015), "Reynolds: You are probably breaking the law right now", *USA Today*, March 29. URL: https://www.usatoday.com/story/opinion/2015/03/29/crime-law-criminal-unfair-column/70630978/

Ridout, Travis N., and Annemarie S. Walter (2015), "Party system change and negative campaigning in New Zealand" *Party Politics* vol. 21, no. 6, pp. 982-992.

Riker, William H. (1982a), *Liberalism Against Populism: A Confrontation Between the Theory of Democracy and the Theory of Social Choice*, Waveland Press.

Riker, William H. (1982b), "The Two-Party System and Duverger's Law: An Essay on the History of Political Science", *American Political Science Review*, vol. 76, no. 4 (Dec.), pp. 753-766. URL: http://www.jstor.org/stable/1962968

Roberts, David (2018), Tweet on Nov. 6. URL: https://twitter.com/drvox/status/1059880801284710400

Roberts, Jacob W. (2014), "The Revolving Door: Public Service Increasingly a Conduit to Lucrative Lobbying Careers", *Southern*

California International Review, June 27. URL: http://scir.org/2014/06/the-revolving-door-public-service-increasingly-a-conduit-to-lucrative-lobbying-careers/

Romance 1998: see Lowi and Romance 1998.

Rosa-Clot, Michele (2007), "This Stalin Frankenstein System: Adoption and Abrogation of Proportional Representation in New York City, 1936-1947", *RSA Journal* 17/18, pp. 201-240. URL: http://www.aisna.net/sites/default/files/rsa/rsa1718/17_18rosaclot.pdf

Ross, Edward A. (1920), *The Principles of Sociology*, The Century Co. Available online at https://babel.hathitrust.org/cgi/pt?id=uva.x000444135;view=1up;seq=5

Rove, Karl (2016), "Unity Won't Come Easy for Either Party", *The Wall Street Journal*, April 27. URL: https://www.wsj.com/articles/unity-wont-come-easy-for-either-party-1461799058

Rucker, Philip, and Robert Costa (2016), "Inside the GOP effort to draft an independent candidate to derail Trump", *Washington Post*, May 14. URL: https://www.washingtonpost.com/politics/inside-the-gop-effort-to-draft-an-independent-candidate-to-derail-trump/2016/05/14/1b04682e-1877-11e6-924d-838753295f9a_story.html?utm_term=.a5c77b866626

Rule, Wilma, and Pippa Norris (1992), "Anglo and Minority Women's Underrepresentation in Congress: Is the Electoral System the Culprit?", chapter 4 of Rule & Zimmerman 1992: pp. 41-54.

Rule, Wilma, and Joseph F. Zimmerman, eds. (1992), *United States Electoral Systems: Their Impact on Women and Minorities*, Praeger.

Ryan, Ivan (with some contributions by Bruce R. Gilson) (date unknown), "Reweighted Range Voting (RRV) – a Proportional Representation voting method that feels like range voting", RangeVoting.org. URL: https://www.rangevoting.org/RRVr.html

Samuels, Katherine (2008), "Single-Member Districts in Austin: An Analysis of Proposed Single-Member District Scenarios", The University of Texas, LBJ School of Public Affairs, December 15. URL: https://soa.utexas.edu/sites/default/disk/AnalysisSMDsAustin.pdf

Sargent, Greg (2015), "Morning Plum: How Republicans will try to blame Obama if the Court guts subsidies", *The Washington Post*, May 22. URL: https://www.washingtonpost.com/blogs/plum-line/wp/2015/05/22/morning-plum-how-republicans-will-try-to-blame-obama-if-the-court-guts-subsidies/

Sartori, Giovanni (1968), "Representation: Representational Systems" in *International Encyclopedia of the Social Sciences*, David L. Sills, ed., vol. 13, Macmillan and Free Press, New York, pp. 465-474.

Sartori, Giovanni (1970), "Concept Misformation in Comparative Politics", *American Political Science Review*, vol. 64, no. 4 (Dec.), pp. 1033-53.

Sartori, Giovanni (1976), *Parties and Party Systems: A Framework for Analysis*, Cambridge University Press.

Sartori, Giovanni (1987), *The Theory of Democracy Revisited*, Chatham House.

Sartori, Giovanni (1997), *Comparative Constitutional Engineering: An Inquiry into Structures, Incentives and Outcomes* (second edition), New York University Press.

Sasse, Ben (2017), "Sen. Ben Sasse Is On The Hunt For 'American Adults'", *On Point* (WBUR), May 15. URL: http://www.wbur.org/onpoint/2017/05/15/ben-sasse-book

Schattschneider, E. E. (1942), *Party Government*, Transaction Publishers.

Scher, Bill (2016), "Nader Elected Bush: Why We Shouldn't Forget", *RealClearPolitics*, May 31. URL: https://www.realclearpolitics.com/articles/2016/05/31/nader_elected_bush_why_we_shouldnt_forget_130715.html

Schickler, Eric (2005), "Institutional Development of Congress", chapter 2 of *The Legislative Branch*, edited by Paul J. Quirk and Sarah A. Binder, Oxford University Press.

Schlesinger, Arthur, Jr. (2000), "Fixing the Electoral College", *The Washington Post*, Dec. 19.

Seelye, Katharine Q. (2016), "Maine Adopts Ranked-Choice Voting. What Is It, and How Will It Work?", *The New York Times*, Dec. 3. URL: https://www.nytimes.com/2016/12/03/us/maine-ranked-choice-voting.html

"Senate, Everyone?" (1961), *Time*, volume 77, issue 14, Mar. 31.

"Senatorial Elections and Primaries, 1906 – 2018", Texas Almanac. URL: https://texasalmanac.com/topics/elections/senatorial-elections-and-primaries-1906-%E2%80%93-2018

Shabad, Rebecca (2017), "What would it mean to erase the debt ceiling?", *CBS News*, Sept. 13. URL: https://www.cbsnews.com/news/what-would-it-mean-to-erase-the-debt-ceiling/

Sharpton, Al (2014), Transcript: Wednesday, August 27, *Politics Nation*, MSNBC.com, August 27, 2014. URL: http://www.nbcnews.com/id/55950524/

Siddiqui, Sabrina (2016), "Republican senators vow to block any Clinton supreme court nominee forever", *The Guardian*, Nov. 2. URL: https://www.theguardian.com/law/2016/nov/01/republican-senators-oppose-clinton-supreme-court-nominee

Slatky, Alec (2010), "Why IRV Produces a Majority Winner", FairVote, July 12. URL: https://www.fairvote.org/why-irv-produces-a-majority-winner

Small Business Majority (2012), "Poll: Supreme Court Citizens United Decision Hurts Small Businesses, Say Owners By 7 To 1 Margin", Small Business Majority, January 18. URL: https://smallbusinessmajority.org/press-release/poll-supreme-court-citizens-united-decision-hurts-small-businesses-say-owners-7-1-margin

Smith, Warren D. (2005), "Reweighted range voting – new multiwinner voting method", RangeVoting.org, Aug. 6. URL: https://rangevoting.org/WarrenSmithPages/homepage/rerange.pdf

Smith, Warren D. (2015), "Approval voting elected the Greek parliament 1864-1926", RangeVoting.org. URL: http://rangevoting.org/GreekApproval.html

Snay, Mitchell (2011), *Horace Greeley and the Politics of Reform in Nineteenth-Century America*, Rowman & Littlefield.

Stein, Jonathan, and Tim Dickinson (2006), "Lie by Lie: A Timeline of How We Got Into Iraq", *Mother Jones*, September/October. URL: https://www.motherjones.com/politics/2011/12/leadup-iraq-war-timeline/

Steinhauer, Jennifer, Mark Mazzetti, and Julie Hirschfeld Davis (2016), "Congress Votes to Override Obama Veto on 9/11 Victims Bill", *The New York Times*, Sept. 28. URL: https://www.nytimes.com/2016/09/29/us/politics/senate-votes-to-override-obama-veto-on-9-11-victims-bill.html

Stern, Mark Joseph (2016), "North Carolina Republicans' Legislative Coup Is an Attack on Democracy", *Slate*, Dec. 15. URL: http://www.slate.com/blogs/outward/2016/12/15/north_carolina_legislative_coup_an_attack_on_democracy.html

Stern, Mark Joseph (2017), "Court Blocks Most of North Carolina GOP's Legislative Coup, Including Election-Board Power Grab", *Slate*, March 18. URL: http://www.slate.com/blogs/the_slatest/2017/03/18/north_carolina_legislative_power_grab_blocked_in_court.html

Stoner, James R., Jr. (2001), "Federalism, the States, and the Electoral College", in Gregg 2001, pp. 51-52.

Sundquist, James L. (1983), *Dynamics of the Party System: Alignment and Realignment of Political Parties in the United States* (revised edition), The Brookings Institution.

Taylor, Andrew (2018), "President Trump's Budget Would Add $7.2 Trillion in Federal Deficits Over 10 Years", *Time*, Feb. 12. URL: http://time.com/5146313/donald-trump-budget-plan/

Tenet, George J. (2003), "Statement by George J. Tenet Director of Central Intelligence", CIA, July 11. URL: https://www.cia.gov/news-information/press-releases-statements/press-release-archive-2003/pr07112003.html

Tideman, Nicolaus (2006), *Collective Decisions and Voting: The Potential for Public Choice*, Routledge.

Trende, Sean (2012), "Did JFK Lose the Popular Vote?", *RealClearPolitics*, Oct. 19. URL: http://www.realclearpolitics.com/articles/2012/10/19/did_jfk_lose_the_popular_vote_115833.html

Tushnet, Mark (2004), "Constitutional Hardball", The John Marshall Law Review, v. 37, pp. 550, 523-53.

Tyrrell, Ian (2008), "What is American exceptionalism?", IanTyrrell.wordpress.com. URL: https://iantyrrell.wordpress.com/papers-and-comments/

Van Boven, Leaf, and David Sherman (2018), "Actually, Republicans Do Believe in Climate Change", *The New York Times*, July 28. URL: https://www.nytimes.com/2018/07/28/opinion/sunday/republicans-climate-change.html

Vital Statistics on Congress (2017), The Brookings Institution, Sept. 7. URL: https://www.brookings.edu/multi-chapter-report/vital-statistics-on-congress/

Wallace, Michael (1968), "Changing Concepts of Party in the United States: New York, 1815-1828", *The American Historical Review*, vol. 74, no. 2 (Dec.), pp. 453-491.

Wallach, Philip A. (2017), "Prospects for partisan realignment: Lessons from the demise of the Whigs", The Brookings Institution, March 6. URL: https://www.brookings.edu/research/prospects-for-partisan-realignment-lessons-from-the-demise-of-the-whigs/

Ware, Doug G. (2017), "Nomination expires for Obama Supreme Court appointee Merrick Garland", UPI, Jan. 3. URL: https://www.upi.com/Top_News/US/2017/01/03/Nomination-expires-for-Obama-Supreme-Court-appointee-Merrick-Garland/4841483472115/

Weaver, Matthew (2016), "Jimmy Carter calls US campaign finance ruling 'legalised bribery'", *The Guardian*, Feb. 3. URL: https://www.theguardian.com/us-news/2016/feb/03/carter-says-campaign-finance-2010-citizens-united-ruling-legalised-bribery

"Why you should vote below the line today" (2018), *The Age*, Nov. 24. URL: https://www.theage.com.au/politics/victoria/why-you-should-vote-below-the-line-today-20181123-p50i0a.html

Wilkinson, Francis (2015), "How Bush v. Gore Led to Obamacare", *Bloomberg View*, June 12. URL: https://www.bloomberg.com/view/articles/2015-06-12/how-bush-v-gore-led-to-obamacare and accessed at https://www.thenewstribune.com/opinion/article26336281.html

Williams, Joe (2018), "Senators Prepare for Messaging and Uncertainty From Immigration Debate", *Roll Call*, Feb. 12. URL: https://www.rollcall.com/news/politics/senators-prepare-messaging-uncertainty-immigration-debate

Wilson, Woodrow (1879), "Cabinet Government in the United States", *International Review*, August. Available online at https://babel.hathitrust.org/cgi/pt?id=mdp.39015004155795

Wilson, Woodrow (1885), *Congressional Government*, Houghton Mifflin.

Winger, Richard (2002), "The Supreme Court and the Burial of Ballot Access: A Critical Review of *Jenness v. Fortson*", *Election Law Journal*, vol. 1, no. 2, June, pp. 235-252.

Winger, Richard (2016), "Georgia Ballot Access Bill", *Ballot Access News*, August. URL: http://ballot-access.org/2016/08/27/august-2016-ballot-access-news-print-edition/

Winger, Richard (2017), "Study Shows How Georgia's Ballot Access Law for U.S. House is Out of the National Mainstream", *Ballot Access News*, May 23. URL: http://ballot-access.org/2017/05/23/study-shows-how-georgias-ballot-access-law-for-u-s-house-is-out-of-the-national-mainstream/

Winger, Richard (2018), "Commentary: How California can keep advantages of the top two primary while curing its defects", *San Diego Union Tribune*, June 8. URL: https://www.sandiegouniontribune.com/opinion/commentary/sd-utbg-california-primary-winger-20180608-story.html

"The Word — It's a Trap!" (2014), *The Colbert Report*, Nov. 10. URL: http://www.cc.com/video-clips/avadrz/the-colbert-report-the-word---it-s-a-trap-

Worland, Justin (2016), "Ethanol Is No Longer the Third Rail of the Iowa Caucus", *Time*, Jan. 28. URL: http://time.com/4186455/iowa-caucus-ted-cruz-ethanol/

"The world v the Donald" (2016), *The Economist: The World If*, May 31. URL: http://worldif.economist.com/article/12166/world-v-donald

Yglesias, Matthew (2018), "Proportional representation could save America", *Vox*, Oct. 15. URL: https://www.vox.com/policy-and-politics/2018/10/15/17979210/proportional-representation-could-save-america

York, Byron (2014), "Another government shutdown? Not gonna happen", *The Oakland Press*, Sept. 8. URL: http://www.theoaklandpress.com/article/MD/20140908/NEWS/140909708

Young, H. Peyton, ed. (1991), *Negotiation Analysis*, University of Michigan Press.

Zimmerman, Joseph F. (1992), "Enhancing Representational Equity in Cities", chapter 17 of Rule & Zimmerman 1992: pp. 209-220.

Index

About the Author

Dan Eckam is a software developer and writer with a deep interest in society, politics, and democratic theory. For many years, he observed American politics and saw connections, unscrutinized by most mainstream commentators, between the two-party system and some of our biggest political problems. Finally, in 2014, he decided to write about them and what could be done to improve our democracy.

He resides in Austin, Texas. This is his first book.